MARKHAM STREET

The Haunting Truth Behind the Murder of My Brother, Marvin Leonard Williams

Ronnie Williams

Edited by Jennifer Hansen

Table of Contents

PART I
Marvin

PART II
The Inquest

PART III
A Cover-up Uncovered

This book is dedicated to the memory of my beloved brother,

MARVIN LEONARD WILLIAMS,

who was murdered in 1960 in the Faulkner County Jail,

and to

our parents, Johnnie and D.V. Williams, who weathered the storms of racism

with dignity and grace,

and who instilled in their children the importance of faith, family,

and the power that love has over hate.

PART I

Marvin

CHAPTER 1

The Letter

My name is Ronnie Williams. I am the youngest of D.V. and Johnnie Williams' eight children. Today, I thank God that I can write this book without succumbing to the anger and hatred I once felt for those involved in my brother Marvin's murder. But in 1984, hatred is exactly what I felt when I learned the facts of Marvin's death. Those facts came from the most unlikely source – a one-armed white man by the name of Charles Hackney who wrote a letter to my parents 24 years after my brother was killed.

I was seven when Marvin died, and I can't recall a single occasion when my parents ever spoke about his death. All I knew was that he tripped on some steps and died from a blood clot. I didn't know why we never talked about it, only that there was an unspoken understanding that Marvin's death was not to be discussed. But the real reason was because my parents always knew the official story was a lie.

It may seem strange that they kept this knowledge to themselves, but in the Deep South in the 1960s they felt they had no choice. Back then it wasn't uncommon for Black men like my brother to be physically abused, or worse, by white police officers. Anyone who spoke out about such an incident was endangering themselves and their family, and my parents had seven other children they wanted to keep safe. So now and then we talked about the good things in Marvin's life, like his military service, how much he loved his family, how kind and handsome he was. But we never, ever discussed his death.

All that changed on August 8, 1984.

That summer I was 30 years old, working in Little Rock for the Arkansas Department of Education. Every morning before work and every evening on my way home from work I stopped by my parents' house to check on them. Our morning visit was a quick check-in, long enough to give Mother a kiss and make sure they were both all right. The afternoon visit was a little longer. First, I'd find and chat with my mother. No matter what she was doing, she always greeted me with the same warm smile and said, "Here comes Mother's baby." After we talked, I'd go find my father and see how his day had gone.

My father had a huge "truck patch," an enormous garden spread across his two acres and the nearby field he leased from a neighbor. That garden was his pride and joy. He worked it daily and often bragged about having one of the best truck patches in the community. When I stopped by in the evening, Daddy was almost always out in the fields. We'd visit about his day, about what he'd planted, the weather, or when the corn would be ready to harvest.

But that Wednesday evening, as soon as I came into view, I could see that Daddy was near the house, watching for me. When he saw my car, he dropped his tools and walked quickly toward Mother, who was already waiting outside the house. As I pulled into their drive, Daddy reached her and they stood together, unsmiling. I knew something serious had happened before I stopped the car. I got out, and they turned without a word and walked to the carport, where it was shady and cool.

The carport was where our family talked, celebrated holidays, and during the long, hot Arkansas summers ate some of my father's sweet watermelons. It was like our sanctuary, with my mother's wind chimes hanging from the beams and making beautiful music in the soft breeze. This was where church deacons lined up on Saturdays to get haircuts from my father (who was, among his many trades, the town's barber) before going to church on Sunday. Meanwhile, their wives sat together and waited for their husbands, sharing community gossip and the latest news about children and grandchildren. So it was natural that if an important conversation were to be had, we would have it there.

When they reached the carport, my mother and father sat down in the lawn chairs they kept there, and I sat across from them. Then my father spoke.

"Hey Son, I've got something here your mother and me would like for you to look at. It's a letter from a guy by the name of Charles Hackney. He says he was in the jail with Marvin and he saw what happened to him."

And then Daddy handed me the letter.

I was completely taken aback. This was the first time in my life either of my parents ever brought up Marvin's death to me. I searched their faces. My father seldom showed emotion, but I heard uncertainty in his voice and saw pain in his eyes. Mother looked helpless, with an expression of total dependency that said, 'Son, we need for you to tell us what to do.'

I opened the letter and read it. When I finished there was silence. Finally, I told my parents I wanted to take it home to read it again and think. I said I'd talk with them the next day about where we'd go from here, and I left.

As I drove down their driveway a powerful feeling came over me that remains with me to this day. It is difficult to put into words, but the best way I can describe it is that I felt a deep stillness and calm come over me, and the spirit of the Lord spoke to me and said, "I have preserved you for this moment."

Those words still resonate in my heart. It was as though God was handing off an assignment to me, as if He was saying, "OK, here is this truth I need for you to tackle. This is why you're here, in this place, and in this moment." I felt certain that whatever was about to unfold was part of my calling, and that I would be equipped to fulfill it.

Before going into my house, I sat in the car and read Hackney's letter again. It was dated August 6, 1984, twenty-four years and three months after the date of Marvin's death. It was addressed to my father, whose first name was misspelled, and the return address was a prison cell in Wrightsville, Arkansas.

Between the moment my father handed me that letter and the moment I opened the door to our house, my world had shifted. But my wife Connie and our two boys, ages 6 and 2, didn't know that. The boys were waiting to play with Dad and tell me about their day, while Connie made dinner. So, I went through the motions of a normal evening, but my mind was far away.

Finally, after the kids were in bed, I went into our bedroom and read the letter a third time. Then I gave it to Connie and asked her to read it.

August 6, 1984

Charles L. Hackney.

B-7. p.o. Box 407

Wrightsville Arkansas

Mr. Delever Williams

Menifee Arkansas

Mr. Williams

This is not an easy letter for me to write. I have wanted to contact you before now, but I just did not do it.

I would like for you to know that it has took me 24 years to get this investigation going. I can assure you that the officials there in Faulkner County knew what happened to your son with in 6 hours after it happened, because I told the prosecuting attorney that morning there in the jail that they beat a Black man there at 2:00 AM. I saw part of it and I could hear more of it but I could not see it. Because I told what I saw my life was thereatened and I was forced to tell lies for these so called up standing people who ran Faulkner County.

Because I was scared. And I was a young man who was dum. Not that I didn't care for my fellow man. But because I knew what could happen to me. I know how you felt because I have lost two of my own. Not that way but just the same they are gone.

In 1962 I did what I could to get this looked into. I agreed to go to Federal Court and tell what I knew. But I never heard anything else about it.

I have lived with it for 24 years. But when I was told that it had been ruled an accident, that was just to much. I do not want to hurt any one by doing what I have did on this matter I hope that you understand. By me seeing what I did caused me some trouble. And the chances are this is going to cause me even more trouble as long as I am here in prison.

I think that I will feel better with my self once this is cleared up and settled but you know as well as I do the rich people go free and the poor people go to prison. That is a bad thing to say about your justic system. But I think that I speak the truth. As long as a man tells the truth he should not have any thing to fear, but I am afraid that is not the way it work every time.

I feel for you and your family, but it was not my doing. I was just a witness. And I would give any thing if I had not have been there that nite.

Yours truly

Charles L. Hackney.

august. 6. 1984
Charles L. Hackney.
B-7. p.o. Box 407.
Wrightsville arkansas.

mr. Deliverawilliams
se.
Menifue arkansas

mr. williams
this is not an easy letter for me to write. I have
wanted to Contact you before now. but I just
did not do it.
I would like for you to Know that it has
took my 24 years to get this investigation
going. I can assure you that the officials there
in Faulkner County Knew what happened to
your son with in 6 hours after it happened.
because I told the prosecuting attorney. that
morning there in the jail that they beat a Black
man there at 2:00 AM. I saw part of it and I
Could hear more of it. but I Could not see it.
because I told what I saw my life was threatened
and I was farced to tell lies for these so
Called up standing people. who ran Faulkner
County.
because I was scared. and I was a young man
who was dum. not that I didnt care for my
fellow man. but because I Knew what Could
happen to me. I Know how you felt. because
I have last two of my own. not that way
but just the same they are gone.
in 1962 I did what I Could to get this
looked into. I agreed to go to federal Court
and tell what I Knew. But I never heard
any thing else about it

I have lived with it for 24 years. but when I was told that it had been ruled an accident, that was just to much. I do not want to hurt any one by doing what I have did on this matter I hope that you understand. by me suing what I did Caused me some Trouble. and the Chances are this is going to Cause me even more trouble. as long as I am here in prison.

I think that I will fell better with my self once this is Cleared up and settled but you Know as well as I do the rich people go free and the poor people go to prison. that is a bad thing to say about your justic system. but I think that I speak the truth. as long as a man tells the truth he should not have any thing to fear. but I am afraid that is not the way it works every time

I fell for you and your family. but it was not my doing. I was just a witness. and I would give any thing if I had not have been there that nite.

C. L. Hackney 80996
B-7 P.O. Box 407
wrightsville arkansas
72183-0407

yours truly

Charles L. Hackney.

Mr. Deluer
Menifee ar
C/o. Post mast

When she finished reading, Connie looked at me and slowly said, "So, your brother was killed? He was murdered?" I think I nodded.

That night I barely slept. Terrible images of Marvin being beaten filled my mind. Why would those officers have beaten my brother? If Charles Hackney told the prosecuting attorney what he heard and saw, why was nothing done about it?

I had no idea how much that letter would change our lives, or that I would be totally consumed with my brother's case from 1984 until this very moment.

What I did know was that Marvin was not an exception. There are thousands of Marvin Williams whose stories will never be told, whose families didn't get a witness letter in the mail, who feared violent retribution if they spoke out, or were never able to build a case because the evidence was deliberately destroyed. In writing this book I am speaking on behalf of all of them.

When I'm asked why I was compelled to write this book, it's all of that history, all those families and victims, and more. It's Marvin, but it's larger than him. It's the anguish on my parent's faces. It's my own fears for my sons and their families. It's what we've lost and what those losses have done to our community and to our country.

For me, change is a heart thing. If we can change the hearts and minds of people, then we have a chance to address systemic racism in America. I hope when you read this story you will think about all the other stories, and you'll want to be part of the movement to make our country a better, fairer place.

But that first night I was reeling. My thoughts jumped from what our family should do, to what advice I'd give my parents the next day. And for some reason, I kept trying to envision where exactly Charles Hackney had been in that jail to have seen and heard what he put in that letter. What was the layout of the jail?

"Where were you?" I asked him silently.

* * *

The next morning, I told my parents I needed more information. But when I came back that evening my mind was made up. I told them I thought Marvin had been murdered and, according to Hackney's letter, officials tried to cover it up. I told them I wasn't going to stop until I got all the facts surrounding Marvin's death.

At this point in their lives, my parents relied on me for many things. I was extremely close to them, especially my mother. All my life she'd been the source of the positive and encouraging words every child needs to hear. I was her only surviving son, so maybe I got a little extra because Marvin wasn't there. As they got older and it became clear to the family that someone needed to take responsibility for checking on my parents, all but one of my sisters lived out of state. So watching over them became my role, and I never questioned it. They expected so little and they'd given us so much.

When I told them what I'd decided, Daddy was the first to respond, his voice filled with sadness and fear.

"Son, I don't want anything to happen to you."

Daddy had lived in the south his whole life. Like all Black men in those days he knew a lot about retaliation, intimidation, and humiliation; about beatings, lynchings, and Jim Crow. He knew what would happen to a Black man who questioned a white man. He feared for me, and he had good reason.

When my sister Donna and I were young, Daddy would sometimes drive us down Sardis Road that runs parallel to Highway 64 south of Plumerville. Each time he took that road, Daddy would slow down and point out one particular tree and say to us, "That's where they would hang Black people."

We knew he wasn't exaggerating because dangling from one of the tree's thick limbs was a large chain on which a noose once hung.

When Daddy was young, a Black man in the Morrilton jail had been taken by a white mob. They brought him to that tree and hanged him. My father saw his body, he saw what the mob had done to him. After that lynching, the chain and noose were left hanging there. The noose finally rotted, or someone took it down, but the chain remained for years. I don't know if it was used again, but it was left there on purpose, to serve as a reminder of what happens to Black men who dared challenge the status quo. Showing us that tree was Daddy's way of warning us about what the world was like.

So, I didn't fault my Daddy for feeling the way he did, but I knew God had given me this assignment, and nothing was going to stop me. I told my parents that, and from that day on every evening was like a debriefing. Mother and Daddy would be waiting for me in their lawn chairs under that carport. "Okay, what do we know and where are we?"

And each day, it was as if a hand was leading me through my steps. I'd never done anything like this before, but I knew my first task was to find the death certificate, and for that I had to go to the Faulkner County Courthouse.

CHAPTER 2

Growing Up in Menifee

My mother was born in 1915, a couple of years before America entered World War I. Her family emigrated from Shelby County, Tennessee and somehow found their way west to Menifee, Arkansas. Eventually, her mother, Sarah, found work as a live-in maid and nanny to a white family in nearby Little Rock. Back then, domestic workers were at the mercy of their employers. They were expected to live on site, with no set work hours and no days off. For them, Saturdays, Sundays, and holidays were workdays like any other. So my mother and her brother, John Otha, were raised by their grandmother, Lucy, in Menifee. On the rare occasions their mother did get a day off, she'd ride the train from Little Rock to see her two children.

Daddy's family was from Monroe, Louisiana. They too made their way to Central Arkansas where his parents, John Henry and Lela Williams, worked as farmers. They had three children, Nina, Tecumseh, and my father, Delavah, the youngest. Daddy, who always went by "D.V.", was born in 1913. From a young age, he and his siblings worked the fields. As a teenager, he was a tremendous baseball player and had opportunities to play in the Negro Baseball League but didn't, or couldn't, pursue them. Yet baseball rewarded him anyway: at a ball game in Menifee where he was pitching, he met my mother.

Back then, baseball was the sport of choice for Black families, allowing young Black men to develop and showcase their athletic prowess, letting families to have fun together, and providing an opportunity for young people to meet. Baseball games often served as a conduit for love and marriage; my mother and father, my brother

Marvin and his wife Bonnie, and my wife and I, all met and fell in love at the baseball park.

Mother used to tell me about how shy and nervous he was when Daddy came to her grandmother's home to get permission for them to date. Since they both worked in the fields during the week, dating meant seeing a movie in Conway on Saturday night. If they didn't have the money to take the train, and they usually didn't, they'd walk the railroad tracks five miles from Menifee to Conway. After the movie they'd walk the track back. They often told us stories about encountering "hobos" along the tracks.

Daddy didn't finish high school, but Mother did. And shortly after she graduated they were married at her grandmother's home, in a porch wedding on Sunday, August 20, 1933, at 5 p.m. The next day they went back to the fields.

Mostly the fields my parents worked were part of what was called the House Bottoms, about three miles south of Menifee. "Bottoms" is a term for low-lying farmland. The House Bottoms was a huge tract, maybe four or five thousand acres near the Arkansas River, owned by a white lady, Miss Mary House. My mother and father were among the hundreds of field hands who worked her cotton and soybean fields.

Every Friday night the exhausted field hands, men and women, went to Miss Mary's home and waited outside until she came out and paid them. Usually Miss Mary paid them with money, which was the agreement. Sometimes, though, she paid them with meat. Mother said it wasn't unusual for that meat to be spoiled, a few times it even had maggots in it. The field hands never knew if they'd be paid in cash or meat.

There's one story we all grew up hearing about those days. One Friday evening Miss Mary House came out and looked at the hundreds of tired men and women gathered there and said, loud enough for them all to hear, "Look at all my darkies. They look like a bunch of black birds."

My mother never forgot that moment. She used to tell that story quite a bit.

Menifee during that time was a bustling community with a population of about five to six hundred residents. It was the economic hub for families of color in Conway County. When we were growing up there were four grocery stores in downtown Menifee, all Black-owned. There were four churches: two Baptist, one Methodist, and one Church of Christ. A Black physician, Dr. McDaniel, saw patients out of his home and employed two Black midwives who assisted at births. There were Black entrepreneurs, like Clarence English who had an auto repair shop, and Leroy Wert who owned a machine repair shop. There was a Black Postmaster who delivered mail and managed the Menifee Post Office. Near the Menifee train station was a Black-owned general store.

As soon as they could, my parents bought a house and two acres in Menifee from Beecher Mitchell, who then became our next-door neighbor. The Mitchell family allowed Daddy to farm nine more acres in exchange for some of the fine produce he raised. That arrangement continued for many years, even after Mr. Beecher died. Every year in late July the Mitchells would come in with their bags and my Daddy would proudly load them up with food during harvest. Any extra that didn't go to feed us he took to Conway and wholesaled.

Mother's full name was Johnnie Olive Willie Bernice Jones. She had an unusual name, and she gave her children unusual names for the time: their firstborn was Emogene, whom we called Emma. She was followed by Ernestine, Marvin, Carolyn, Verna, Barbara, Donna, and me, Ronald.

Times were always hard, but Daddy and Mother knew how to make ends meet. Until I was a junior in high school, we raised everything, and I mean everything. Every year around Thanksgiving, Daddy would kill a pig or two. Our neighbor, Mr. Holloway, would salt the meat for us and hang it in the smokehouse and we'd have bacon and pork. We lived off that for the year.

Mother raised chickens and ducks, so we always had eggs. She had a big chicken house as well as small coops for the broody hens and their chicks. Whenever we needed meat Daddy would go out and kill a chicken. Mother raised so many chickens that even after feeding our family of ten, she had enough to sell to people in the community to make a little extra money.

Some of that "extra" money went to keep us all in the nicest clothes she could find. All our clothes came from the thrift store. Mother would look for the better brands and she'd take them home and wash, starch, and iron them. They looked so good, and we were always dressed well. In fact, I didn't know I was poor until years later, when I went to Hendrix College as a freshman.

My father was an exceptional gardener. He grew boysenberries, strawberries, corn, green onions, peas, purple hull beans, watermelon, cantaloupe, kale, turnip greens, sweet potatoes, and more, all neatly growing in their own sections. Peanuts were a specialty of his. When they were ready, we children would pull them and position them on their stalks to dry out. Then we'd put up bags of peanuts to snack on through the winter. I loved peanuts, and I think Daddy grew them mostly as a special treat for us kids.

Through the years, Daddy added on to the property. Near the house he built a tornado shelter where he kept Mother's canned goods. Underneath the house was a crawlspace, and Daddy got down there and dug it out to create a big holding area so he could store sweet potatoes where it was cool. Behind the house he built two smokehouses where he stored meat, bacon, and hams.

What Daddy grew, Mother canned. And if Daddy hadn't grown it, she was very particular. On summer weekends we'd drive west on Highway 64 through Plumerville to Morrilton and stop at all the fresh produce stands until she found what she liked. When peaches were in season, we had to drive all the way to Clarksville to get this one kind of peach she wanted. It had to be that special kind of peach, and when she found it she bought it by the bushel, so she could can jars of peach pie filling for the winter.

Around 1959, when I was about 6, Mother started doing domestic work. In 1967, she took a second job as lead cook at my school. Her day started at 7:15 making the school breakfast and then lunch. Mother was a wonderful cook. When I was in elementary and junior high, white businessmen would stop at our school, which was all Black, to eat lunch just so they could have my mother's cinnamon rolls, or her pigs in a blanket, or her famous vegetable soup every Friday. When she got off that job about 2:30, she went to Morrilton and Conway to clean houses for some prominent white families. She'd get home about 8 or 9, sometimes with leftovers from school to warm up for us.

Mother was the glue of the family. One of her favorite sayings was "Son, I may not have a quarter in my pocket, but nobody will ever know it." She was the can-do person and the encourager. She built us up by telling us how she saw us. "Hey son, you're going to be a leader." I can't tell you how many times she told me that. In my memories, my father was quieter and more cautious with his praise and with his affection. He had all these kids to feed and raise and, especially after Marvin died, he had to be careful. He didn't want to lose any more.

Ours was very much a religious home. Mother was raised Methodist and Daddy, when he did go, was Baptist. But after he started dating my mother, Daddy found his way to the church. In our home, not going to church was not an option. If you were a Williams kid, you were going to church on Sunday morning and back again Sunday night at 5 for Baptist Training Union, or BTU, which had an adult class and a section for children. On Wednesday night you went to mid-week prayer meeting. At home, my Daddy read scripture, we discussed scripture, and we prayed out loud. Over the years, Mother and Daddy both taught Sunday school.

Family dinners were a huge deal in our family, especially Sunday afternoons. There was always conversation around the table. My parents and the older kids talked about things in the community, sometimes a little gossip, or what had happened on their jobs. Whether he was working in the fields or later on working for the railroad, Daddy was often away during the week. As often as she could, Mother made it a point for everyone to sit down and spend time together over dinner. Family dinners are a tradition in my family to this day.

My sisters did housework and canning and some of the farming, but most of the farm work fell to Marvin when he was home, and later to me. When I was young, Daddy and I would go across the freeway to get the two mules he co-owned with another neighbor, Mr. Lee Wert. We'd drive those mules back to our fields, and that's how we tilled the fields. Eventually, he went in with a friend and bought a tiller. Even then, we worked sunup to sundown breaking the ground to plant, weed, and tend those fields, and they were as neat and perfect as any you'd find. You'd never see a blade of grass in Daddy's fields. Not one.

Daddy raised his own potato slips, or starter potato plants. When they were ready he'd separate them one by one, then he and I would go out in the field together. He'd furrow in long rows and then make an indentation with his hoe where the slips should go. I'd follow behind him with a bucket of potato slips, placing one in each hole, making sure the roots pointed down, pouring water in the hole, and packing the hole back with dirt.

That was hot, painful, miserable work. And it was in that potato patch, when I was about ten or eleven years old, that I had my big 'Aha' moment: If God would point me in the direction of higher learning, I swore I'd never look back.

* * *

Growing up Black in Menifee, Arkansas in the 1940s and 50s was extremely difficult. My parents often talked about how hard it was for them. Back then, the only work a person of color could reliably find was in the fields in summer as a day laborer, usually chopping, pulling, and picking cotton. If you weren't in a cotton or soybean field, the only other option was domestic work as a household servant, washing clothes, cleaning houses, cooking meals, and caring for the children of white families.

My parents wanted more for their children, and they instilled in us a serious work ethic. While other kids were playing, my siblings and I were working. When we weren't working someone else's farm, we worked our own. It was a never-ending process. Marvin, like the rest of us, longed for the day when he could leave the farm and move on to bigger and better things.

Marvin and his friends had to travel long distances to find work as field hands. Many white farmers contracted with people from the Black community to bring workers to their farms. Clarence English was one of several black 'transporters.' He had an old bus he'd fill with farm workers from Menifee to take to Scott and Biscoe, some 85 miles away. Farm workers preferred towns like Scott and Biscoe because the white farmers there provided living quarters for their field hands to stay in during the week. In truth, these were nothing more than shanties, but staying over spared the exhausted field workers the long, hard ride back and forth every day. That was worth it, even if it meant not seeing your family the entire week.

When they were working the fields, Emma, Ernestine, Carolyn, Verna, Marvin and my father left before dawn Monday mornings. They'd work all week and come back Friday night. My siblings and my father worked like dogs for those long farming seasons to earn enough to get us through the rest of the year. Daddy and the girls were paid 50 cents a day, $2.50 for the whole week. But when Marvin worked, he made 75 cents a day, he was that strong and fast. All of them contributed what they made to support the family, no one ever thought this money was for them. There was one time, though, that my sister Carolyn remembers our parents let Marvin keep all he'd earned for one week. He used that money to buy Christmas gifts for all of us.

Field work back then was awful, and that word doesn't begin to describe it. You'd start at 6 a.m. when it was still dark and the fields were blanketed with dew. Walking through the thick, wet foliage of rows of cotton or soybeans left your clothes soaking wet. You couldn't see the ground, you couldn't even see your feet. It's a miracle none of us were ever snakebitten.

Once the sun came out, the fields dried up and got dusty, and that dust clung heavily to your wet clothes and lay like a thick plaster on your skin. By 11 a.m. you were dirty, stinky, and caked in mud. And then came the hardest part of the day, scorching hot, no gloves, and seven more hours of work ahead of you chopping.

When you chopped, you used your own hoe. You'd be out there chopping grass with it, breaking up the dirt, preparing the field for planting, and eliminating the weeds on every row – and those rows were long. In time, the ever-present blisters on your hands turned into callouses. Marvin started working in the fields when he was about ten years old. By the time he was 12 or 13, my sister Carolyn says his hands already looked like an old man's.

About 6 that night, you'd go back to your shanty, sore and bone-tired. There were no showers or baths for the workers. For dinner, Carolyn recalls that Mother and Daddy would bake sweet potatoes on Sunday night for all of them to take with them to the fields. Those sweet potatoes were their primary food for the week.

Carolyn was the closest in age to Marvin, and they had the closest relationship. To this day she often talks about what they experienced in those fields. As I was writing this book, she'd often call and ask how it was going, and talk about how hard they had to work, especially Marvin.

Once harvesting season was over, which typically lasted into early fall, Marvin and my sisters could focus on academics. Before integration, young Black men and women were bussed into Menifee from all over the county to go to Conway County Training School. CCTS as it was called, taught kindergarten through 12th grade. Probably 50 buses came from all over bringing students to that school. That went on until 1966 or 67, when some of those young people were able to go to schools in their own towns. Marvin and all my siblings went to CCTS, and his name is still inscribed on the sidewalk on the hill going up to that gym.

Mother was a brilliant woman, so much so that several of the white women she worked for asked her if she had a college degree. Marvin was like her in that way. He excelled in so many subjects that he was promoted to a higher grade several times and graduated high school at the age of 15. Mother often talked about the many conversations she had with Marvin's English teacher, Mrs. Jo Willie English. Mrs. English would say to her, "Mrs. Williams, Marvin is a genius. Please make sure he goes to college." Unfortunately, Marvin never made it to college.

A new level of oppression really kicked in during the 1950s. That was a tough decade for Black families in the Deep South. In 1954, a Black man named Isadore Banks was lynched in Crittenden County, Arkansas, way out east of Menifee. Banks was a WWI veteran and a prosperous Black landowner, which was nearly unheard of in our state. His burned body was found tied to a tree, and his murder made statewide and national news, sending a terrifying message to Black families in our state. Of course, his killers were never found.

The next year, Emmett Till, a fourteen-year-old African American boy, was visiting cousins in Mississippi when he was kidnapped, beaten, tortured, shot and then thrown in a river. His body was sent home to Chicago, where his mother held an open casket funeral. She told journalists to take photos of her son's mutilated corpse, so the country could see what had been done to him, and they did. In 1955, Jet magazine, a Black-owned magazine with a national Black readership, published those photos. I doubt my parents ever saw that magazine, but they would have heard about the case and the photos. They would also have heard that the two white men who confessed to Emmett Till's murder were acquitted.

Then, in 1957, the Little Rock Central High School crisis happened only forty miles down the road from Menifee. The president of the United States had to send federal forces in to prevent a white mob from attacking Black children who were trying to go to school.

These incidents epitomized the ever-present violence Black people lived with across the country, and especially in the Deep South. Meanwhile, the relentless oppression, intimidation, and degradation that happened every day in a thousand ways never made the news.

The 1950s was also the decade when job opportunities started to open up in cities like Philadelphia and Chicago. Large concentrations of Black people there were doing relatively well. Of course there was still racism in the north, and plenty of it. Even so, Black people could have a better quality of life, you didn't have to work the fields, or sharecrop, or deal with the conditions that existed in the south.

As soon as they could, my two oldest sisters left and moved north. First was Emogene, who married early and moved to Kansas City. Ernestine soon followed, moving to Detroit, Michigan, where she lived for the rest of her life.

In those days, Black men didn't have careers as sportscasters, but that's what Marvin aspired to be: a professional sports broadcaster. He was so good at it that he was often asked to broadcast local baseball games in bigger communities like Conway, Morrilton, and Little Rock. He got quite a reputation for that. Then Mr. Clermon Mitchell, a friend of the family who lived in Milwaukee, Wisconsin, invited Marvin to broadcast games in that city, where Negro baseball flourished. This was a thrilling opportunity for Marvin, and he went with high hopes.

Across the country, Baseball was THE sport for Black families. We didn't have professional basketball or football leagues, but there was a national baseball league for black players. So that was the thing families did. Anywhere there was a Black community like Menifee, you'd find hundreds of people at the park for a Saturday afternoon or Friday evening baseball game. The games ended when it got too dark to play because there were no lights. The sport was immensely popular and on game night, there'd be cars parked all along the road and packed into the park. There'd be makeshift food stands, usually some boards set up between trees, selling fried fish and sodas.

To Marvin's deep disappointment, nothing ever materialized from his trip to Milwaukee, which wasn't surprising. It would have taken an act of God for a Black man in the 1950s to have excelled in a profession dominated by white men. So he returned to Menifee, to a hard life of plowing, chopping, and harvesting crops for white farm owners.

CHAPTER 3

A Chance to Get Away

After graduating early from high school, Marvin decided his best opportunity for leaving the south and finding a better life would be to enlist. Although he was only 15 years old, he looked and acted older. So he told recruiters he was 18, and joined the Navy. Black men in the military in the 1950s weren't treated with anything near the same respect as white men, but Marvin knew nothing could compare to what Black men and women were experiencing daily in the south. Plus, it would give him the opportunity to travel the country and make all of us proud.

After completing basic training, Marvin was stationed in San Diego for six months. He loved it. But just when he thought he'd found his place in society, someone from Menifee reported his age to Navy officials who determined he was too young to serve, and therefore had to be discharged.

My parents believed they knew who turned Marvin in. Just like during slavery, you had Black people who got paid to recruit and deliver field workers. Transporters got paid for each worker they brought, and if they brought someone like Marvin, who was known as a very good worker, they were paid more. A Mr. Woods from the community was a transporter for some of the white property owners, and often took Marvin to the fields before he enlisted. Woods enjoyed a better-than-average lifestyle for Menifee, and my parents always used to say, "We know it was Woods who reported Marvin's age." I'm not sure how they knew, but people talked, and everyone knew Woods always made a nice bit of extra money off Marvin.

Back home, Marvin packed away his Navy uniform and pulled out the old work clothes he'd worn to the fields. I can only imagine what my brother felt going back to the miserable labor he'd so desperately tried to get away from.

After a couple of years working in the fields again, Marvin was finally of age. The military was in his blood now and he couldn't wait to get back. Menifee was a small community, and Marvin had a close-knit group of about 10 boys he'd grown up with. His closest friend, C.R. English, and six other boys from the community were enlisting, including his friends Homer and Robert Delph, Allen Powell, Elbert Heaggans, Joe Flakes, and our cousin John Ellis Green. All of them wanted to get out of the south, and there was no way Marvin was going to be left behind. This time, however, he wanted to enlist with a different branch of the military – the United States Army, where he could become a U.S. Paratrooper.

C.R. English was already stationed in Germany when he got a letter from Marvin saying he wanted to re-enlist. For the next few months C.R. heard nothing from Marvin. Then one day he was sitting in his barracks and saw the shadow of a tall Black guy standing in the doorway. He remembers looking up and thinking, "This cat looks sure looks like Marvin Williams." And it was.

Marvin had trained at Fort Campbell, Kentucky, then made his way to Munich to serve with his best friend. Years later, when I called C.R. and asked him about those days, the first thing he asked was if I was writing a book about Marvin. I could hear the emotion and relief in his voice when I said yes. Immediately, he started talking about my brother.

"Marvin did it all," C.R. told me. "There was nothing the army could throw at him that he couldn't master, physical or mental."

C.R. described Marvin as tough and "a bit of a daredevil." The idea of jumping out of planes intrigued them both. In training jumps over different parts of Germany, Marvin was always one of the first to jump, while others were forced and, in some cases, even refused to leave the plane.

In their downtime, C.R. and Marvin loved boxing, and Marvin became an excellent boxer. But his real passion in Germany was basketball. He loved to play pick-up games with his army buddies. Since there weren't many guys in their unit who stood at six feet, four inches tall, Marvin used his height to his advantage. C.R. laughed when he said he always got a kick out of watching how Marvin dominated those pick-up games.

But there was one thing C.R. wanted me to understand about my brother, one thing above all else: "Marvin was an excellent, disciplined soldier who was respected by his peers as well as his commanding officers. And he was considered a leader by all of them."

Those are C.R.'s words. Knowing how we were raised and what our parents instilled in us, I wasn't surprised to hear that he was a disciplined soldier. Discipline and hard work came easy for Marvin, it was part of our family culture. What did surprise me was C.R.'s comment about how others respected Marvin.

To be considered a leader among U.S. Paratroopers was quite an accomplishment for anyone. But for a Black man in the 1950s to be perceived as a leader in that battalion by his fellow soldiers and his commanding officers was truly impressive. Marvin had to be more than a good soldier to earn that kind of respect. He had to be exceptional.

After Marvin died, C.R. would come to Menifee at least once a year, usually around Independence Day. Whenever he came to town, he stopped by to visit Mother and Daddy. Mother always shed a few tears when she saw C.R. And on each visit, he went out of his way to see me. He called me "little Marvin." He'd come up and shake my hand, then he'd put his hands on my shoulders and say, "You look just like Marvin." That meant so much to me. I could hear the genuineness in his voice. Everyone in our family knew that C.R. and Marvin were more like brothers than friends.

* * *

After being honorably discharged from the United States Army in 1958, Marvin returned to Menifee. Not much had changed. The south was still the south, and opportunities for Black men and women were few. But our family was so excited to have him home, he was our hero!

I remember seeing Marvin in his uniform when we picked him up at a bus station in Conway. Everything about him was in order. His shirt was starched, his tie was tucked away, and his shoes were glistening from a good hard shine. I can still remember the sour apple hard candy he brought for us little ones. I was standing near my mother and when she saw Marvin, she said, "Here comes my big Sonny." She was so proud of him.

Marvin achieved something no other member of our family had, including my parents. He took such pride in wearing the uniform of the US Army. It was a symbol of accomplishment and a source of pride for everyone who wore it, but especially for young Black men from the south who longed for America's acceptance.

C.R. had been discharged months earlier and took a job with the Cook County Jail in Chicago. He reached out to Marvin several times, trying to get him to move to Chicago where jobs were plentiful and where racism, while it certainly existed, was not as overt. He could get Marvin a job with the jail system, he said, all Marvin had to do was pack his things and hit the road. Sometimes I think about how things might have been different if Marvin had accepted C.R.'s offer... who knows? The what-ifs are haunting.

But Marvin chose to stay in Menifee, near his family. I know he felt very close to my mother. And since he'd grown up hunting, fishing, and playing baseball with my father, they had a special relationship Daddy couldn't have with the girls. Maybe he felt the same sense of responsibility to our parents that I did in later years. Whatever it was, instead of leaving, he took a job painting buses with Wards Bus Manufacturing Company in Conway, six miles east of Menifee. His job was inside a building and not in a cotton field, so it was a major upgrade from field labor. Thomas Johnson, a longtime employee of the company and a close friend and relative of our family, helped him get that job.

Marvin loved his job with the bus company. It was a reliable position and the pay was substantially more than white farmers paid field hands. In addition to a secure job and higher wages, Marvin worked side-by-side with some of his high school buddies, like Robert Oliver, Robert Delph, Allen Powell and Joe Flakes. Wards was a major employer in the area and a number of people from our community worked there, so Marvin was comfortable in that environment.

Marvin was 14 years older than I was, and once in a while he'd come get my sister Donna and me and take us to see a movie at the Rialto Theater in Morrilton. As with all theaters in the south, we had to go in through a separate entryway designated "colored," then up a secluded stairway to the balcony. On one of these trips, Donna and I had found our seats when I looked up and saw Marvin at the top of the stairs, scanning the crowded balcony trying to find us. When he spotted us, he looked so relieved. Then he came down and gave each of us a quarter to buy a soda and some popcorn. Back then, twenty-five cents went a long way. To this day, I remember how worried he was that his little sister and brother wouldn't be able to buy snacks like everybody else.

Another time he took me for a ride in his car. I don't recall where we were going, but I remember being fascinated with how he shifted the gears. I was mesmerized watching him move those gears from one place to another. I can still see him smiling as he looked down at me, saying, "What's wrong?"

I wasn't the only one who adored Marvin, all his siblings did. He was the third child and the oldest male, and we all looked up to him. Through the years so many people who knew him have told me the same thing, "There was something special about Marvin." For lack of a better word, he was impressive. He had an authority about him, even before he enlisted.

I remember my mother telling us about the time she was fixing something and needed my sister Ernestine to hold a curtain rod steady. But Ernestine was having attitude issues, and each time Mother would get the rod in the right place and step away, Ernestine would shift it or drop it a little on purpose. Mother kept asking her to stop and hold it still, but she kept on doing it. Then Marvin walked in.

"Ernestine, did you not hear Mother tell you to hold that rod still?" he said calmly. And she did.

For social life, young people had to go to the nearby city of Conway. There were four places in Conway young Black men and women could gather without fear of being harassed by law enforcement, although that wasn't guaranteed. There was the movie theater on Front Street, where blacks had to enter through the rear of the building and up the staircase to the balcony; and Mountain View Park, where Blacks could play baseball; and there were two diners, the Sunset Café and the Deluxe Diner, both on Markham Street. These last two were popular gathering spots for Blacks. If you wanted to meet someone from the opposite sex, Markham Street is where you'd go. And that's where Marvin and Bonnie spent much of their time getting better acquainted.

Not long after they met, Marvin was playing a baseball game in Conway, and after the game they talked. Bonnie had heard him broadcast a game and she says that was the icing on the cake for her. After a serious courtship, they married and moved into a small, two-bedroom house on the south side of Menifee, across the railroad tracks and near the cotton fields where Marvin worked as a young boy. The house was a little rundown, but it was all he could afford at the time. I remember my parents taking us there and Donna and I would play in a tire swing he'd made for us in his front yard. I loved playing in that old swing.

Within a short time, they celebrated the birth of their son, Ricky. A few months after Ricky was born, Bonnie was pregnant again with their second child, Sharon, a baby Marvin would not live to see.

CHAPTER 4

Everything is Wrecked

The early evening of Thursday, May 5, 1960 was like any other. My father was finishing his work in the garden and my mother was in her chicken house gathering eggs when Marvin dropped by to visit, which he did most evenings after work. He quickly said hello to all of us and then made his way to the chicken house to see Mother. She greeted him with the same words she repeated every time she saw him, "Here comes my big Sonny."

That night was the Conway County Training School's high school prom. Our sister Verna was Homecoming Queen and Marvin had promised to be there. He was in a bit of a rush when he came by because he'd taken his friend Allen Powell, who was having car trouble, to Morrilton to pick up a shirt. His visit with us had to be quick because he still needed to go home and dress. Years later, Mother remembered kissing Marvin's cheek and giving him a big hug that night before he hurried home to see his family.

Bonnie was seven and half months pregnant and didn't feel like going to the prom, but she was fine with Marvin attending because our sister, Verna, was Homecoming Queen. The prom was a community tradition, and everybody would be there, including alums of the high school. Years later, Bonnie recalled that before he said goodbye that night, Marvin told her he loved her and kissed her, and then he kissed Ricky.

At home that evening, as we were finishing dinner, Daddy heard a weather report about possible tornadoes in our area. Daddy called Marvin and told him to bring Bonnie and Ricky to our Grandma Lela's house, which was near our house, so he could pick up all three of them and bring them to our house where they'd be safer in case there really was a storm. Little did Daddy know that would be one of the best decisions he'd ever make.

According to Carolyn and Verna, the prom was a great success. It was held in the gymnasium which was filled to capacity with hundreds of students and alumni. I remember Carolyn telling me how much fun they had that night, singing, dancing, and greeting old friends and classmates. Everybody was getting down to the hit music of that day. When "Goodnight Sweetheart, Goodnight" was played, Carolyn remembers Marvin coming over and asking her friend, Maggie Powell, to dance. That turned out to be the very last song of the prom, because as soon as it was over the principal made an announcement on the public address system that he needed to cancel the prom due to a tornado warning issued for the area.

This was not something hundreds of young men and women who'd waited the entire year for this event wanted to hear. One of Marvin's friends suggested they go to the Sunset Café. Marvin was reluctant, as he had to be at work the next morning. But a few of his friends convinced him to go, saying that if he'd take his car, one of them would drive while he rested on the passenger side. They told him they wouldn't be there long, so he agreed.

Later, Emma Jean Handley, who'd also danced with Marvin at the prom, remembered him bringing his car around to the gym and getting out and saying, "Any of you who want to go to Conway better come on."

Marvin had driven Allen Powell and his wife, Maggie, to the prom, so they got in the front seat with him. Then Marvin's friends Joe Flakes, Robert Oliver, and Robert Delph got in the back. Somewhere on the way to Plumerville, Joe Flakes, who'd had way too much to drink, fell sound asleep.

Marvin drove Allen and Maggie home to Plumerville before heading to Conway. Allen later recalled that they talked about Marvin coming over the next day to paint Allen's car. After dropping Allen and Maggie off, Marvin said he was tired, and asked Robert Delph to drive to Conway. Marvin moved over to the passenger side of the car and Robert Delph got behind the wheel and drove. Soon, Marvin fell asleep.

When they got to the Sunset Diner on Markham Street, Robert Delph roused Marvin who said he was too tired and would stay in the car and sleep. Joe Flakes was still passed out in the back seat. So Robert Delph and Robert Oliver got out and went into the Sunset Café, which was already full of people.

A few minutes later, our cousin John Ellis Greene was headed into the Sunset Café when he saw Marvin's car parked on the street outside, with Marvin asleep in the passenger seat. He tapped on the window to see if Marvin wanted to come in with him. Marvin sleepily told him he'd be in shortly, so John Ellis went on in, assuming Marvin would follow in a little while.

About 15 or 20 minutes later, someone came in and told Robert Delph that Marvin and Joe had been arrested. When John Ellis heard that, he went outside to see if it was true. He found Marvin's car empty, and one of Marvin's shoes lying in the street.

Our sister Verna went to the Sunset Café after the prom as well, but she has no memory of it. We have photos of her as Homecoming Queen that night, and Marvin there to see her crowned. Those were the last photos of him alive.

* * *

Back at our house in Menifee, the weather took a turn for the worse. Around 10 p.m. it really started to change. I remember the sound of the wind blowing harder and harder. I was only seven, too young to understand what tornadoes were all about. But I remember clearly how all at once everything seemed to stop. There was an eerie silence. No wind, no rain, no thunder. Just silence. Then suddenly a loud noise, like a freight train, came barreling toward us. I was in the hallway near our living room when Daddy yelled, "Lie down on the floor!" I fell on the floor, closed my eyes, and felt our home move as if it were on wheels, traveling across the ground while the walls started to come apart.

There was a roaring sound, and then everything stopped. I smelled something strange in the air, maybe gas from broken lines, I don't know. After the house stopped moving, I slowly opened my eyes but couldn't see anything because of the water running down my face. I pulled myself up from beneath all the debris and cried for my mother and father. One by one, I heard the voices of each member of our family, and then I heard my mother calling out, "Where is my baby?" I cried louder and louder and she and my father made their way to me. She grabbed me and hugged me to her and in the intermittent flashes of lightning my father saw my face and yelled, "We have to get Ronnie to the hospital... He's bleeding badly." That's when I realized that what I thought was water was actually blood from a huge gash on my forehead, which later required 40 stiches to close.

Remarkably, our 1956 four-door Chevrolet was still standing only yards from the house. The tires were flat, but none of the windows were shattered. Daddy crammed all of us into that Chevrolet – Mother, Grandma Lela, Barbara, Bonnie, Ricky, Donna, and me – and then jumped in and drove west on those flat tires until he found a neighbor to take us to the hospital.

To this day, I don't know who took us to the hospital. I wish I did. For whatever reasons, that person didn't take us to the closest hospital in Conway. Instead, he took us to the hospital in Morrilton, almost twice the distance in the opposite direction. As I think back on it, I believe it was God's hand distancing us from the most painful of our losses, which was yet to come.

Bleeding, bruised, and homeless, my family had just survived the most terrifying experience of our lives. All that we owned, and all that was left of our property, were the clothes on our backs, but we were all alive and together. The only unaccounted ones were Carolyn, Verna, and Marvin. Since they were out of the direct path of the storm, my parents assumed all their children were safe.

The hospital decided to keep me overnight to make sure the wound was closed and there were no signs of infection. I was released the next morning, Friday, May 6, and someone drove us back to Menifee. We went directly to our home to see what was left and found it completely destroyed.

That tornado was about a quarter of a mile wide and it tore through the center section of Menifee. Our house and Grandma Lela's house were directly in its path. Grandma Lela's house was literally gone, as if it had vanished; we never found a thing from it. Our home was demolished, and although we searched the site, there was not one thing we could salvage from the wreckage - no clothing, no shoes, nothing. The tornado even killed our pet dog, Bullet.

Daddy's nephew, JC McDaniel, and Thomas Johnson, a relative and the man who'd gotten Marvin the job at Wards, found us at the site and invited my parents to come stay with them. We'd have to divide the family, but since they lived across the street from each other we'd still be close. My parents agreed and JC took all the children and Bonnie and Ricky to his house. Donna and I were thrilled with the arrangement because his two youngest kids were our ages, and we were excited about having play time with our cousins.

My parents stayed behind at our homestead with Mr. Johnson. And it was there, later that afternoon, that Mother's nephew, John Ellis Greene, found them and told them Marvin was dead.

Somehow, they brought my mother back to Mr. Johnson's house, and my father and Mr. Johnson left for Conway to find out what happened.

My sister and I were outside Cousin JC's house playing when we heard a piercing scream from the Johnson's. I ran across the street to see what had happened. As I got closer I could hear Mother screaming and crying uncontrollably. I knew something was terribly wrong. I looked for Daddy, but he was nowhere to be found. Someone told me Mr. Johnson had taken him to Conway.

I couldn't understand why my mother was crying and my father wasn't there to console her. Lenora Johnson, Mr. Johnson's wife, was sitting next to Mother on the living room sofa with her arms around her, trying to comfort her. All I heard was Mother repeating over and over again, "Marvin is dead. Marvin is dead." Then all of us started to cry. I was too young to understand, all I knew was that I couldn't bear to see my mother hurting this way.

Marvin's wife Bonnie remembers going numb when she found out Marvin was dead. She was seven and half months pregnant, she and her baby boy had just survived a tornado ripping apart the house they were sheltering in, and now her husband was dead. Bonnie was only 17 years old, and her world and her life were shattered.

Our sister Carolyn was married by then, and lived nearby with her husband, Willie. Later that afternoon, Robert Flakes drove Marvin's car up to Carolyn and Willie's house. He parked it, then knocked on their door. Carolyn answered, and Robert had to tell her that Marvin was dead. She didn't believe him. She told him, "No, no he's not, there's his car." And he said, "No, I brought the car home." That's how she found out.

As news of Marvin's death started to circulate within our small community, people from all over Menifee converged on the Johnson's home. They wanted our parents to know how much they loved Marvin, that they were praying for our family, and that they felt his loss keenly, too. Seeing how much my mother was hurting, I doubt she ever remembered how many people came that day and the next.

When my father returned from Conway, his face was filled with grief. All he'd learned was that Marvin had died in the Faulkner County Jail, and his body had already been sent to the Arkansas Crime Lab in Little Rock for an autopsy. Some people he knew told him that a Coroner's Inquest had already been scheduled for the very next day. Had those people not told Daddy about the inquest, he would have missed it.

To this day, it still upsets me that no official from the City of Conway or from Faulkner County ever contacted my parents to inform them of Marvin's death. Not that day. Not the next day. Not one person, not one time.

That callous behavior didn't make sense, not even in those overtly racist times. Years later, we learned that several hours before John Ellis found my parents and told them their son was dead, officials from Faulkner County were driving all over the place, including to Menifee, to build their cover story. One of the men they talked to that day was Joe Flakes, who'd been arrested with Marvin and released that morning, and who lived near us. These officials had been right there in our small town where everyone knew what had happened to us and where we were staying. But at no time that day, as they drove all over the county finding and instructing witnesses, did any official take the time to inform my parents that their oldest son was dead.

CHAPTER 5

The Cover-up Begins

A round 9:30 on the morning of Friday, May 6, 1960, my brother Marvin Leonard Williams, age 20, died alone in a cell in the Faulkner County Jail.

When he was found hours later by the jailer, Marvin's body was lying face down on a bunk. His head was turned toward the cell door. Above his right eye was a deep gash, as well as a cut on his upper lip. The flesh around the deep gash was bruised and swollen. There was bruising across the bridge of his nose and a swollen area near his hairline. His kidneys were bruised and bleeding. The backs of his hands were bruised. On the back of Marvin's head, behind his left ear, was a wound that was four inches long and one-and-a-half inches wide where his skull had been fractured. This injury, which would have caused him unimaginable pain, was what killed Marvin.

Between 1 and 3:30 p.m. Friday afternoon, Marvin's bruised and battered body was removed from his cell and taken down the street to McNutt's Funeral Home. The owner of the funeral home, Robert A. McNutt, also happened to be the Coroner of Faulkner County. Because my brother died in a jail, an autopsy was required. But Robert McNutt ignored that protocol and did a perfunctory examination of Marvin's body. Then he arranged for Marvin's remains to be immediately embalmed.

Our cousin John Ellis lived near the Sunset Café. Sometime around midday on Friday he saw Marvin's car still parked on Markham Street, in the same spot as the night before, and he knew something was wrong – Marvin should have been bailed out by now. Alarmed, John Ellis went to the jail to check on him.

Officer Bill Langford was behind the desk when John Ellis came in. Nearby was Officer Iberg, one of the officers who'd arrested Marvin and Joe. When John Ellis asked about my brother, Langford told him that Marvin had an accident and was dead. Then he said, matter-of-factly, that Marvin's body had been taken to McNutt's Funeral Home. Stunned, John Ellis asked what happened. In response, Officer Iberg stepped forward, unsnapped his holster, and put his hand on his gun, turning so that John Ellis could clearly see what he was doing. It was an unmistakable threat. John Ellis left.

Back then, everything was segregated, including funeral homes. White funeral homes only handled white bodies, and Black funeral homes only handled Black bodies. Thrower Funeral Home, in Morrilton, routinely handled Faulkner County cases that involved a Black person's corpse. If Thrower's was full, the logical back up would be one of several black-owned funeral homes in Little Rock, which wasn't that far away.

But Marvin's body was not taken to Throwers, or any other black funeral home. It was taken to McNutt's, which was a white-only funeral home. This was unheard of.

And John Ellis knew that.

As soon as he left the jail, he rushed to McNutt's, a few blocks away, and asked at the front desk where Marvin's body was. When he was told it was already in the back, he went straight to the back room where two white men were preparing Marvin's body for embalming.

John Ellis was a formidable man, close to Marvin in height and a little stouter. Like Marvin, he had an inner strength and force of character.

"Stop! You can't do this!" he shouted at the men. "His parents don't know he's dead, they have to give permission! You're not allowed to do this, I'm going to drive to Menifee right now and tell them what you're doing!"

Remarkably, they stopped.

For a Black man's body to even be in McNutt's was completely out of the ordinary, as was the hurried order for immediate embalming. And as soon as they saw Marvin's body, these men would have known how he died. They might not have known exactly who did it, but they had to suspect the police were involved. They also knew that once a body has been embalmed, crucial information and evidence is forever lost.

So when John Ellis barged in, his threat hit home. They stopped. At 3:30 that afternoon, Marvin's body was sent from McNutt's Funeral Home to the Arkansas State Medical Examiner in Little Rock for an autopsy.

This would have been a very different book if John Ellis Greene hadn't intervened when he did. If he hadn't acted when he saw Marvin's car, if he hadn't gone straight to the jail and then rushed to McNutt's, if he hadn't had the courage to barge in and confront two white men so forcefully that they backed down. If he hadn't done all those things, then Coroner McNutt would have had my brother's body hastily embalmed. And the full truth would never have come out.

To this day, I am awed by John Ellis's courage. He loved Marvin and he protected him to the end.

CHAPTER 6

McNutt

Forced to send Marvin's body to the Arkansas State Medical Examiner, Robert McNutt made one last attempt to control the situation. He wrote the following cover letter that accompanied the body:

> "Dear sir, the above captioned, Marvin Williams, died in the Faulkner County Jail, prisoner of the City of Conway, Arkansas. He was committed about 1 am today. His home is in Menifee, Ar., where the storm struck at about the same time that he was arrested. His baby was hospitalized by the storm. [*This was a mistake. I was hospitalized. Marvin's son Ricky was fine.*] It is not believed that this man was in the storm. He was arrested for drunkenness. He had to be supported to walk. The injury on his forehead was caused by a fall at the foot of the courthouse steps on the way to the jail which is on the top floor of the courthouse. Please determine the cause of his death by autopsy and notify me as soon as possible the results of your findings so that I can file the death certificate for record." Yours truly, R.A. McNutt, Coroner of Faulkner County."

A healthy 20-year-old man is dead. No sworn statements had been taken, no inquest had been held, no autopsy had been done, but Coroner McNutt made it clear that he'd already determined the cause of Marvin's death.

Cover-ups of police brutality were familiar and frequent in the south and across America. When a Black man died suspiciously in police custody, it was easy for officials to concoct a cover story, usually one that blamed the victim in some way. Then all they had to do was find a corrupt prosecutor, judge or doctor to rubber stamp their story with official approval.

In the cover-up of Marvin's death, Coroner Robert McNutt and his perfunctory report were supposed to be that rubber stamp. But now Marvin's body was going to the State Medical Examiner in Little Rock, who would issue an autopsy report. According to standard procedure, that autopsy report would be shared at the official Coroner's Inquest into Marvin's death. And if the autopsy report became public, the truth would also be known.

So now the officials involved had a problem: How to prevent the autopsy report from becoming public? The solution they landed on was to call for an official inquest the very next day, even though it was a Saturday, and convene a sympathetic jury to find that the death was accidental. Then they'd close the case before the autopsy report came back and the truth would be buried with Marvin.

Normally, a Coroner's Inquest is a public proceeding announced in advance in the newspaper. Inquests are often scheduled weeks after the death to allow time for an autopsy to be completed, a jury to be chosen, and anyone with relevant information or any other interested party to be notified.

Of course, that's not what happened for Marvin.

The Faulkner County Prosecutor was George Hartje, Jr. In an unprecedented move, and without any public notice, Hartje called for a Coroners' Inquest into Marvin's death the next day and neither he nor Coroner McNutt notified anyone in our family. But word moved fast in the Black community. Someone let my father know about it, and the word continued to spread. It must have come as a shock to Hartje and McNutt when the inquest started and the room began to fill with Black people.

The inquest into Marvin's death convened at 1 p.m. Saturday, May 7, 1960, with the Faulkner County Prosecuting Attorney, George Hartje, Jr., and Faulkner County Coroner Robert McNutt presiding. The jury of 12 well-known white businessmen from the City of Conway included: Harold Newton, Harold Johnson, George Harton, Robert Jones, Billy Belote, E.A. Montgomery, Raymond Kordsmeier, Cecil Bell, C. Homer Jones, Herman Winters, B.S. Graddy, and Buel Womack.

The purpose of the inquest and the job of the jury was to determine if Marvin Williams' death was accidental or not. If he died accidentally, the case was closed. If foul play was involved, there'd be an investigation and probably a trial. Of course, the latter finding was unlikely, because by the time the inquest started, the Prosecuting Attorney George Hartje and Coroner Robert McNutt had both taken an active role in the cover-up of my brother's murder.

But that wasn't known for another 24 years.

PART II

The Inquest

What follows is a summary of the actual inquest based on original testimony. Portions have been edited for clarity and brevity.

CHAPTER 7

The Inquest Begins

Prosecuting Attorney George Hartje, Jr. opened the inquest into Marvin's death by addressing the jury.

Hartje: "You have been summoned together as a coroner's jury to look into the facts surrounding the death of Marvin Williams. He is a Negro who was put in jail Thursday night, and who was found dead in the jail Friday at noon. His body has been sent to Little Rock for the autopsy. The autopsy will tell us exactly what caused his death. There has been some question about foul play on the part of the police, or something to that effect, and that's particularly what you as a coroner's jury have been summoned here to look into – to see if there is any evidence of foul play on the part of the police in the death of Marvin Williams. Now his body is outside in an ambulance. It is standard procedure for the coroner's jury to view the body prior to us beginning our introduction of the evidence or prior to hearing any of the witnesses concerning his death. Now, Mr. McNutt, do you plan to leave it in the ambulance or maybe bring it… "

Coroner Robert McNutt: "At the appropriate time, or whenever we need we can bring it into the back room and the jury and those who should can view the body."

I knew the inquest transcript would be difficult to read, but Hartje's initial reference to my brother's remains as "it" spoke volumes. To these men, Marvin's body was a thing, an object of little or no value. And that's how they spoke of it, even though our father sat in front of them hearing every word, including when Hartje suggests the jurors go ahead and view Marvin's body so they can "get it over with."

The jury went into a back room, viewed Marvin's body, and was seated again.

The first witness was Marvin Iberg, one of the two City of Conway police officers who arrested Marvin. He was sworn in and Coroner McNutt asked him to tell the jury everything he knew regarding Marvin's arrest. Instead, Iberg began his testimony by recounting a completely different arrest he made earlier that night of another young Black man, Curtis Macon. Here is his complete testimony:

"Night before last at approximately 12:45 or earlier in the night, the chief and I made an arrest up here – uh – we uh – it was a young subject [Curtis Macon] who was arrested for being drunk and disturbance. We knew the subject real well and we carried him back to his house. We got – when we got back to his house his father said if we would release him to him he would keep him inside the house and he wouldn't be out anymore that night. Well, we did that and about 12:45 Harve Macon, the boy who the one it was, Harve Macon come down to the police station and said the boy got very belligerent at that time and he couldn't control him. He wanted to know if I'd go up there and get him and place him in jail, and I asked Harve to go with us and he did. We picked the boy up and placed him jail and returning Harve to his home, in front of his house there was Chevrolet car sitting in front of his house, parked on the wrong side of the street with two fellows in it and we got out to check to see what they were doing there, and we found them to be in a drunken condition and the fellow in the front seat, which was Marvin Williams – I personally tried to wake him up and was unable to and I called Mullenax to help me. We continued trying to wake him up and was unable to and we took him out of the car. We lifted him out and he was so heavy that I was unable to hold up my side and he never did say anything at all, and we let him down to the street his knees touched the street and I got a better hold under his left arm with my left hand. I got ahold the seat of his pants with my right hand so I could hold his weight up. We placed him in the back seat of the police car on the left side and went back and wakened the other subject [Joe Flakes] and he was able to make it to the police car on his own power with very little assistance, we just held him to keep him from falling, and we put him in the police car and continued on to jail. At that time there was a very bad cloud coming up in the west and then it started blowing and raining real hard when we got to the jail. But before that we, uh, I realized the condition of the one that we couldn't wake up and in my own mind I knew we would have to carry him. I radioed in to ask Langford just to leave the police station and go with us, and he did. We picked him up at the police station and went on to the jail. When we got over there Langford took the jail keys and took the boy [Flakes] out that was in the left back seat and he walked inside the courthouse on his own power. Bill [Mullenax] and I tried to wake this Williams and was still unable to and we had to partly drag him out of the police car, but uh, when we got him on the outside and the rain and cool air hit him the boy come to and stood on his own power for just a matter of seconds and I thought he was going to be all right at that time so we slackened our hold on him and he fell forward and his head struck the second step on the west side of the courthouse door steps. So we picked – we reached we tried to catch him before he hit the ground but was unable to. We picked him up and carried him on into the light and he had a small gash in his forehead, I don't remember where now, I know it was in his forehead, and he did bleed just a little. He had a light colored top coat and it didn't look too bad at that time. We took him on up to the jail, before we got there we stopped at Joe Martin's apartment and woke him up and told him that there was a storm a'coming and we took the boy on up and placed him in jail and he laid down on the bunk on his own power, we just helped him in jail and he laid down on the bunk on his own power, we just helped him to keep him from falling and that's all I know of about it. We did go back twice that night to check on him to see if he was bleeding or anything and he was not. The chief and I went up there and checked him and turned him over and he wasn't bleeding or anything and he was – he appeared to be asleep, he was snoring at that time."

Hartje: About what time was that?

Iberg: Sir I suppose it was, I don't know for sure, but it was approximately 2:30.

Hartje: Now was this the same night they had the storm at Menifee, and Guy and Greenbrier?

Iberg: Yes sir.

Hartje: And tornado?

Iberg: Yes sir.

Hartje: Where did you say the car was at the time you picked him up?

Iberg: It was parked on the wrong side of the street just almost directly in front of Harve Macon's house.

Iberg goes on to say that Marvin was in the front passenger seat and the other man, Joe Flakes, was laying down in the back seat with his feet up in the window.

Robert McNutt: Was his [Marvin's] condition such that he could even resist arrest – he was asleep when you found him?

Iberg: Yes sir. No, sir, he never said a word at any time.

Bill Mullenax, an officer with the City of Conway and the other arresting officer, testified next. If the transcript did not identify him, you'd think it was Officer Iberg all over again, their stories were so similar. Strangely, Mullenax also began by recounting the arrest of Curtis Macon. Then his story follows Iberg's closely, with one key difference: when Mullenax first mentioned the location of Marvin's car, he said it was "parked on the left," which meant it was parked on the correct side of the street. Then, stammering, he corrected himself and said it was "parked on the east side of Markham Street, just about in front of Harve Macon's house."

By the time the inquest occurred, the officers and officials involved had crafted a cover story about Marvin's death that hinged on certain key details. One of these was the location of Marvin's car. The officers had no cause to approach Marvin's car in the first place, so they created one by saying Marvin's car was illegally parked in front of Harve Macon's home, and that this had bothered Harve Macon so much that he asked the officers to check on the car.

In 1960, the police did not have to be good liars to be believed. They only had to concoct a story and stick to it. So both officers began their testimony with the same lengthy explanation of how after they'd arrested Harve Macon's son, Curtis, earlier that night, Harve asked them to check out Marvin's car.

Next to testify was officer Bill Langford, who states that he was called to escort Joe Flakes into the Courthouse and take him upstairs to a cell, leaving Iberg and Mullenax alone with Marvin in the dark parking lot. Langford also described encountering Iberg and Mullenax on the stair landing a short time later as they were bringing Marvin up to his cell.

> Hartje: Did you notice any cut or abrasion on him when they brought him up?
>
> Langford: I noticed he had some blood on the front of his shirt.
>
> Juror George Harton: Do you know whether the boys were having any trouble getting this Williams up the steps?
>
> Langford: No sir, not that I saw, sir, none whatsoever.
>
> Harton: In other words, they just assisted him?
>
> Langford: Yes sir, that's right.
>
> Hartje: Was he able to walk, or?
>
> Langford: He was walking with their assistance.
>
> Hartje: They were helping him keep his balance?
>
> Langford: Yes.

The next witness is Joe Martin, Deputy Sheriff and the Jailer for Faulkner County, whose testimony would become central in our investigation. This was the most painful testimony for me to read. It must have broken my father's heart to hear.

> Jailer Joe Martin: "Marvin Williams was put in jail around 12:45 or 1:00 o'clock a.m. somewhere in that neighborhood and Iberg and Mullenax woke me up and told me of some of the storm and they locked him up. About fifteen or ten minutes after he had been locked up, he was crying and shaking the door up there.
>
> "If you've ever been up there by them doors, them doors are loose and they're steel, shake them and it will echo plum down that hall. So I go up there and talk to him and he told me to call his dad and let him pay him out and I got to talking to him. He told me he worked for Ward Body Works and Wade Howell (Marvin's supervisor at Ward's), and that he painted and he needed to get out to go to work at 7:00 o'clock

in the morning. I told him I'd get him out at 7:00 o'clock and I said you go on over and lay down, so he went over in the corner of the cell and layed down on the bottom bunk and I never heard another word out of him.

Jailer Martin said he was then called to the nearby town of Greenbriar, where he stayed until 7 a.m., when he returned to the jail and went to see how many inmates there were. He lists five: Joe Flakes, Curtis Macon, Charles Hackney, Lou Cogbill, and Marvin Williams.

Jailer Joe Martin: "I carried breakfast to two of them and coffee to two of them. And I went around Williams, he was still asleep on the bed and he was snoring, and so I didn't go in the cell with him. I come on back down and I went back up and got my pans.

"About 9:30 or 9:00, somewhere in that neighborhood, Prosecuting Attorney George Hartje called me to bring Cogbill over here to question about a little old deal we have, and I brought him over here. I went up to get Cogbill and I looked in there and Williams was still on this bunk asleep.

At noon, the jailer said he went back to the jail to get Charles Hackney and take him to Prosecuting Attorney Hartje's office, presumably at Hartje's request.

Jailer Joe Martin: "And I went in to see Williams and wake him up or something, and his arm here was cold and I felt it and didn't feel no pulse and I felt of his neck and there wasn't none and I pulled his shirt tail out and his back was warm and I go downstairs and call the Sheriff and he had me call Mr. McNutt (the Coroner) and the doctor, and they come over to see him.

Prosecuting Attorney Hartje asks the jailer a series of questions about Marvin's position on the bunk, whether he was moving or making any sound, and Joe Martin replies that once Marvin lay down on his bunk at 1:15 or so, he never moved. At 7 a.m. he was in the same position he'd been at 1:15 a.m, and other than "snoring," Marvin had made no sound.

Marvin was lucid when he talked to the jailer around 1:15 a.m. He shared specific and accurate details about where he worked, who his manager was, and what time he needed to get to work the next day. When asked how Marvin sounded in that exchange, the jailer said, "he sounded natural," but when a juror asked if he got the impression Marvin was drunk, Jailer Martin answered, "Yes sir, he was drunk." But he never explained what gave him that impression – the smell of alcohol, slurred speech, unstable on his feet, etc. – and no one asks him.

Another juror, Robert Jones, followed up.

Jones: "Was his head bleeding the first time, Joe, when you went up there?"

Jailer Joe Martin: "I just remember a gash up here or some blood some-where on his head, I don't know, it was dry then."

If the officer's story about Marvin falling on the courthouse steps fifteen minutes earlier was correct, then that had to be some of the quickest drying blood any of us had ever seen.

Jones: "Was it a bad gash?"

Martin: "No sir, it wasn't, it looked like a little ole gash about an inch long, it looked just like a skinned place, I never paid no attention to it, I never got close to it."

Jones: "He didn't complain about it hurting?

Martin: "No, he never said a word about it."

Juror Raymond Kordsmeier: "The blood on the steps and places like that, would you know how much there was on the steps?

Martin: "I didn't notice. I didn't notice any blood on the steps and I've been up and down those steps quite a few times.

Kordsmeier: "Was there any blood in the cell other than his own?

Martin: "No sir, I don't recall any. Now I believe there's one drop in there, that's all I've seen in there.

Finally, Martin was asked who was closest to Marvin's cell. He answered, "the boy across the hall from him, and that hall's about eight feet wide. There was a boy in it."

That "boy" was Charles Hackney, who 24 years later wrote my parents about what he saw that night.

At this point, jurors have been asked to believe the following:

- Within a 30-minute time frame, Marvin went from a drunken stupor so severe that he couldn't stand, walk or communicate on his own, to standing up unassisted in his cell and explaining clearly that he worked at Wards Body Works, his supervisor's name was Wade Howell, and that he had to be at work at 7 a.m.

- Jailer Joe Martin spoke with Marvin face-to-face and barely noticed a gash on his forehead that another officer testified had bled so much it bloodied Marvin's shirt, yet the jailer was observant enough to notice "one drop of blood" somewhere in the cell.

- On the night a tornado a quarter-mile wide hit part of their city and nearby communities, Officer Iberg and Chief of Police Hensley were so concerned about a "small gash" on a black inmate's forehead that they returned twice during the busy night just to check on him.

My brother pleaded with Joe Martin to call our father because Marvin knew what was in store for him if he didn't get out of that cell. He knew, probably because Iberg told him, that they were coming back later that night to hurt him. Joe Martin promised to wake my brother at 7 a.m., but he did not. Nor did he enter the cell to wake or check on him at 9 a.m. when he brought coffee and breakfast to the other men.

CHAPTER 8

Joe Flakes

The next to testify is Joe Flakes, who was arrested with Marvin. Joe testified that he was so drunk he didn't know where he was or who was with him, and that he fell asleep in the car long before they got to Markham Street. The last person he remembered being in the car with him was his cousin Allen Powell, so he thought Allen was the person he was arrested with.

Joe described how Marvin was already in the back seat of the police car, slumped against the door with his face turned away from Joe, when Joe got in the police cruiser. During the drive to jail, Marvin did not say or do anything.

The police drove to the courthouse and told Joe to get out, and Officer Bill Langford took him upstairs and put him in a cell with Curtis Macon. Later on, the other officers brought Marvin up to a different cell.

Joe Flakes: "Sometime later in the night I heard Marvin crying, so I lay up there and listened to him and finally he quit and went to sleep. Some officer came up there the next morning and said, "We're going to wake him up so to tell him about his father." The officer never could get no sense in Marvin, so he just left. I guess about two hours after he was gone, Marvin commenced to keeping up some funny racket, and this other boy that was up there with us, what was his name?

Hartje: Macon.

Joe Flakes: "Macon, he listened along and Marvin keep on making it and he carried that on about ten, fifteen minutes I guess. Just kept on making a little funny noise, so we tried to call him and call him and never could get any answer. After awhile he just quit and the jailer came up there and went in there and tried to wake him up, and he said, "I believe this boy's dead." When he told me that I asked him to let me out to go see. I went over there with Marvin and he was dead."

Joe is asked about the sound Marvin was making.

Hartje: About how far was the cell you were in from the cell he was in?

Flakes: Oh, I guess just the wall between us.

Hartje: Could you see into his cell?

Flakes: No, I couldn't see into his cell.

Hartje: Now, you say some time during the night you heard him making some noises?

Flakes: He was crying during the night. That was in the morning he was making the noises.

Hartje: When you say he was crying, was he just sobbing like a person would cry? Or was he trying to say anything or making any… words or anything like that?

Flakes: No, he wasn't making any words, he was just crying.

Hartje: Can you estimate what time this morning you heard him making the noises? Was it after breakfast or before?

Flakes: It was after breakfast… around 9:30 I guess.

Hartje: 9:30? Now, what kind of noises would you say he was making?

Flakes: Well, he was – a little wheeze like, whing noise.

Hartje: Can you imitate that noise he was making?

Flakes: No, I can't.

Hartje: Could you try?

Flakes: No, I couldn't try.

Hartje: Well, was he making it with words like I'm doing now, or was he whistling, or --?

Flakes: It was more like a whistle. He would start real low and he'd get louder and louder.

Hartje: Was it like a man having trouble breathing or something like that?

Flakes: I guess you could call it that.

I can't tell you how difficult this was to read. They were almost certainly describing Marvin's last attempts to breathe – his death rattle. And my poor father had to sit there and listen. It must have broken his heart.

Hartje: And it wasn't until noon when you went over there that you knew it was Marvin Williams instead of Allen Powell?

Flakes: Well, I asked who it was when I went over there.

Hartje: And did you see any marks on his body around his head or anything like that? That looked like he'd received a pretty good lick?

Flakes: Yeh, he had a gash over his right eye.

Hartje: Did he have any other marks on his head or body that you saw?

Flakes: No, no more than his hand, his hand was a little bruised.

Hartje: His hand was bruised?

Flakes: His hand was bruised and uh - - he had a gash over his – I supposed it was his right eye – a gash up there, and there was some blood in his ear.

Hartje: Some blood in his ear? Did it look like it came from his ear or maybe dripped down into his ear?

Flakes: Well, it was dry. I couldn't very much tell where it came from.

Hartje: How long were you with the body… how long were you there?

Flakes: Oh, I'd say around fifteen or twenty minutes.

hartje: You make any effort to see if there was any marks on him or anything like that?

Flakes: No, he was lying face down, and then they came and got him. I didn't move him or nothing.

Hartje: You didn't move him?

Flakes: No sir.

Hartje: Could you tell whether his body was warm or cold or anything?

Flakes: It was cold, 'cause I went over there and felt his pulse and he was cold.

Juror George Harton now asks Joe if anyone had gotten into a fight or quarrel in the hours prior to Marvin's arrest. This is a line of questioning Hartje and others return to repeatedly. Joe insists he saw no one fighting that night.

Before Joe Flakes leaves the stand, George Hartje brings up the bruises on Marvin's hand again.

Hartje: … You say he appeared to have a bruised hand. How do you attribute that bruised hand?

Joe: Well. He just had a little – uh skinned place on his hand.

Hartje; Had a skinned place on his hand?

Flakes: Skinned place on his hand. Didn't amount to anything.

Hartje: Got any idea how he got that skinned place?

Flakes: No, I wouldn't know where he got it.

Hartje; Did you say that you were with him all the time at the prom or you were not with him all the time at the prom?

Flakes: Well, just off and on, both of us was there together. He didn't get beat up at the prom.

The obvious cause of Marvin's bruised hands is that he fought back against his attackers. Years later, we realized this was correct, and that he might have seriously injured one of them – a fact Hartje would have been aware of during the inquest. Through his repeated questions, Hartje was making sure Joe would not talk about Marvin fighting back at the jail.

After Joe Flakes, the next man to testify is Charles Hackney. In the letter he wrote my parents, Charles Hackney confessed that he lied on the stand during the inquest because he'd been threatened to never tell anyone that he saw and heard Marvin being beaten.

Hartje: Did you hear this fellow make any noises that night one way or another?

Charles Hackney: Yes, sir.

Hartje: Or that day? What did you hear?

Charles Hackney: Well, it, it seemed like he was crying and mostly a groan. It went on for I guess about – well, it woke me up… and I asked that boy that slept right there by me if he heard that fellow cry and he said he didn't. And I was talking to those two boys that was in there that got out this morning and they told about him crying, and I told them that I heard somebody crying up there that night. It sounded like he was in a – oh – strain or something.

Q.: How long did that last?

A.: Well, as long as I was awake there. I guess it was about fifteen or twenty minutes.

Q.: You know whether or not anybody came up there when you heard him crying?

A.: Not while I was awake they didn't.

Q.: Did you hear him rattling the doors?

A. Well, those pipes are loose back there in the back and I couldn't tell whether it was the door rattling or the pipes. I wouldn't say about that, 'cause I ain't sure.

Q.: Did you hear him making any noises this morning after the sun came up?

A. No sir.

Juror Robert Jones: Did you hear any kind of disturbance up there the other night?

A.: No more than just that racket from him.

Lou Cogbill, who also testified 25 years later that he was also threatened if he told the truth, took the stand next, saying he heard nothing, saw nothing, and knew nothing.

Then McNutt calls Harve Macon, Curtis Macon's father, who lived next door to the Sunset Cafe.

The official story depended on two critical details only Harve could confirm –that Marvin's car was illegally parked in front of his home, and that he asked the officers to check out the car. But in his testimony, Harve Macon rebuts the first point, and never says the second.

> Harve Macon: "… all I know is they [the officers] went to the car and opened the front door and this boy that was in the front seat, they tried to wake him up. Well, he didn't wake up – I don't reckon he woke up – and they pulled him, drug him out of the car and tried to stand him up and he didn't stand up. They tried to walk him to the car and he didn't walk. They picked him up and carried him to the car and put him in the back seat.
>
> Juror Homer Jones: Harve, how long had that car been parked over at your house?
>
> Harve Macon: Well, I don't know.
>
> Q.: Was it there when – when the police took your boy to jail?
>
> A.: Well, I don't remember.
>
> Q.: You don't?
>
> A.: Sure don't.
>
> Q.: But you did see the officers load both these boys in the police car?
>
> A.: That's right.
>
> Q.: You were there?
>
> A.: That's right.
>
> Q.: Did you see – did either of these boys cause the, cause the officers any trouble?
>
> A.: Sure didn't.
>
> Q.: …the one that was carried, they couldn't wake him up at all?
>
> A.: Well, he didn't – he didn't act like he woke up to me. I was standing on my porch.
>
> Q.: In other words, they more carried him rather than him getting out on his own power.
>
> A.: That's right.

Q.: And what time of night was that?

A.: Well, I would think it was somewhere around 1:00 o'clock. That's what I figured it was. It may not of been that late, or it could have been later, but that's as near as I can remember.

Coroner McNutt: Did you know either of the boys?

Harve Macon: No, I didn't know either one of them.

Hartje: ...did that car stay up there in front of your house?

Harve Macon: Well, the car was there the next morning. It wasn't in front of my house.

Hartje: But it was there close to your house wasn't it?

Harve Macon: Close to my house.

Juror Homer Jones: How close were you, Harve, when the officers took these two fellows out of this car? How close to them were you?

Harve indicates a distance in the courtroom that was about 30 feet.

Harve's porch was about 10 feet from the street. If Marvin's car was 30 feet away, then it was legally parked across the street and the officers had no cause to approach it. Furthermore, Harve lived next door to the Sunset Café and across the street from the Deluxe Café, two of the most popular weekend gathering spots for young Black men and women. There were always cars parked outside his house, near his house, and across from his house. He would have been accustomed to cars parked outside his home at night, so why Marvin's car would have bothered him was a point that was never raised during his questioning.

Instead of following up on the discrepancy in the location of Marvin's car, Hartje asked Harve if his wife was with him and if she saw anything. Harve answered no, she was not with him. Emphasizing this point, Hartje asks if Harve's wife can add anything his testimony. Harve says no, she can't. After making certain the jury heard that Harve's wife was not a witness to Marvin's arrest, and could not add anything to Harve's testimony, Hartje asks the jury if they would like her to be called. Logically, the jury declines, and Harve is dismissed.

Years later, Harve Macon's wife, Ora Macon, would testify that she was with Harve that night, and she did see Marvin and Joe arrested. She would also indicate that her husband, Harve, had probably been threatened and coached on what to say by the police.

CHAPTER 9

Marvin's friends testify

With the inmates and Harve Macon's testimony completed, Prosecuting Attorney Hartje and the jurors discuss bringing in Marvin's friend Allen Powell to testify. And that's when George Hartje casually directs a question to my father, as if Daddy were no more than a disinterested observer in the courtroom.

Hartje: Mr. Williams, have you seen Powell?

D. V. Williams: I seen him this morning.

Hartje: …This is a little bit off the record, more or less, but… what has Powell told you?

D. V. Williams: Well, it was my understanding that he said he was at Conway with them, and he knows my boy was arrested with Flakes, but that was all he knew about it.

Q.: Where was he and what was he doing when they were arrested?

A.: Well, I didn't ask him. He just came down and told me how sorry he was when he heard that the house was tore up.

Q.: What kind of a fellow is this Allen Powell?

A.: Well, as far as I know he's a pretty good youngster, I don't know anything about him.

Q.: How old is he?

A.: Oh, I guess around twenty. I've never knowed him to be in any trouble around here.

Juror B.S. Gaddy: When was the first time Powell talked to you?

D. V. Williams: It was yesterday about 7:00 o'clock. It was a little before I went –

My father is interrupted by Conway City Attorney Robert W. Henry, who apparently has been in the courtroom the whole time. Henry objects to my father testifying without being sworn in, so Daddy is sworn in and McNutt asks if the jury would like to question him.

Juror Homer Jones: I'd like to ask him some questions. Was Marvin the kind of a boy that ever got in trouble? Had he been in any trouble or was he belligerent when he got to drinking?

Here is my father, appearing at a coroner's inquest, hoping to receive justice for his dead son. His family had just survived the tornado that demolished our home, and Daddy was still wearing the same clothes he had on when the tornado struck. Even though this hearing was held in 1960, when race relations in this country were at a low, certain social behaviors like offering condolences would have, or should have been normal – especially after the double tragedies of losing a son and a home. It's notable that not a single official or juror in the room expressed any sympathy for my father. No condolences, no words of encouragement, no nothing. Basic human decency should have moved someone to say something, even if they didn't mean it, but no one did.

Instead, the next step in the strategy was to attack Marvin's character. And juror Homer Jones, whose attitude throughout the inquest is anything but impartial, is more than willing to lead the charge.

D. V. Williams: He's never been in any trouble that I know of. Before he married, he'd come home or something late, but I wouldn't have no trouble out of him.

Juror Homer Jones: Well, let me ask you this, and I know you don't like to talk about it and we don't either, but it might be important. Did he pretty well often get on these drunks or was it something that was just once and a while?

D. V. Williams: Well, not regular that I know of.

Homer Jones: Not regular? Has he ever been in jail?

D. V. Williams: Might have been.

Homer Jones: Not that you know of? And you don't know of him having any trouble with anybody else there?

D. V. Williams: Not in Menifee.

Homer Jones: Or at drinking parties or anything like that?

D. V. Williams: Not to my knowing.

I don't know how my father held his peace, but he did. Marvin was not a belligerent troublemaker, nor was he given to going on 'drunks' or attending 'drinking parties.' No one who testified suggested that he was. If Homer Jones, or any of them, had really wanted the truth as to whether Marvin had been drinking that night, all they had to do was wait for the autopsy report.

I love my father's response, "Not to my knowing." Daddy was a man of great faith, integrity, and common sense. He knew nothing bad about his son, but he also knew that when young people go to events like a high school prom and reunion, drinking may occur. Sadly, it would be 25 more years before he found out that Marvin was not drunk the night he died. In fact, Marvin had not drunk any alcohol that night at all.

Daddy went to this hearing hoping for justice, but he was forced to sit on that stand and listen as his dead son's character was attacked, and Marvin's remarkable life story was deliberately distorted. My brother was reduced from a proud veteran, hardworking husband and father, and beloved son, to a belligerent drunk, because that's what the official cover-up required him to be.

Next, Prosecuting Attorney Hartje asks my father a leading question.

Hartje: Has anybody told you that the police beat your son up, or anything like that?

D. V. Williams: Well, I heard that, and so far as knowing the truth, I don't know.

Hartje: Who was it that told you that?

D. V. Williams: Well, ah, Flake he – he didn't said whether they beat him up, but he said Marvin was in good condition when he was with him until they deposited him into jail and…

Q.: The same Flake as this in here?

A.: ...that there wasn't nothing wrong with him when they put him into jail, and they hadn't been into nothing that night.

Q.: Did Flake indicate to you that the police had maybe beat your son up?

A.: No, he didn't say that.

Q.: He didn't?

A.: No, he didn't say that.

Q.: Has anyone else indicated to you that might have been what happened?

A.: Well, I heard the rumors, but as for knowing – I don't know.

Q.: Do you know of anyone that was in a position to know, or anyone that we could call that would know something one way or another?

A.: No, I don't.

Q.: None of the people that have talked to you, you would consider accurate or knowing what they were talking about, or were they just repeating something they heard?

A.: To my way of seeing it, they's just repeating something that they heard. Not eye witnesses.

The sinister nature of this exchange cannot be overstated. Hartje is asking for the name of anyone who knew or said that Marvin was beaten to death by the police. By asking repeatedly for a name in open court, he was issuing a clear threat – to my father and to every black person in that room. His goal was not to get the truth. His goal was to find and stop whoever was telling it.

My father leaves the stand and juror George Harton asks the crowd if anyone else has heard rumors about Marvin's death. Eugene Landers, a respected teacher who knew our family, answers.

Landers: I had some students that came by mention they heard the police had done something to this boy to cause his injuries, to cause his death. ... Talking to Mrs. Kuykendall and I mentioned that I was quite surprised, I said I couldn't believe it. I was, and I am.

Juror Harton: Those Pine School children didn't call names?

Within hours of Marvin being found dead in the county jail, word of his murder had spread across the community and into the schools. Eugene Landers heard about it and couldn't believe it. His comment about his students' emotional response to the news is a glimpse into the impact Marvin's death had on the community.

> Landers: "They were quite despondent when they came back."
>
> Juror Harton: "Eugene, you can see what we are trying to do."

And in the nuanced way Black people have spoken truth to power for centuries, Eugene Landers responds:

> Landers: "Yes, I see. I understand what you are trying to do."

Eugene Landers, like every Black person in that courtroom, knew exactly what the white officials were trying to do; they were trying to cover-up a murder and silence anyone talking about it.

> Harton: If nobody can name names to us, what are we going to learn about this thing? You didn't get the names of the children that told you that?
>
> Landers: No, I didn't.
>
> Juror Homer Jones: They had just heard –
>
> Landers: Some of the people, some of the fellows who were in the jail at the time, heard this boy hollering, "Oh, stop it." That is what I was getting at.

Landers has just shared that someone who was incarcerated with Marvin that night said they heard him yell, "Oh, stop it!" as he was being beaten by the police. Anyone who knew Marvin well, especially our father, knew how much pain he had to be in to utter those words.

> Harton: There were five boys in jail that night and we have heard every one of them.
>
> Hartje: No, we haven't heard [Curtis] Macon.

Eugene Landers: That's why I can't decide – if this rumor got out, as I said to Mrs. Kyukendall, it seems that somewhere something's wrong. Nobody believes they'd have to beat Marvin if he was that drunk.

Harton: Mr. Martin said that at 7:00 the next morning, you know, after all this had transpired, there were five boys in jail and all five of those boys have been here except one and the one that's lying back there dead.

Unknown Member of the Jury: But these rumors got out.

Juror Harold Johnson: But nobody knows where it came from.

Eugene Landers: I don't know if the girls do or not.

Juror Harold Johnson: But they didn't know? They just heard it?

Eugene Landers: Yes, they said they heard it and I said, "Oh, you don't know what you're talking about," just like that. And then another one came around and mentioned it again, and I said, "Oh, just be quiet," and "You know that you're not sure." Then I went into the office and that's when we got with Mrs. Kuykendall talking about the prom and she mentioned that we have a person who is dead in jail, and… and then I found out that it was – it was here in Conway. I wouldn't think of them doing anything like that.

Juror George Harton: You heard Harve's testimony?

Landers: I've heard them all and that's why it was quite a surprise to me.

Landers leaves the stand and the next witness called is Curtis Macon, Harve Macon's son who was in jail when Marvin was killed.

Hartje: What time were you put in the jail Thursday night?

Curtis: I don't know, it was about 10:30 or 11:00 o'clock.

Hartje: 10:30 or 11:00 o'clock?

Curtis: Yeah, that's right.

This time contradicts the officer's testimony. For the cover story to work, Curtis had to be arrested around midnight. So Hartje quickly makes sure the jury hears that Curtis was drunk.

Hartje: Were you drunk that night, Curtis?

A.: Yes.

Hartje: Did you hear anything out of the ordinary all the time you were over there in the jailhouse?

A.: I was asleep.

Hartje: Well, did you hear anything after you woke up the next morning?

A.: Well, I heard some coughs… and the next thing was snoring real loud.

Hartje: Were you there when the deputy found Marvin Williams?

A.: Yeah.

Hartje: And did you go over there in the cell where Marvin was?

A.: Yes.

Hartje: Did you see any cuts or abrasions or bumps or bruises on him?

A.: No, I didn't see no cuts on his face, 'cause he was laying on his face.

Hartje: Did you see any blood over there?

A.: Well, it looked like some was running out of his mouth.

Hartje: Do you know of anything that would show evidence of the police beating him up or any brutality or anything like that on the part of the police?

A.: No.

Hartje: Have you told anybody that there was any brutality or the police beat him up or anything like that? Is that what you think happened?

A.: I don't know. I was asleep when the others got there.

And again, juror Homer Jones interjects to protect the cover story's timeline.

Juror Homer Jones: Curtis, then to the best of your knowledge you don't even remember when you were locked up, do you?

Curtis Macon: I can remember when they taken me to jail. I can remember that.

George Harton: You remember going all the way from home to jail?

A.: Yes sir.

Q.: Which one of the men arrested you, Curtis?

A.: It was Marvin Iberg.

Q.: Just the one officer?

A.: He nods affirmatively.

Q.: And your daddy went with him and you to the jail?

A. That's right.

Prosecuting Attorney George Hartje then calls Joe Flakes back to the stand, reminds him he's still under oath, and tries to get him to say that he's the one who started the rumors about the police beating Marvin.

Hartje: Now, Joe, have you said anything to Mr. Williams or have you told anybody that the police beat up Kenneth Williams – uh – Marvin Williams that night?

Joe Flakes: No, I didn't swear they beat him up.

Hartje: You didn't swear they did? Do you think that they did?

Joe Flakes: Well, I think that's what happened, 'cause there was nothing else wrong with him.

Hartje: There wasn't nothing else wrong with him? When did you see him?

Joe Flakes: I seen him, when they was taking me out of the car, in the back seat. There wasn't anything wrong with him then.

Hartje: And when did you see him next?

A.: Next time I saw him he was dead.

Hartje: And that was at 12:00 o'clock noon the next day?

Joe nodded.

Hartje: Now, Joe, you told the jury a minute ago that you didn't even know who that was in the back seat there. Are you telling the jury you looked close enough to examine him to see if there's anything wrong with him and still didn't recognize that it wasn't Allen Powell?

A.: Well… I could tell in the cell there was blood all over his shirt. He had a cut, a gash kind of up over his eye. Like he'd been hit with something. But I knowed myself he hadn't been in no fights.

Officers Iberg and Mullenax both testified that the injury on Marvin's forehead happened *after* they arrested him, but Hartje is laying the groundwork for suggesting it happened in a fight at the prom before his arrest. Of course, if that was true, then Iberg and Mullenax were lying about his fall on the steps.

Joe says again that Marvin wasn't in any fights, and the implicit threats start.

Hartje: How many people have you talked to, Joe, and mentioned the possibility or said that the police had beaten him up or something like that?

Joe Flakes: I haven't talked to anybody.

Hartje: You haven't talked to anybody? I think you just got through saying you talked to Mr. Williams, didn't you?

Joe Flakes: Yeh, I told him the word was that his son was dead and he already knew it.

Hartje: Now, Joe, did you hear anything that night or anything like that?

A.: No more than him crying at night.

Hartje: How long was it from the time they took you up there until the time they brought Marvin up there?

A.: I guess about five minutes.

Hartje: About five minutes. Did you hear him holler or anything during that period of time?

A.: No, I didn't. Sometime along in the night I hear Marvin crying.

Juror Robert Jones: If you think they beat him up, when do you think they did it? I mean, about what time?

Joe Flakes: Well, I wouldn't say that he was beat, I would say he was -- down while he was over at the courthouse.

Juror Robert Jones: Between the time - -

Joe Flakes: Between the time they carried me up and brought him up.

Anyone listening for the truth could have heard it, if they wanted to. Joe was telling the courtroom that Marvin was beaten while Iberg and Mullenax had him alone in the dark parking lot.

Juror George Harton: They didn't have any trouble with him over there where they found you all in the car?

Joe Flakes: No.

Q.: He didn't cause any trouble to nobody?

A.: No, 'cause he was already in the car when I got in there.

Q.: Do you know when they took him out of the car to go in?

A.: No, all I know is they brought him up about five or six minutes after I was put in the cell.

Apparently, juror Raymond Kordsmeier is listening, because he questions why Marvin went from being able to drive to being unable to even sit up in the back of the police car. But Hartje and McNutt interrupt him and ignore the question.

Hartje: We're particularly interested in any kind of police beating he might of gotten or anything like that. ... And evidently any talk like that is stemming from you and we'd like to know what –

Joe Flakes: Well, now I didn't swear to no beating or anything.

Coroner McNutt: Did you start the rumors?

Joe Flakes: No, I didn't start them.

Hartje: Have you been talking to folks of a possibility that the police beat him up?

Joe answers that if anybody has said that it's their own opinion, not his.

Juror Raymond Kordsmeier, still trying to understand what happened to Marvin, asks if they could have been in a car accident or if Joe saw any "blood in the car or any indication of any fight or violence taking place in the car?"

Joe: No, there wasn't. Nothing left in there but one of Marvin's shoes.

And again, the truth is in the details: No conscious man goes to jail wearing one shoe.

Then Thomas Johnson, who accompanied my father to the inquest, spoke up and said he could shed some light on the condition of the car. After being sworn in, he explains that he co-signed the note on the car with Marvin because Marvin wasn't yet 21 when he bought it. When the man they bought it from heard that Marvin was dead, he came and got the car. But before he took it, he and Thomas Johnson looked it over. The condition of the car, Thomas Johnson said, was exactly as it had been when Marvin bought it. No blood, no dents, no sign of an accident.

Juror C. Homer Jones speaks up, and again insinuates Marvin was a drunk.

Juror Homer Jones: Thomas, as far as you know, what kind of a boy was Marvin Williams? Did he get on these drunks pretty regular to your knowledge or not?

Thomas Johnson: Marvin was kind of by me like he was to his daddy. If he did, I didn't know nothing about it.

Homer Jones: You didn't know about it? And you worked with him what, five or six days a week?

Thomas Johnson: Yes sir. And he was the most mannerable boy that I've ever been around. I've made the remarks to my wife that he would mind me better than my own children. He was good to get along with and a fine painter.

Hartje: Have you heard these stories about the police beating up Marvin and things like that?

Thomas Johnson: Now I couldn't tell you, uh – directly. I've heard rumors.

Hartje: Do you know of anyone that was in a position to know anything definite about it, that we could call?

Thomas Johnson: I do not.

Juror E. A. Montgomery: You hear those rumors nearly any time they arrest anybody and put them in jail.

Hearing that, Thomas Johnson asks if he could be allowed to say something, and Hartje tells him to go ahead.

Thomas Johnson: I have never been arrested, but I've been stopped, and I've seen lots of people arrested. When the police say you drunk and you say you ain't, the next thing is a lick. It's best that you don't say anything, you just don't, unless you want to get your head... I – I like everybody, I'm a friend of humankind. I love the colored people and I love white people and I love all and the only thing I'm trying to do is to help you people. And I don't have any personal strings to pull.

Juror Homer Jones: Thomas, you've heard this testimony here haven't you? All of it?

Thomas Johnson: Yes sir.

Juror Homer Jones: One of them was completely out, the other one they aroused and he went to the car. His own testimony said these officers did not abuse him in any way. They just - - they have to be firm ... Now, the thing I am trying to clear up here is, if there is any faint suggestion that the officers mistreated this boy, why would they do it? He was completely out, he was helpless. They had to carry him. They carried him from his own car to the police car. They had to carry him up the steps and put him in the jail. I'm trying to ask you...

Thomas Johnson: Well, it doesn't seem like he offered no resistance whatever or anything. That he - -

Homer Jones: He was completely helpless. Now, I mean, why would there be any reason or any room for any abuse, is the thing I'm trying to get at?

Thomas Johnson: I'm wondering the same thing.

Once again, juror Homer Jones acts more like a prosecutor than a juror. When Thomas Johnson described how Black men arrested by the police are likely to be hit no matter what they say, Homer Jones trivialized that violence, saying the police "just have to be firm."

Throughout this inquest, the real story of Marvin's death is told by courageous Black men like Thomas Johnson. When he says if the "police say you drunk and you say you ain't, the next thing is a lick," he's telling the jury what happened to Marvin. When he, Eugene Landers, Clemen Wilson, and others say it "makes no sense" for the police to hit a man who can't defend himself, they're telling the jury that's what happened to Marvin.

But the jury wasn't listening.

CHAPTER 10

"A Delicate Balance"

At this point at least three jurors, Raymond Kordsmeier, B.S. Graddy, and George Harton, seem to have reservations about the official story, and they start to speak up.

> Juror Kordsmeier: Are we concerned with the actual responsibility or cause of death, so far as it relates to the time of his arrest and death?
>
> Coroner McNutt: The autopsy will determine the cause of death, and we have a verbal report from that only. We will have a written report next week.
>
> Juror Kordsmeier: I mean, are we interested in maybe people unknown who may have been actual witnesses?

Raymond Kordsmier seems exasperated. Here they are midways through the hearing and he wants to know why they aren't talking about the cause and time of Marvin's death? In using the term "actual witnesses," he makes it clear that he thinks there's more to the story than what the police have said. If he believed the officers' story, then he'd already heard from the "actual witnesses."

> Coroner McNutt: "Yes, if there's any way for us to determine that, we need to do that... It is the duty of the Coroner's Jury, I think, to defi-nitely place responsibility if it can be done, but we definitely want to find out, I think the purpose of this is to determine whether or not

there was foul play and if possible, to what extent the law enforcement officers were responsible for his injuries."

If Coroner McNutt felt this way, he could have suspended the inquest for one week until they got the autopsy. Hartje doesn't like where this is going, so he interrupts with a long-winded history lesson.

Hartje: "The Coroner's Jury is an archaic organ of the law. Its history dates back into very ancient time. It primarily was convened when they found somebody dead and they didn't know why. The question was then, did he die of natural causes or did he die of foul play? Back then they had no embalming system or anything we have, they found the body, the body would decompose rapidly, so they would get this jury together to look at the body to see if there was any evidence and to hear what witnesses they could find, then put him away and if there were evidence of foul play at that time an investigation would continue until such time as they could either find nothing or find someone that had done him in.

Unimpressed, Raymond Kordsmeier repeats his question, this time more bluntly.

Juror Kordsmeier: "We're not trying to find out whether the police department is responsible for the death?"

Hartje: We're trying to find out if there's any evidence of foul play. Is there any criminal responsibility for this man's death.

Juror George Harton: This evidence that's lying back there, that we just seen, can that be talked about here?

Hartje: Yes sir.

Coroner McNutt: It can be talked about. The - - all we have is the verbal telephone diagnosis.

Harton: Would there be any reason why you shouldn't tell this whole thing here what you told us back there?

Coroner McNutt: No. The state pathologist who performed the autopsy called last night and gave me this information. Dr. Fox is the man who did the work, and he says that there was a fracture of the skull in the left temple region. Epidermal Hematoma, that's a blood clot. And laceration in the front of his head. Now that's all I have here, but his written report will come next week and it will be more detailed than this, and after they have an opportunity to make a microscopic examination we'll get a detailed report weeks from now that will be pages long.

Twenty-five years later, Dr. Fox testified that he did not remember making such a call.

Juror Harton: You didn't have a verbal statement about the cause of death?

Coroner McNutt: Well, the cause of death is the...

Hartje: Blood clot in the temple region.

Juror Homer Jones: Above the left ear?

Coroner McNutt: Concussion.

Harton: Not the injury on the...

Hartje: Not the injury on the forehead.

Juror Harton: In other words the one back here (indicating behind his left ear) is the one that killed him, not the one right here (pointing to the location of the open gash on Marvin's forehead).

Coroner McNutt: That's right, the injury back here is the one that killed him.

Hartje now gives the jury his theory about what caused the four-inch fracture to the back of Marvin's skull, without referencing any medical findings to support it.

Hartje: Now there are two possibilities, either he was hit back there or instead of a concussion there is a repercussion. You hit a sudden blow to this part of your head, the brain has a tendency to move in that direction and snap back evidently, and when it snaps back it causes a concussion back here, and it's very frequent, very ordinary, for the concussion to be on the opposite side of the head from wherever the blow is. Unless there is a fracture of the skull.

71

Hartje's theory is ludicrous. Of course there was a fracture! It was four inches long and was caused by multiple forceful blows to the back of the head. Continuing to express concern and doubt, Juror George Harton says:

> Harton: This blow that we haven't heard any evidence about, I mean this concussion that we don't know too much about, is there any indication that it was caused by a separate blow? Is there any indication that there was more than one blow on that head?
>
> McNutt: Well, now, that may be one of the things that we can't find out. We want to find out if we can.
>
> Juror Kordsmeier: Did they make a report about the uh - -
>
> Juror Harton: The autopsy doesn't show that there was a second blow, or more than one blow?

To their credit, jurors Harton and Kordsmeier keep asking about a possible blow to the back of Marvin's head that Hartje and McNutt don't want to talk about. So Hartje reverts to stating that Marvin was drunk, as if that would explain a four-inch fracture in the back of his skull.

> Hartje: No, but that will come with the later report. This report says nothing about it, but the later report will show an alcohol content in the blood stream, it will show the condition of his heart and liver and various vital organs and several other things like that.

Then Robert McNutt makes this jaw-dropping statement addressed not to the jury, but to the Black men and women in the courtroom.

> Coroner McNutt: "I think that all of you folks here know why we're trying to be unusually careful in this instance, because of the delicate balance between your people and ours. We're not wanting trouble, and neither are you folks. These rumors can cause trouble, and we are trying to get at the root of this, so that it's possible to stop those rumors. It is very important to us. Conway has enjoyed a very good relationship with your people, and we want to continue it that way. Is there anything else now, is the jury ready to…

In other words, there are white people, "our people," and there are Black people, "your people." And there is a "delicate balance" between the two that is so fragile it could easily be upset by "rumors." The subtext is clear: If anyone in the Black community says white police officers killed Marvin, the white power structure will retaliate. For their own safety, Black folk better not upset that "delicate balance."

Coroner McNutt said he wanted "to get at the root of this," but that root was the systemic racism that permeated every aspect of our lives. He protected, nurtured, and was a direct beneficiary of that insidious root, a root that never seems to die, but instead keeps spreading underground, pushing up poisonous new shoots over and over again.

Hartje suggests a recess to allow them to find Allen Powell, and juror George Harton asks if they can recess until the following Saturday. This would have meant the autopsy results would be available when the inquest reconvened, so Hartje and McNutt completely ignore him.

> McNutt: Does the jury feel like it can render a good decision with the evidence that we have? Do you feel like you need the testimony of this other witness to come to a decision?

McNutt's words "good decision" were a familiar prelude to injustice for Black men and women. The officers who murdered my brother were about to get away with it, and my father had to witness the cover-up playing out before his very eyes, while his dead son lay in a back room nearby.

But just before the jury recesses, Raymond Kordsmeier raises this question:

> Juror Kordsmeier: Let's say that the autopsy comes back and says that the man was not drunk.

Thank you, Raymond Kordsmeier for this question, may God rest your soul! Hartje is not prepared for it, and as usual, responds to the question by repeating it as a question.

> Hartje: Suppose it comes back and says it was not?
>
> Juror Kordsmeier: Yes. Well, we got a man that's unconscious and not drunk. Now, that's just presupposing.
>
> McNutt: Yes.

Kordsmeier: What happens, I want to know.

Raymond Kordsmeier just described the elephant in the room: What if Marvin wasn't drunk, but was rendered unconscious while in police custody?

> McNutt: "Well, now… that's ah…"

> Hartje: "We have ample evidence before us that he was. And we got all the policeman to say he was, and we got Macon who says he was, and we got Flakes that says he'd been drinking wine and whiskey all evening. Now, I understand what your thought is, but I don't think that's one of the bridges, I don't think we're going to have to cross."

> McNutt: It would be that the man was unconscious from something else besides what he had been drinking, but that doesn't mean the police were the cause of his unconsciousness.

To be clear, there is no such "ample evidence." Neither Harve nor Curtis Macon said that Marvin was drunk. Flakes admitted to his own drinking, but did not say Marvin was drunk. The only "evidence" was lying in the back room – it was Marvin's body.

The first paragraph of Dr. Fox's report on the autopsy of Marvin Williams says, "A tattoo was present on the right forearm. This was of a parachute with "US Paratrooper" on its border." If that one piece of information had been shared with the jury, it might have changed the way they saw my brother. But Hartje and McNutt could not allow the jurors to see my brother as a man who bravely served his country, and none of my brother's remarkable life story was shared.

McNutt's response to Raymond Kordsmeier's question about what it would mean if Marvin was not drunk is as desperate as it sounds. He's throwing everything against the wall to see what sticks. It's a familiar tactic: If the truth begins to emerge, bury it in alternative facts. Sadly, it was effective, and Raymond Kordsmeier becomes hesitant to press forward on the issue of Marvin's alleged intoxication.

> Juror Kordsmeier: "Well, I'm not concerned, I mean as far as that question is concerned, it's who might have caused his unconsciousness or his ability to act at that time? Is it a fact that it was from alcohol and not from some other cause?"

Juror B. A. Montgomery: "Well, I think we need that other witness. That's who I think we need."

Juror B.S. Graddy: "Well, I don't see where it's much important to us whether he was drunk or whether he wasn't. We're trying to find out what the cause…"

Coroner McNutt: If there was foul play.

Juror B.S. Graddy: That's right, and if he was drunk, that gives nobody, the police or anybody else, any right to abuse him.

If only the jury had been able to hold on to that one clear truth that B.S. Graddy just stated: No matter what Marvin's condition, no one had the right to abuse him.

McNutt: The autopsy report will reveal the answers to your questions, but – but – that will probably, possibly in the preliminary report, possibly in the detailed report, which will come much later.

George Harton: That's something we won't have by seven o'clock?

McNutt: We won't have that by seven o'clock.

At this point the jury recesses for almost two hours.

CHAPTER 11

The Courage of Those Who Loved Him

At 7 p.m., the jury reconvened, and Allen Powell was sworn in.

> Hartje: Were you with Kenneth Williams Thursday night? Marvin
> Williams, rather, Thursday night?

This is one of numerous times that George Hartje calls Marvin the wrong name, underscoring his utter lack of respect for my brother. Allen Powell explains that Marvin took him to the laundry in Morrilton early in the evening and then the two met up again when Marvin took Allen and his wife, Maggie, to the prom with him. Hartje then asks if Marvin had been drinking. Allen hesitates and then says, "I'd say – yes, he'd been drinking." Hartje asks what they talked about in the car after the prom.

> Allen Powell: Our conversation was about painting my car. He was
> supposed to of painted my car today.

And now the same insinuating questions are directed to Allen. How much drinking did he do that night? Who was in the car with him? Was Marvin drunk or in a fight?

> Juror C. Homer Jones: Allen, what was Marvin Williams' condition
> the last time you saw him?
>
> Allen Powell: Marvin's condition the last time I saw him, I mean he
> was in good condition, 'cause he drove the car and he carried me and

my wife home and I wasn't afraid to ride with him and I wasn't afraid for my wife to be a'riding with him.

Juror C. Homer Jones: What time of night was it?

Allen Powell: I don't know exactly what time it was 'cause I don't have a watch, but it was late after the prom got out at Menifee School and I heard the prom got out about 12:00, but just exactly, I don't know.

Then a series of questions comes from Robert W. Henry, the City Attorney for the City of Conway.

Robert Henry: Now Allen, do you know of or have heard of Marvin and Joe Flakes having any trouble?

Allen: Not that I know of.

Robert Henry: Had they been friends a long time?

Allen: I think they have been. They came to school together a lot.

Robert Henry: You say you did not come to Conway that night?

Allen: No, I did not.

Robert Henry: You don't know of your own knowledge whether Marvin and Joe got any trouble?

Allen: No. Personally, I found Marvin very easy to get along with, drunk or sober, and he never did much drinking. I'd never known him to try to fight, he was easy to get along with. He would sleep most of the time when he was drinking.

It didn't take much effort in 1960 for a cover-up like this to work, but an essential step was to reduce Marvin to something less than the man he'd been. So Henry's first question implies he was a drunk who got into fights, and that there may have been an altercation between Joe and my brother, even though there was no evidence or testimony to suggest this.

Then George Hartje gets back to what he really wants to know: Who is spreading the rumors?

Hartje: What have you heard of his death?

Allen Powell: I heard that he died in jail.

Hartje: You heard that the police beat him to death?

Allen Powell: I heard that it was possible that he had been beaten while he was arrested.

Hartje: You heard that it was possible that such had happened?

Allen Powell: That's right.

Hartje: Have you run across anybody that says definitely that it did happen?

Allen: No, I didn't run across anyone who said it definitely did happen.

Hartje: Did you run across anyone who would have occasion to know that such is possible to have happened?

Allen: No.

Hartje: Did you talk to Joe Flakes?

Allen: I saw him a short while in the morning and again this afternoon.

Hartje: What did Joe say about it?

Allen: Joe said he thought that it was me in jail instead of Marvin and he was crying and he saw that it wasn't me.

Hartje: Was Marvin a pretty fast driver?

Allen: No. No. I didn't think he was.

Hartje: But if the prom was over at 12:00 o'clock and he carried you all home and the police picked him up between 12:30 and 12:45, they had to come pretty much directly to Conway, didn't they?

Allen: Well, I'm not sure what time the prom was over, and I'm not sure what time Marvin carried me to my mother-in-law's. And I couldn't be sure whether he came straight to Conway, whether he stopped, I couldn't be sure.

Robert Delph, who was in the car with Allen and Marvin and who drove to Conway, is sworn in next, and Hartje begins his questioning by again forgetting Marvin's name:

Hartje: When was the first time you saw Robert Williams – Marvin Williams that night?

Robert Delph: It was about 9:30.

The questions continue: Who was in the car? Did you have anything to drink that evening? Where did you park the car? Why did you come to Conway? On and on. In response, Robert Delph explains that when they got to the Sunset Café, he and Robert Oliver got out and went in, leaving Marvin and Joe Flakes asleep in the car.

Hartje: Where were you when the police picked these two up?

Robert Delph: I was in Son Thomas' place. [Son Thomas owned the Sunset Café.]

Hartje: Did you see the police come and pick up these boys?

Robert Delph: No, I didn't. Someone came and told us about it and I went to the door and looked and they was gone by that time.

Hartje: How come you to leave the car there all night?

Robert Delph: Well, I was afraid to move the car 'cause I was…

Hartje: Do you have the keys to the car?

Robert Delph: No, I don't.

Hartje: But you did the driving from Menifee to Conway?

Robert Delph: That's right.

Hartje: How come you to do that, was Marvin in any condition to drive?

Robert Delph: He was. He just told me he was sleepy and for me to drive.

Hartje: Was he asleep when you got here to Conway?

Robert Delph: He was.

Hartje: How long had he been asleep?

Robert Delph: I don't know exactly when he went to sleep.

Hartje: Was Joe asleep too?

Robert Delph: Yes, Joe was asleep.

A little later, juror B. S. Gaddy asks about the location of the car.

Juror Gaddy: Where did you park the car after you got to Conway?

79

Robert Delph: Across from Son Thomas' place.

And once again, the crucial detail that provided cause for the police to approach Marvin in the first place is refuted. If Robert parked the car across the street from the Sunset Café, then it wasn't in front of Harve Macon's home, and Harve Macon would not have asked the police to check it out.

Juror C. Homer Jones picks up on this.

Juror Homer Jones: That wasn't where it was when the police picked them up, was it, Robert?

Robert Delph: Yes, that's where it was. That's where I parked the car.

Hartje quickly moves the line of questioning back to Marvin's character.

Hartje: Did you all have any trouble that night one or another?

Robert Delph: No. No trouble at all.

McNutt: Was there any cause for anyone else hitting Marvin Williams with something?

"Anyone *else* hitting him with something" is a strange way for McNutt to pose his question, unless he already knew someone who had struck Marvin.

Robert Delph: No there wasn't.

Robert Henry: There was time for that to happen, wasn't there?

Robert Delph: I don't know.

Juror George Harton: Robert, tell me, how long were you down here in Conway before somebody said these boys were picked up?

Robert Delph: About fifteen minutes or so. Something like that.

Robert Delph goes on to say that he stayed in town until the rain from the tornado stopped, and then he went over to the jail to find out what happened to Marvin. But when he got there, he couldn't find anyone.

At this point, Robert Delph is told to stay in the courtroom and Joe Flakes is brought back to the stand, where he reiterates his earlier testimony, again admitting to being extremely drunk. His questioning culminates in this exchange:

Robert Henry: Do you remember testifying this afternoon that [Allen Powell and Marvin] were dressed almost exactly alike, so you just mistook the two?

Joe Flakes: Yea.

Henry: In your estimation do Marvin and Powers – Powell, look a lot alike?

Joe Flakes: Well, not exactly.

Robert Henry: And yet I believe you testified you got close enough to him to see that he was hurt?

Joe Flakes: See if he was hurt?

Robert Henry: Didn't you testify that?

Joe Flakes: You asked me if there was anything wrong with him. I say there wasn't nothing wrong with him. I didn't see nothing wrong with him when he was in the car.

This was a game that Robert Henry, and all the Robert Henrys of the world, excelled in: Discredit the Black man. Confuse the witness. Hide the truth behind a maze of distortion and lies. And then divert attention. And it worked.

Coroner McNutt: This is plenty evidence it looks like to show that they were in such condition that they hardly know what was going on.

Coroner Robert McNutt had seen my brother's body at his funeral home. He knew exactly what happened to Marvin, and he was part of the cover-up. Yet he still declares there is "plenty of evidence" that the Black men in Marvin's car were in such a drunken stupor that they did not "know what was going on."

Then, unexpectedly, Raymond Kordsmeier did what the facilitators (McNutt, Hartje, and Henry) should have done. He asked if it was possible for anyone here to come forward and say what they wanted to say.

Hartje: Oh, I don't know of any reason why they shouldn't one way or another if anybody got anything they'd like to add.

Coroner McNutt: As long as it will contribute to the evidence.

The first person to accept this invitation was Clemen Wilson, a Black man who lived less than a block away from the Sunset Café. No one in our family knew Mr. Wilson, but I would love to have met him because what he did next took amazing courage. Knowing his life could hang in the balance for challenging the white establishment, he stood before this crowd and told the truth. Once again, the Black witnesses tell the true story of what happened to Marvin.

> Clemen Wilson: "Well, I'd like to say something. Myself and Joe Woodson and Alice Nickles and also Stan's daughter, was sitting on the bench there in front of Joe Woodson's store when this boy [Curtis] first got out of jail. He came straight to us and he says to us, "Did you all hear about the law a'beating that boy to death in the jail?"
>
> We said, "Who?" and he called the boy's name and I said, "Well, I don't know him," and Alice Nickles said, "Yes, I know him, but at the same time she mistaken the boy for one that lives in Mayflower. They kept on talking about the boy and she said, "Oh, no, that boy lives in Menifee."
>
> Now this Macon boy told us that he saw this boy after he was dead. So, me, Joe, Alice, and Stan's daughter, we hadn't heard anything about it. That was along 12:00 o'clock and he told us that he saw the boy and blood was running out of the boy's ears. That was the Nigger boy told us. So we hadn't heard anything about it whatsoever until he come up there with it, and he was just out of jail."

I can only imagine what Mr. Wilson's statement did to the atmosphere in that room. Curtis Macon had testified to one thing before this jury, after saying another thing to four Black people right after he left the jail.

> Hartje: Were you here this afternoon to hear Curtis Macon's testimony?"
>
> Mr. Wilson: I was.
>
> Coroner McNutt: What's your name?
>
> Mr. Wilson: Clemen Wilson.
>
> Coroner McNutt: Speak loud enough to hear it on record.
>
> Mr. Wilson: WILSON, CLEMEN WILSON"

George Harton: Clemen, do you remember Curtis testifying that there was dry blood on his ear and that it might have come from… on his forehead there you know, and it might have come from out of his ear, already dried?

Mr. Wilson: When, this afternoon? I do remember him saying something about dry blood, yes.

Homer Jones: He hasn't been sworn in has he?

Hartje: No, he has not.

Homer Jones: I think he ought to be sworn in.

So Clemen is sworn in and McNutt tells him to repeat what he just said, which Clemen does. I would have understood if Clemen Wilson felt intimidated and kept his mouth shut. He wasn't the only one sitting outside that store who heard what Curtis Macon had to say. But he was willing to put himself at the center of this injustice. He does not waver, he does not stumble, he just speaks the truth. That is a man who deserves to be lifted up, and I do so with the greatest respect and admiration.

Juror Billie Belote: Did he say that he saw them hit this boy?

Mr. Wilson: He didn't say he saw it. He say they beat him to death. He didn't say he saw.

Belote: Did he say he had heard it?

Mr. Wilson: He told us that he heard a terrible racket 'cause Joe Woodson and I begged him to remember. Joe asked him, "Well, what did the boy do?" He said he heard the boy saying, "Oh, oh, oh." He didn't say that he saw them beat him, but he told us that they did do it. See, he heard that racket.

Juror Belote: This racket, where he hear the racket at? Outside or - - -

Mr. Wilson: No, he was in jail. He was in jail when he heard the racket.

Juror Homer Jones: That boy testified here this afternoon that he didn't hear anything.

Hartje: He said he didn't hear anything from 10:00 o'clock at night on, I think that's what he said, or 11: 00.

Although he probably didn't realize it, Hartje just repeated Curtis Macon's statement that he was already in jail two and a half hours earlier than the police said he was.

> George Harton: His daddy had him arrested, but Curtis didn't think
> he was drunk enough to be down there. Do you remember him testi-
> fying this afternoon that he didn't know anything that happened to
> Williams down there at the jail?
>
> Mr. Wilson: I most certainly did. I really did. Yes, I did.

Then comes a clear threat to Mr. Wilson from a juror the transcript describes as "unidentified." For some reason, the transcriber could not, or chose not to identify the person who made this comment.

> Unidentified: Right there (pointing at Mr. Wilson) is where it all
> started. That's where all off colored rumors start.
>
> Mr. Wilson: Now that's what I know about it. I did not know the boy,
> but some -
>
> Juror B.S. Graddy: But some of these did know the boy?
>
> Mr. Wilson: So that's all I know, but I do know the boy came straight
> to us and told us that. And there was four on the bench.
>
> Juror George Harton: Would there have been any reason why he would
> hesitate to tell us that, if he had known that?
>
> Mr. Wilson: How was that, sir?

Clemen Wilson is incredulous that Harton would ask such a question. Everyone in that courtroom knew why Curtis Macon, or any Black man, would be terrified to tell city officials that he heard white police officers beat a black man to death.

George Harton lived in Conway, Arkansas, twenty minutes west of Little Rock, where three years earlier the President of the United States had to send federal troops to prevent a white mob from attacking nine black children while they were attempt-ing to enter Little Rock Central High School. I wish I could have asked him where he was during that crisis, as the rest of the nation watched white mobs attack and beat black journalists, hurl racial epithets at innocent black children, and threaten

Black families in central Arkansas. All these abuses occurred while local law enforcement stood by and did absolutely nothing. Without federal intervention one can only imagine what history would have recorded about the Little Rock Central High School crisis.

Every Black man knew the 'system' would never accept his word over that of a white police officer, nor would it protect him from what would follow if he dared to speak up.

> George Harton: Would there have been any reason that you know of why he would have told us this afternoon, here under oath, that he didn't hear anything, that he was asleep all that time? Would he have any reason for that?
>
> Mr. Wilson: No, I don't know.

Why did George Harton spend so much time quizzing Mr. Wilson on what Curtis Macon did or did not say during his testimony, when all they had to do was bring Curtis back to explain? Juror Billie Belote had similar thoughts and asked if Curtis was still available.

Hartje could easily have sent officers to the Macon's home a couple blocks away to have them return, but he had no intention of going down that path. The Macons had said what they were instructed to say, and Hartje knew that if he brought Curtis back to the stand to answer questions they hadn't prepared him for, it could jeopardize the cover-up.

> Hartje: I don't think he is. Curtis Macon. Now, they asked me this afternoon if... if I needed them anymore and I told them no, and I don't imagine they've come back.
>
> Juror Raymond Kordsmeier: C.W., which story would you be more likely to believe? The one this afternoon or the one yesterday at noon?
>
> Mr. Wilson: Well, to tell the truth, Mr. Kordsmeier, I couldn't say either. But the way I see it, he [Curtis] had no reason for coming up to us off-handed, without anybody saying anything to him, and telling us that. It would seem more that what he said to us would be the truth, 'cause he hadn't any reason to come straight to us and tell us about that.

Kordsmeier knew Clemen Wilson well enough to call him "C.W.," and he asks him a direct question. Clemen Wilson answers courageously, telling the all-white jury and the all-white officials that he believed Curtis Macon told the truth when he said my brother was beaten to death by police officers.

Juror Homer Jones: Did he act like he was excited when he came up there and told you that?

Mr. Wilson: He didn't seem like he was. No, he did not.

McNutt: Well, you heard the testimony this afternoon that Marvin Williams was in a stupor or - - or almost unconscious when they took him out of the car, they had to support him, they had to carry him. All the testimony support that. Now, what reason would they have for striking him at all?

And here Clemen Wilson joins Eugene Landers and Thomas Johnson and Marvin's friends when he says:

Mr. Wilson: I don't see any reason. I wouldn't see any reason whatsoever for hitting a man who's helpless and can't help himself, what reason would they have? I don't see no reason.

McNutt: It doesn't seem reasonable.

Clemen Wilson sat through the entire proceedings and listened to all the testimony. He'd heard everything that was said that day. And when asked, he truthfully says his piece, while remaining humble and respectful enough to avoid the danger of being labeled "uppity," a term which most certainly would have created problems for him and his family.

McNutt: What time was he put in jail?

Mr. Wilson: Who?

McNutt: Macon.

Mr. Wilson: Oh, I don't know.

Hartje: He was put in around, between 10:00 and 11:00 pm, I think.

Once again, Hartje undermines the officer's cover story, which depends on Curtis being arrested around midnight. Even the prosecuting attorney who helped craft the story couldn't keep it straight.

So Juror Homer Jones, who seems to have made it his mission to protect the officer's cover story, reminded Hartje of where Marvin's car was supposedly parked.

And then Allen Powell raised his hand and asked to speak to the jury again.

CHAPTER 12

Allen Powell and Henry Beard

When Allen comes back to the stand, he discusses Marvin's condition, and then he tells the jury about three Black men who were beaten by the Conway police for no good reason.

> Allen Powell: I have a friend that lives in New Hope settlement. His name is Beard and he works somewhere in Conway, and a year ago this Beard got beat up down here, at the police station. I was under the understanding that one night Owens, he got beat up down here and he hadn't had a drink, and I was under the understanding that a guy by the name of Charles Brewer that lives out in the hills, got beat up down here one night."
>
> Hartje: Is that what people have told you or do you know anything about it?
>
> Allen Powell: Brewer told me out of his own mouth that he got beat up. Owens told me out of his own mouth that he got beat up, and so did this other boy. Beard and Brewer, they were just telling me that today and, in fact, it hasn't been an hour ago, before this court started, Beard was telling me about himself. Now how true I don't know, but this is something they've told me.

Only 48 hours earlier, Allen was with his good friend Marvin. Now Marvin's battered body was lying in the next room. Allen had had enough. In a hostile environment filled with contempt and disdain for Black men, he wanted the jury to know that officers within the Conway Police Department had a history of beating Black men, and he named three actual victims.

After hearing Allen's testimony, these alleged victims should have been called to testify. But they were not. Instead, McNutt's next question shows what Black people were up against: No matter what a white officer does to you, you must have deserved it.

> McNutt: What was the reason that they got beat up, were they resisting arrest or what?
>
> Allen: I don't know the reason, but I hear Owens say that he passed a car on the hill and the police asked was he drunk and he said no. He said they hit and kneed him onto the floor, and he got up again and they asked him was he drunk and he said no. Now that was the reason I heard. Now the reason that Brewer was telling me about, he said he was sitting in his car and the police came up and got him and asked if he was drunk. He told them no, he wasn't drunk but he'd been drinking. He said they asked him again and he told them no but that he'd been drinking and one of the police, I don't know who, said "Well that makes me a liar." And Brewer said "No, it don't make you a liar," and he said the police hit him in the mouth with a flashlight. He asked the police why he did it or something to that effect, and then him and the police tied up together in the car. Two more police came up and he say he jumped out to run then, but they halt him and he stopped. That was the understanding I had from Brewer and that was the understanding I had from this other boy. Now Beard here, I don't know what - -
>
> George Harton: Do you know the names of the officers that beat up these two boys?
>
> Allen: No, I don't. I don't know any officer on the Conway Police force.
>
> Harton: You didn't hear their names called? The other boys didn't ever know their names?
>
> Allen: I don't know whether they called their names or not, they said it was the police, that's all.
>
> Harton: You know whether it was state policemen or Conway Police?

Allen: I would think it was Conway police because they was speaking about being in the city at the time, but I heard no names. I don't know.

Juror Homer Jones: What was the reason, if all these things happened, would there have been any reason that they wouldn't make a complaint? If they were being treated in that manner without any reason for it? Do any of them drink?

Once again, a white man wants a Black man to explain why Black victims of police brutality would not file complaints with the police who brutalized them. Any Black man or woman who endured the 1950s understood that to sign a complaint against a white person in authority, particularly police officers, was signing your own death certificate. Everyone in that courtroom knew police departments in the south operated with absolute impunity in how they treated the Black community. When were white youth, sober or drunk, stopped by police officers without cause, beaten with flashlights and blackjacks, or harassed on a daily basis? Never.

These twelve men took for granted the privileges white men and women enjoyed. The question was an empty one, to answer it truthfully would have endangered Allen and enraged every white man in that courtroom. And Homer Jones knew that.

Allen: No, I don't know why they didn't make a complaint or why there was no complaint made. Like I say, I don't know whether they was drunk or not. But all the same, I know what they told me out of their mouth and I know about one particular boy who lives in Plumerville who I was telling about, and I very seldom ever see him take a drink. That's why he was talking about it, because he said he hadn't had a drink.

Juror Robert Jones: Well, what's your opinion about it? Do you think the police beat Marvin up?

Allen Powell: I have no way of knowing.

Juror Robert Jones: I mean your opinion.

Allen: My opinion, the way I heard of Marvin's condition, I think that they did.

Robert Jones: Why would they beat him up and not lay a hand on Flake?

Allen: Well, the way I understand it, and the way Flake told me today, I asked him how could they beat Marvin and didn't beat you? He said, "I had vomit" and "I was sober than Marvin." And he said, 'I was roughed up a little bit, but the police didn't hit me."

Robert Jones: Well, if Marvin was out, why should they – he wasn't resisting them?

Allen: Well, in my opinion they didn't know he was out. I would think they was trying to sober him up. They may have thought Marvin was just faking or something, and they beat him up.

Hartje is not pleased with this line of questioning nor with Allen Powell's responses. He reverts to attacking Joe Flakes' credibility.

Hartje: How much confidence would you put in a man's statement who drove from Menifee to Conway with two men and didn't know it, and thought another man was in the car who had gotten out in Menifee, and from his own statement had considerable to drink? Do you think that man is worthy of belief?

Allen Powell: By me living in the community with most of these boys and being raised up with most of them, I'd say under the circumstances some of the boys, they may be confused 'cause they was drinking. Like some of the boys, they didn't care who they came to Conway with. They didn't care who else was in the car with them, and I can see their point because the same night I didn't care who else was in the car with me and my wife, cause I didn't think I was coming to Conway. I may would have come to Conway if Marvin had asked me to come. But instead of Marvin asking me like usually he do, when I got out of the car he said, "Allen, you going to Conway?" And I said, "No, I'm going to stay at home with my wife tonight." And he says, "I think that's the right thing for you to do since you got your wife, to stay at home with her." And he said to me, "Allen, be careful," like that. Then he says it again, and I opened the door to the house and my wife had already gone in, and he called me again and he said "Allen, be careful," And I say, "Okay, Marvin."

Coroner McNutt: Why would he caution you so, over and over?

Allen: I don't know. In my opinion, when he cautioned me to be careful, he knew what was about to happen to him.

Montgomery: How did he know what was going to happen to him?

Allen: I mean, you don't have to know what's going to happen, you get those feelings sometimes that things are not right.

As a man of faith, I believe God speaks to us in many different ways. Like Allen, I believe on the last night of his life Marvin had a premonition of what was to come. We don't have to have all the specifics to listen to that "inner voice." Marvin's caution to his friend was prompted by what his inner voice was saying to him on the night of his death.

Harton: He was a little tight? Marvin. We had some testimony he had somebody to drive.

Harton is asking if Marvin didn't want to drive because he was drunk.

Allen: Well, I have been with Marvin a lot. Marvin don't like to drive too well, especially this car, 'cause it was hard to manage. I was with him a lot and he was awful nice about letting other boys drive his car, 'cause he just didn't like to drive. Most of the time, when he had someone else in the car that could drive, he would let them.

Montgomery: Was you with Marvin before the prom?

Allen: For a while.

Montgomery: Early in the evening at Delph's house?

Allen: No, not at Delph's. Me, his wife and my wife, his baby and my two babies, we all were at my mother-in-law's early in the evening.

Montgomery assumed, as Joe Flakes had in his earlier testimony, that Marvin was among those who gathered at Homer Delph's house to drink wine and whiskey before the prom. But Allen was at the gathering and said, "no I don't remember Marvin being there because early in the evening when I was at Delph's house, I don't think Marvin was off of work at that time." Robert Delph, Homer Delph's brother who was at that gathering, also testified that he did not meet up with Marvin until he arrived at the prom around 9:30 p.m.

George Harton: Did you go straight from there to the prom?

Allen: No. Marvin went home to get dressed early and I went home to get dressed.

Homer Jones: Several of these witnesses here have testified that they was pretty well oiled up. Was there any trouble up there at the prom?

Allen: I didn't see any trouble at the prom. In fact, this is the first prom that I've ever been to and didn't see any trouble.

Homer Jones: You didn't see it if there was?

Allen: I didn't see any trouble.

Homer Jones is sowing doubt by suggesting that Marvin got his injuries in a fight at the prom. But why? Both arresting officers testified Marvin sustained his injuries during a fall at the Faulkner County Courthouse. The one rules out the other: either it was the fall on the courthouse steps, or the new theory that Marvin was injured in a fight nobody knew anything about.

Allen's testimony was rich with information, including a detailed accounting of what he and my brother did in the hours leading up to Marvin's death. Looking closer at it, I realized how much of a "giver" my brother was. During his final hours on this earth, Marvin had done a lot for his family and his friends. It was as if he'd written a "to do list" he needed to complete before leaving us for the last time.

Here are my brother's last movements on Thursday, May 5, 1960:

- 3 p.m. – He finishes his shift at the Ward Bus Manufacturing Company in Conway.

- 3:30 – 4:00 p.m. – He arrives at his mother-in-law's home in Conway to pick up his pregnant wife, Bonnie, and their fourteen-month-old son, Ricky, and take them home.

- 4:00 – 5:00 p.m. – While driving to their home in Menifee, Marvin was stopped by Allen, who tells him he's having car trouble and asks if Marvin will take him to Morrilton to pick up a shirt from the laundry for the prom. Marvin agrees, and drops Bonnie and Ricky off at Allen's mother-in-law's home to wait with Allen's wife while he and Allen go to Morrilton.

- 5:00 – 6:30 p.m. – Marvin drives Allen to Morrilton to pick up a shirt. Then Marvin and Allen return to Allen's mother-in-law's, and Marvin picks up Bonnie and Ricky and heads home.

- 6:30 – 6:45 p.m. – Marvin drops off his family at their home in Menifee, and then drives to our house.

- 6:45 – 7:15 p.m. – Marvin comes by our home, as was his custom, embraces my mother, and says hello to the rest of us. Then he goes back to his house. (Before Mother passed away, she often talked about her last visit with Marvin. She specifically talked about the softness of his skin when she kissed him on the cheek for the last time).

- 7:15 – 7:45 p.m. – Marvin goes home to get cleaned up and dress for the prom.

- 7:45 – 8:00 p.m. – Because of a tornado warning, Marvin takes his family to Grandma Lela's house.

- 8:00 – 9:00 – Marvin drives back to Plumerville to pick up Allen and Maggie Powell to take them to the prom, then drives to the prom.

- 9:00 p.m. – Marvin arrives at the Menifee prom.

- 11:30 – 11:45 p.m. – The prom at Menifee is stopped early due to a tornado warning issued for the area. His friends ask Marvin to take them to Conway, and he reluctantly agrees.

- 11:45 – 12:15 p.m. – Marvin drives Allen Powell and his wife home to Plumerville and drops them off. Marvin asks Robert Delph to drive his car to Conway while he rests. Marvin falls asleep and Robert Delph drives to Markham Street in Conway.

- 12:15 – 12:30 a.m. – They arrive on Markham Street and park across from the Sunset Cafe. Marvin says he will stay in the car and sleep while Robert Delph and Robert Oliver go inside.

On the last night of his life, Marvin was doing what he was known to do – spending time with his family and helping his friends.

Next, Allen is asked repeatedly why Joe Flakes would tell him the police "roughed him up a little bit," while testifying to the jury that the police had treated him nice.

Allen Powell: Only explanation I would figure is that by him knowing me he would tell me that, 'cause he knows I'm not going to bring any harm to him.

B.S. Graddy: That's the statement we made here this afternoon. We're not trying any of you people on anything you've done. That's none of our business. We're trying to find out what has happened to a friend of yours, and if there was any trouble or anything of that kind, well, that's what we're trying to find out. And if you were drunk, that's between you and the law... but if you know, or any of the rest of you people in here have anything definite on what might have happened to this boy that was killed, well, we'd like to know about it to try to keep it from happening anymore. Do you know anything definite about it? That's what we'd like to find out.

Note the tone behind these offensive words. "We're not trying YOU PEOPLE on anything you've done." Incredibly, Allen just gave the jury the names of three black men who were beaten by the Conway police, the same police department that arrested Marvin. But the jury did not want to hear from any of those men Allen named, not even the one who was present at this hearing. When B.S. Graddy refers to my brother as "this boy that was killed" instead of "this boy who had the accident" he's revealing what he knows to be "definite." He knew, as they all knew, that murder was the truth they were sworn to find but would never accept.

Undeterred, Allen continued to defend my brother's character.

Allen: Well, like I said, I don't know anything definite. There's a difference between being drunk and drinking.

B.S. Graddy: That's true. That's true.

Allen: I don't know anything definite, 'cause I wasn't here and I didn't go to jail with the boy. When I left the boy he seemed happy and everything was normal. I expected to see him the next day, talking about how he enjoyed the prom. In fact, I was supposed to see him the next day 'cause he was supposed to have painted my car today. I was supposed to bring my car down to Walker's this morning because we had a game scheduled to play over at North Little Rock and I wanted my car painted for the game."

And with that final description of the day my brother should have had, a day he would have spent doing a favor for his good friend instead of lying bruised and broken and dead, with that final memory they never shared, Allen had given Marvin and our family all he had. Allen truly honored his friend that day. I know my brother would have been proud of him.

> Hartje: Now, have you told this coroner's jury everything you know that's pertinent to this Marvin Williams? Have you told them everything you know from your own knowledge and everything like that?
>
> Allen: I told them everything that I thought I know and everything that I have heard concerning Marvin Williams.

Once again, Hartje says, "this Marvin Williams," as if describing an object rather than a human being. Hartje was angry with Allen's testimony and his attempts to humanize my brother. He and his associates viewed Marvin's death and any attention it received as something that contaminated their pure city, and it was their responsibility to clean it up so they could return to business as usual.

But there was little Hartje could do to silence the sound of Marvin's blood crying from that back room where his body lay. Then, again, the unexpected happened: A voice from the back of the room said, "I would like to say something."

The voice belonged to Henry Beard, one of the three men Allen Powell testified were beaten by Conway police. Hartje and his friends could not ignore Beard's raised hand, and he is sworn in.

Henry Beard was an unwelcome surprise for George Hartje and Robert McNutt. A high school baseball champion and veteran of the Korean War, Henry Beard was a local celebrity who played in the Negro Baseball League. As a catcher with the renowned Kansas City Monarchs, he caught for the great pitcher, Satchel Page. Every person in that room, including all the jurors, knew who Henry Beard was. Perhaps this was why Henry Beard was allowed to give such detailed testimony, including a description of the weapon with which Marvin was probably killed.

> Beard: "Powell testified a moment or two ago that the Macon boy told him the police beat this boy to death. Macon told me the same thing. I was kind of hurt about it, because they beat me up once before, and it really hurt me cause the kid was a nice boy. He was a real nice kid. He wouldn't hurt anybody. He might have got off the wrong tract once

and awhile when he was pretty tight, I'm not doubting that, but he was a wonderful kid and I don't believe whatever the two officers who roughed him up and killed him said… because he wouldn't do anything like that. I'd known him personally. We played basketball against each other and we were what you might say pretty good proteges. But when they told me about it, it really hurt me. I couldn't tell you how it hurt me, because most people wouldn't understand. You see, I'm an athlete and whatever hurts me it hurts me in a special place."

Homer Jones: "What did you get beat up for?"

Throughout this proceeding, Homer Jones drives the police narrative more than any other juror. Not only does he support the cover story, he knows the details of it better than the officials who helped devise it. He repeatedly pushes witnesses to name anyone who might be "starting rumors," and more than once he makes it clear, as he does here, that police beatings of Black men must be the victims' fault.

Maybe Homer didn't have the capacity to understand that by asking this question, he was acknowledging that police beatings happened regularly. Or maybe he didn't care. He expresses no outrage, no concern, no anything. He doesn't even question Mr. Beard's truthfulness. He just casually says to him, "Why did you get beat up?"

Beard: I'll tell you what happened to me. I was down across the bridge one night coming towards Conway, and the boy who was driving was going about 55 or 60 miles an hour. So this police, he was state police, his name's Stewart. So he told me stop and he says, "You boys was rushing it pretty fast." I said, "We slowed down before we got over the speed limit." He says, "Whichever the same, you was rushing it pretty fast and we got to go to the police headquarters in Conway." So he asked this boy who was driving, Troy Perkins, how fast he was going, and Troy says, "Well, I was going about 55 or 60, I try to stay under the speed limit." The state police, he say, "Well, I know the police, the cops," that's the way he said it, "I'm going to tell you the facts. They're pretty hot between here and Mayflower. So around Plumerville, I'd try to keep it within the speed limit." So Troy says, "I'll try and keep it within the speed limit." So the state policeman says, "We'll carry you over to the police headquarters."

So we got over there, and the police, Jordon, asked me, "How fast were you going Henry?" And I says, "Oh, we was going about 55 or 60. He lives right west of me, and he wouldn't go over the speed limit." And then Jordon says, "I don't want to call you…" Can I quote what he said? Am I free to say this?

Hartje: Yes, you can. If he just wants to get it off his chest or something like that.

McNutt: It's far removed from what we are doing here.

Beard: Yeh, you know, this leads up to this case.

Hartje: Well…

Beard: So Jordon told me, "How fast was he going?" And I say, "55 or 60," and he says, "Henry, you a damn liar. I'm going to whip your ass if you don't tell how fast he was doing." And so, I'm just a human being, see, and you only live for long, so I told him, "I'll tell you how fast he was going, but don't jump on me, I haven't done anything." And he says, "You don't tell a damn lie no more. If you do I'll whip your head."

So I said, "Well, it's been whipped before, you won't get no cherry." That's what I told him. So he tells me, "I'm going to carry your ass to jail. You're a smart Nigger." That's the very words he told me. I had two years on one of the best police forces in the world, and I know the law from the word to stop, see. I don't bother anybody, but he told me, he says, "I'm gonna whip yo' damn head. You're a smart Nigger."

Homer Jones: Henry - - -

Beard: And so I said, "Well, you don't get no cherry."

Homer Jones: Henry, what did he hit you with?

Beard: A blackjack. I'll tell you the model. It's a A-32, that's the way the Army describes it. A short model - a little short one. It's one of the shorter ones. It has a inside core. It's leather, with a inside core of rubber around the wood with a small wood sponge.

Billie Belote: Now, this was a state trooper do this?

Beard: No. This guy Jordon did this. The state trooper told Jordon, "He's just drunk, he don't know what he's doing. Don't bother him like that." The state trooper, he was nice. He held up for me. He said, "Just carry him to jail." Now I really wasn't drunk, but the state trooper thought I wasn't myself.

Juror Billie Belote: Well, how does this tie in with this case we're talking about today?

Beard: Only thing I'm interested in is justice. Like I told this man here, that doesn't tie in with this case none whatsoever. The only thing that I know that would tie in with this case is what the Macon boy told me – that the police killed this kid. That they beat him to death. And he told me the same thing that he told Powell.

George Harton: Did he tell you he saw them do it?

Beard: Well, he told me that when the Williams boy was coming to jail he thought he heard him hollerin.

B.S. Graddy: When he was coming to jail?

Beard: That's right.

In his testimony, Henry Beard does three remarkable things:

- He testifies that Curtis Macon told him the police beat Marvin to death.

- He gives the serial number and description of a type of blackjack similar to the weapon that killed Marvin.

- He described his own beating by a Conway police officer who used this model of blackjack, making it clear that it was carried and used in this way by the Conway police.

- He provided the name of an Arkansas State Trooper who was a witness to his beating.

And he did all this knowing the danger he could be putting himself in.

Beard's testimony coming after all the others should have been enough to change the course of the inquest. It should at least have convinced these twelve men to wait for the autopsy report before coming to a decision.

But it wasn't.

How could the jurors not see the nexus between my brother's death and Beard's beating? The only difference between the two cases was that one man died and the other lived to tell what happened to him. The dots connecting these two cases rested solely within the city police.

McNutt had heard enough from Henry Beard, and he goes on the attack. This is the moment I've been waiting for. It was always there hiding beneath the surface, but I was surprised McNutt would verbalize it on the record.

> Coroner McNutt: Now let me tell you something. The police are, whether you believe it or not, the police are our friends.
>
> Beard: That's right. I like to think that.
>
> McNutt: Now listen, I was stopped by a state trooper one time when I was starting on a vacation, just this side of Menifee, and I was going a little bit too fast. And a state trooper whissed right around us and my wife and I were talking about how he was exceeding the speed limit, and then we wondered what would happen if headquarters knew he was driving that fast. It wasn't long until we run onto a car that he was after and he had pulled him over and stopped him. Well then, we slowed down and went around and – innocent like, and then we wondered how he'd go about stopping someone. Well, it wasn't long until he stopped us next.

"Now let me tell you something" was McNutt's way of letting Beard know he was sick and tired of his testimony. Beard had crossed the line and hit close to home, and McNutt needed to put him in his place. He wanted everyone to know that the behavior of these racist, abusive officers would be ignored because, after all, they gave tickets to white people, too. Most importantly, he wanted it known that the police were his friends. He worked with them, went to church with them, and socialized with them.

And sometimes, he even covered up crimes for them.

McNutt's lame story about a speeding ticket he got from a state policeman while traveling in Western Arkansas was the true diversion. It had no relevance to the abuses Black families were experiencing at the hands of police officers employed by the City of Conway. For him to equate getting a speeding ticket with Beard getting slammed in the face with a blackjack or my brother being beaten to death was unconscionable. But then, as I've reminded myself so often, these men had no consciences.

Beard's response to McNutt's statement was spot on –

Beard: I have no worries about this state policeman. He was very nice, he even went to an extreme to help me, see. Because the city police they were really roughing me up. They were giving me a hard time. He asked them to stop.

Hartje: Mr. McNutt, may I suggest this.

McNutt: Alright.

Hartje: I don't know if the rest of them got a chance to eat supper or not, but I didn't, and Henry hasn't got anything that's pertinent to this hearing.

Beard: No, only thing I have is what I say about what Curtis Macon told me.

Hartje: I've heard about it all my life, and if you don't know anything pertinent to this particular issue, and the rest of you out there, if you don't know anything pertinent to this particular issue, don't speak up. If you know anything about Marvin Williams and his particular episode, let us hear about it. But, Henry, take your seat back over there now, and let's proceed with this particular hearing right here.

Beard just testified under oath that Curtis Macon told him the police beat Marvin in the jail and he heard Marvin screaming in pain. Nothing could be more relevant to Marvin's case, but Hartje dismisses Beard's testimony as not "pertinent to this particular issue."

Apparently, a critical mass of African Americans attended the inquest. Otherwise, Hartje would not have said, "And the rest of you out there." It gives me some comfort to know our father was not alone that day, and that he was surrounded by Black men and women who showed up to offer their support to our family and to bear witness to the travesty of the proceedings. Though they were powerless against this injustice, their presence spoke silently the words which have become a rallying cry for Black men and women today: Black lives matter!

Hartje knew no one would question his tactics. His dismissive "I've heard about it all of my life" was a message to every black person in attendance that no matter what these police officers may have done to them, he did not care. He was sick and tired of hearing Black people moan and groan about police brutality. As his friend and co-conspirator Robert McNutt said, the police officers "are friends of ours." No way in hell was he going to prosecute them, no matter what they might have done.

Of course, if Hartje "had heard about it all of his life," that should have sent a message to this jury about the extent to which these abuses were occurring, but it did not move them. To him, my brother's death was an 'episode.' It was "his particular episode."

For a long time, this term just would not leave me. "His episode" suggests that Marvin in some way contributed to his own demise, it was "his." The word trivialized the brutality my brother endured. This was the first time I heard someone describe a murder as an episode, a word typically associated with a story or TV show, rather than a murder, a word that allows greater flexibility to present alternative facts and direct the jury's attention away from the police.

What Prosecuting Attorney George Hartje, Jr. did not know was that God had archived this "episode" for future viewing.

> McNutt: We have no more witnesses so, if the jury is ready, we'll go into session and see what your verdict is. We will need to have the room cleared and let the jury be here alone.
>
> Juror George Harton: What about Oliver? What about Oliver, he might - -
>
> Juror B.S. Graddy: He's not available, is he?
>
> Hartje: He's not available and he was in the café with Delph. He went in with him and stayed with him.

Then Homer Jones makes one last attempt to bring back the person he now believes is "spreading rumors" about what the police did to Marvin.

> Juror Homer Jones: I wonder if during the time we're back here, if it'd be possible to locate this Macon boy that made this testimony here and then we've got...
>
> Hartje (to Joe Martin): Reckon you can run him down?
>
> Joe Martin: He shouldn't be too hard to find. We'll have him back, I think.

And that is where the transcript ends. Two witnesses testified under oath that Curtis Macon told them the police bludgeoned my brother to death and that he heard Marvin cry out in pain. But Curtis Macon, who lived only a few blocks away, was never called back to the stand.

The courtroom is cleared, and the jury deliberates, and then comes to a decision: Marvin Williams died from a concussion, and "testimony under oath did not reveal any foul play."

All twelve jurors signed the statement.

Here are the last entries in the transcript of the Coroner's Inquest of May 7, 1960:

"All persons other than the coroner and the Coroner's Jury thereupon retired from the hearing room and the jury thereupon deliberated upon its decision. Following such deliberation, the coroner called said hearing to order and the following proceedings were had."

By Robert McNutt: "Coroner's Inquisition, State of Arkansas, County of Faulkner. An inquisition taken the 7th day of May, 1960 at Conway, Arkansas in said County of Faulkner, by Robert A. McNutt, Coroner of said County upon the dead body of Marvin Williams, Negro male, aged 21, of Menifee, Conway County, Arkansas, says that said Marvin Williams came to his death by concussion of the brain as revealed by autopsy done by the State Pathologist. Testimony under oath at a Coroner's Inquest did not reveal any foul play from the time of his arrest until the time of his death. The following jurors signed this statement: C. Homer Jones, E.A. Montgomery, B.S. Graddy, Harve Newton, Billie F. Belote, Raymond Kordsmeier, Cecil Bell, Herman Winters, Buel Womack, George G. Harton, Robert E. Jones, Harold Johnson.

In testimony whereof the said Coroner has hereunto set his hand the day and year aforesaid.

R. A. McNutt, Coroner

BY ROBERT W. HENRY:

The foregoing ten records, being both sides therof, compose the entire transcript of this inquisition. This shall be preserved by Robert W. Henry, City Attorney for the City of Conway.

CHAPTER 13

My Summary

What was going through the minds of these twelve jurors as they waited to sign a document they had to know was a lie? Did they consider that signing it would make them complicit in the coverup? Did the few who expressed doubts finally decide to just go along, even though they knew it was not the whole truth? Or did they just not care?

Only God knows.

As I wondered about this, my mind took me to the word of God, to the book of Genesis, chapter 18. Abraham is pleading to the Lord on behalf of the cities of Sodom and Gomorrah, cities known for sinfulness. The Lord was planning to destroy these two cities, but Abraham intervenes and asks the Lord this question: "Will thou also destroy the righteous with the wicked?" After a series of exchanges between Abraham and the Lord, the Lord's final response is, "I will not destroy this city if you can find me 10 righteous men." (Gen 18:32.).

Twelve men signed off on this document. Where was that one righteous man? That man of courage who only had to insist on waiting one week for the autopsy report? That man who was willing to say, "I will stand for what is right in the eyes of God, even if it means I stand alone."

Several jurors raised challenging questions during the proceeding. Their questions were dodged with pompous words, subsumed in a blame-the-victim theory, or simply ignored. Several jurors recognized that some testimony disputed critical details of the cover-up. A few may have known the truth. But in the end, all twelve men set aside their consciences and preserved the status quo. By signing they supported the system that held their world in place.

The transcript they signed states that my brother's death was caused by "concussion of the brain as revealed by autopsy done by State Pathologist." But the jury did not see the autopsy report, because McNutt and Hartje said it was unavailable and might take weeks to be completed.

In fact, the autopsy was already completed. It is dated May 6, 1960, the day Marvin died and the day *before* the hearing was held. If jurors had been allowed to see it, they would have known that it stated the cause of Marvin's death was a massive fracture to the base of his skull.

These men knew what they were doing when they signed this document, just as they knew that the normal process for scheduling an inquest had been ignored for a reason. Nothing about this inquest was normal, it was rushed, it was held on a Saturday, it did not include the autopsy report. None of the men involved in this case ever thought the truth of my brother's death would come out. But the Gospel of Luke tells us, "For nothing is secret, that shall not be made manifest; neither anything hid, that shall not be known and come abroad." (Luke 8:17).

The tenor of the times was to sweep these "episodes" under the rug as quickly as possible and return to business as usual, as if nothing had happened. After all, it was 1960, and no one who had any power to change the outcome cared that a Black man was beaten to death in police custody.

* * *

After reading the inquest transcript, my spirit was not at peace. Beyond the inconsistencies in the cover story, there were things I couldn't get out of my mind.

1. Why couldn't Marvin walk to the police car on his own? The description of his arrest didn't make sense. The autopsy findings proved that Marvin was not intoxicated, so there had to have been another reason why he couldn't walk under his own authority.

2. Why did Iberg and Mullenax take Marvin and Joe Flakes through the west entrance of the courthouse, rather than the south entrance? I entered the Faulkner County Courthouse many times as a young boy. The south entrance was the direct route up the stairwell to the third floor, where the jail cells were located. It was illuminated and was

generally used by city and county officers when transporting prisoners to and from the jail, especially at night. The west entrance was secluded and dark and was the furthest from the jail. It was not the logical entrance to use to transport two men to jail, especially not in bad weather.

3. The officers testified it was a rainy, stormy night and "the wind was blowing awful hard." So why didn't they all go inside the building at the same time? Nothing prevented the three officers from bringing Marvin and Joe in at the same time. Instead, officer Langford was told to go ahead and take Joe in, while Iberg and Mullenax stayed behind with Marvin.

4. Iberg and Mullenax's descriptions are suspiciously similar: they loosen their grip at the same time, they heard the thunder at the same time, they realized the rain hit Marvin and he came to at the same time, they saw him fall and reached for him at the same time, and so on.

5. To find out if the open gash above Marvin's right eye could have come from a fall on the steps, I went to the steps on the south entrance of the courthouse. The west entrance steps are now covered by a ramp, but both entrances had the same steps. Laying down on the ground, I placed my forehead on the second step from the bottom, the step the officers said was the one Marvin hit his forehead on. No matter how I turned, I could not find a way that Marvin could have sustained the strange triangular bruising and gash on his forehead from that step.

6. The officers' response to the forehead injury was bizarre. Both testified Marvin was not seriously injured and there was little or no bleeding. But if that were true, why would Iberg bring the chief of police, C.O. Hensley, to the jail two separate times after Marvin is incarcerated "to check on him?"

7. The tornado came through the middle of Conway and was about a hundred yards wide. It stayed on the ground for half a mile, causing terrible destruction and killing one person. Why would Iberg and Hensley take the time to "check on" a Black prisoner after a severe tornado tore through part of their city?

8. Why was Marvin isolated from the other inmates? Like everything else, jails were segregated in the 1960s. The Faulkner County jail had one cell for white men, one cell for Black men, one cell for white women, and one cell for juveniles. Black women were placed in the women's cell or were put with the Black men. Joe Flakes and Curtis Macon were put in the cell for Black men. But Marvin was put in the white women's cell, the cell described in the transcript as having been designed to provide a little privacy.

There were six bunks in the cell for Black men. Joe Flakes and Curtis Macon occupied two, leaving four available bunks. There was no reason for Marvin to be isolated, unless the officers were planning to do something to him they didn't want anyone to see.

9. Why didn't the jailer, Joe Martin, check on my brother in the morning or react to the blood from his ear and mouth? Why was he so calm after finding my brother dead in his cell? He testified Marvin was found in the same position he'd been in all night, on a bunk on his stomach with his head turned towards the cell door entrance. Joe Flakes saw blood in Marvin's ear. Curtis Macon saw blood running from Marvin's mouth. This blood would have been seen by anyone looking in on a prisoner as Joe Martin said he did. A normal response to seeing blood running from an ear or mouth would be concern. But Joe Martin's response was, "I felt he was just snoring."

10. Why was it necessary for Joe Martin to take Lou Cogbill and Charles Hackney to see George Hartje the next morning, before he checked on Mavin? Was it because Hartje needed time to ascertain what these two white inmates heard and saw before the word got out that Marvin was dead? Did he also need time to threaten them and tell them what to say on the stand?

11. Who was the person Charles Hackney referred to when he said, "...I asked that boy that slept right there by me if he had heard that fellow cry and he said he didn't." That's not how he'd refer to his childhood friend, Lou Cogbill. If it had been Lou sleeping next to him, would he not have said, "I asked Lou if he heard these sounds?" But he says, "this other guy," which suggests there was a sixth person in that jail

whose identity was hidden from the jury. (Later we learned that this was true.)

12. On page 15 of the coroner's transcript, Robert McNutt asks Joe Martin, "Did he – uh – vomit or show other signs of being sick?" Joe Martin replies, "He hadn't vomit when I was up there at 12:00" (the time he allegedly found Marvin dead in his cell). "He had vomit before daylight." But how would the jailer know Marvin vomited before daylight when he testifies that he left around 1:30 a.m., and returned after 7 a.m., well after daylight?

13. Why did Joe Martin allow Joe Flakes and Curtis Macon to enter Marvin's cell? Why did neither of them say anything about seeing any vomit? They testified they saw blood in Marvin's ear, and blood running from his mouth, but no vomit. If Joe Martin saw vomit in that cell before daylight, as he claims he did, and it was not there when Joe and Curtis entered that cell at noon, then Marvin's cell had been cleaned.

14. Why had someone tried to clean Marvin's shirt and dinner jacket? In addition to the testimony about blood in his shirt, Dr. Fox's autopsy report indicates that Marvin's white dinner jacket had "pinkish colored stains of water mixed w blood" but he makes no mention of blood on Marvin's shirt. What happened to all the blood? If someone attempted to clean his clothes, it happened at McNutt's Funeral Home.

15. Why wasn't Joe Martin ever asked who called him to go to Greenbriar, or what he did there during his six-hour absence from the jail? This time span conveniently takes him out of the courthouse when Iberg and chief Hensley return twice to Marvin's cell.

16. Why was my brother taken to a white funeral home which never took Black bodies, when there were two Black funeral homes nearby that always took Black bodies?

17. Why was there such a rush to embalm my brother's body before his wife or parents were informed of his death?

18. And finally, the one concern that stands out above the others is this: Why was Chief of Police C.O. Hensley, who went into my brother's

cell twice the night he died, absent from this critical hearing? Why wasn't he called as a witness? Why didn't he attend?

As I pondered these questions, the spirit of the Lord spoke to me. It was one of those spiritual moments that is very difficult to explain. All I can tell you is that the Lord revealed to me what happened to my brother when those officers approached his vehicle.

Marvin had to go to work the next morning, which would have been Friday morning. At 1 a.m. he was asleep outside the Sunset Café, in the front passenger seat of his Bel Aire, when officer Iberg woke him up. I'm convinced my brother said something that offended Iberg, a dangerous thing for a Black man to do then and now. Of course, what might be considered offensive to a white police officer could have been anything – even something as simple as, "What do you want?"

I believe my brother was assaulted at least three times that night. The first time was outside his car near the Sunset Café. He was unable to walk from his car to the police car because he'd been struck at least once, probably with a blackjack. This would account for the bruised area near his hairline and explains why he couldn't walk.

The second assault occurred in the secluded, dark parking lot on the west side of the Faulkner County Courthouse. When Langford took Joe Flakes into the jail, Iberg and Mullenax stayed behind with Marvin. There, in the rain and wind, they took their time with him.

The next time Langford saw Marvin on the stairs inside the courthouse, Marvin had the deep gash to his forehead, probably also made by a blackjack. The blackjack used by Conway police then was a flat weapon with a metal core surrounded by hard leather, stitched along the sides. If you turned it on its side and struck someone, it could open a gash. It could also create the very distinctive bruising and marks around this wound that were described in the autopsy. Even so, according to the jailer's testimony, between 1:15 and 1:30 am. Marvin was lucid, able to stand, walk, and carry on a detailed conversation under his own power.

About an hour later the third assault occurred.

The only known events that occurred in Marvin's cell between 1:30 a.m. and 9 a.m. were two visits by officer Iberg and Chief of Police Hensley. According to Iberg's testimony, the first visit occurred around 2:30 a.m. That's when they pulled

Marvin out of his cell and beat him to teach my brother a lesson. And that's when I believe my brother fought for his life.

Marvin was 6 foot 4 inches tall, a former U. S. Paratrooper, and an excellent boxer. The two men had weapons and Marvin was already injured, but I believe Marvin knew what was coming and fought back, and that's when Chief Rod Hensley sustained an injury, possibly to his face. This would explain the bruising on Marvin's hand, and the rageful force with which he was beaten by Hensley and Iberg, again and again. And it would explain Hensley's conspicuous absence from something as important as a coroner's inquest to review the conduct of his department's police officers. It would explain Prosecuting Attorney Hartje's glaring failure to call Hensley as a witness, and the fact that no one, not Hartje, Robert McNutt, or Robert Henry, nor any juror, makes any inquiry or statement about the chief's whereabouts. Chief Hensley wasn't called because Marvin had given Hensley an injury that would have been visible to the jury.

The facts of Marvin's death are clear and verified by autopsy: He died from a four-inch fracture to the back of his head caused by multiple blows delivered with extraordinary force. There was nothing accidental about his death.

Here's a list of all the things that don't add up:

1. Marvin was arrested for sleeping in his car, which is not a crime in this country.

2. Marvin was denied medical attention after his alleged fall on the steps.

3. The jailer, Joe Martin, promised to wake Marvin at 7 a.m. the next day but then inexplicably decides not to, and then does not even check on him in his cell.

4. On the morning of Marvin's death his body was sent to a white funeral home.

5. Coroner Robert McNutt ignored protocol and ordered Marvin's body be hastily embalmed.

6. No city or county official ever made any effort to contact Marvin's wife or parents to notify them of his death.

7. The City of Conway conducted a judicial inquiry on a Saturday within 24 hours of a suspicious death in their jail.

8.   The City of Conway proceeded with the inquest without any public notification.

9.   The Coroner's Inquest concluded its findings without ever seeing the autopsy report, or calling as a witness the physician who prepared it.

10.   This hearing began and concluded its work in just one afternoon and evening.

11.   Marvin Iberg and the chief of police returned twice to Marvin's cell on the night a tornado struck their city and county.

12.   The testimony of the two arresting officers was nearly identical, and they used the same or similar phrases repeatedly.

13.   One witness is taken into the courthouse upon arrival. The other, Marvin, is kept outside with the two arresting officers.

14.   The jailer testifies that Marvin vomited before daylight. But there was no vomit in Marvin's cell at noon. Someone cleaned the cell.

PART III

A Cover-up Uncovered

*"For there is nothing covered, that shall not be revealed;
neither hid that shall not be known."*

CHAPTER 14

Life After Marvin

Robbed of justice by a corrupt system, my parents did what countless African Americans have done for centuries: They leaned on their faith, trusted God, and moved on. But they never forgot.

Our family stayed with cousin JC and the Johnsons for several months while Daddy rebuilt our new house – on the same spot where the old one had stood. Bonnie and Ricky moved to Conway to live with Bonnie's mother. Two months and fourteen days after Marvin was killed, Bonnie gave birth to their daughter, Sharon. Once the house was finished, Mother and Daddy would often go pick up Ricky and Sharon and bring them home to spend the weekend with us.

Marvin's death had a lasting impact on our community. By 1960, the Second Migration was well underway. African Americans from the south were already moving to urban centers in the north and midwest. The chronic abuse and intimidation of Black men and women in the South fueled that population shift, along with the belief that Black people could have a better life and job outside the South.

Meanwhile, during the Central High School crisis, Arkansas became infamous for the violent racism of both the white mob and our governor, Orville Faubus. That crisis may have shocked the nation, but the white voters of Arkansas felt differently. Governor Faubus was re-elected in a landslide the next year and as soon as he could, Faubus shut down Little Rock schools for an entire year to prevent further integration.

So Black families in Arkansas might hope for change, but we weren't holding our breath.

About three years after Marvin was killed, when I was ten, Mother took me to Detroit to visit my sister Ernestine for a week. Her home was like a dream to me. She lived in a suburb of the city, in a beautiful neighborhood with manicured lawns. Her one-story home was so nice; it had a fenced backyard and air conditioning. That week in Michigan was eye-opening for me. I saw that Ernestine had a wonderful life, as my sisters Emogene and Carolyn did later in Kansas City. Experiences like this cemented the belief that the quality of life and the opportunities for Black people were much better outside the Deep South.

Before Marvin's death, Black people in Arkansas were already moving north. But after he was killed, it seemed like departures from Menifee and surrounding towns increased. It was as though the community collectively reached the same conclusion: If they could kill Marvin Williams, no one was safe.

Eventually most of Marvin's friends left Arkansas: Robert Delph, Homer Delph, Joe Flakes, Robert Flakes, Allen Powell, John Ellis Green, William Gault, even Curtis Macon. With his friends gone, and with my parents and older siblings never speaking of Marvin's death, I grew up loving my brother's memory and believing his death was a tragic accident. Our lives went on.

By the time I was eleven years old, I was working the fields in the Morrillton and Plumerville Bottoms with my sisters. The transporter for those landowners was Mr. Jeff Coleman, who lived in the community. He drove us to and from the fields in a covered pickup truck retrofitted with benches. We'd load into that truck promptly at 5:30 a.m. with our hoes, and he'd pack us in like sardines until there were about 25 of us inside. There was never enough room on the benches, so whoever got on last had to sit on the floor.

After picking us up, the transporter made only one stop – at a store owned by the farmer whose fields we'd be working. Every day we had to stop by that store. They opened it early for the field hands, and we'd quickly buy lunch, maybe a can of sardines or spam and a soda. Then we'd load back up and get to the fields about 6 a.m. and work until 6 p.m.

The days were scorching hot, and the only break we got from the sun was if we could find a shade tree to eat our lunch under. Sometimes Mr. Coleman came back at lunch with his large water container and one metal dipper, but we couldn't count on that. Most days he dropped us off and came back at finishing time.

By the time I was working the fields we were making $5 a day. And still, every Friday evening, we had to go to the landowner's home in Plumerville and wait until he or his wife came out and handed us our $25 for the week.

Most weeks, we had no idea where we were going when we got in that truck. If the transporter you worked for got an order from a landowner for 40-50 "hands" to work cotton, and another 40-50 to work beans, that transporter would say, "Yes sir, I know exactly where to get them," because wherever he got a bid, that's where you went. How long you stayed and worked a tract depended on the size of the field and the crop. Plumerville Bottoms was thousands and thousands of acres. We could be there a month or more, and then move somewhere else.

Everything in the South was determined by the cotton crop, including the school year which was structured so Black families could go pick and pull cotton in August and September. I did some picking cotton and let me tell you, it was tedious and dangerous and worse than chopping. Picking cotton meant you'd pick one plant at a time, all down your row, row after row. You'd work each stalk on each plant, using both hands and going from branch to branch. All day long you'd pull the white, fluffy cotton from the sharp, spiky bolls, trying not to let the spikes jab your fingers and hands – which was nearly impossible. Most pickers had gloves, which helped, but no matter how tough and calloused your hands were, at the end of a day picking cotton your fingers were bruised and usually bloody.

After you pulled a handful of cotton, you dropped it in a burlap sack that hung by a strap around your neck and shoulders. You dragged that burlap sack behind you all day as you worked. Daddy was strong and he'd pull a huge bag, the amount of cotton he was able to pick was enormous. But the rest of us were smaller, so we had smaller bags. Once you could hardly drag it anymore, you took it to the weighing station in the middle of the field where it was weighed and the pounds were recorded next to your name. The men at the weigh station dumped your cotton into the truck and then gave you your bag back, so you could go back and do it again. It was a hard life, and many Black families who worked those fields really suffered. Some had no shoes, and everyone got terribly sunburned.

When you were chopping you were paid by the day, but for picking cotton you were paid by the pound. There were good pickers, and then there were the rest of us. If you were a good picker, you made a lot better money. Of course, you never knew if you were being paid for everything you picked or not. Sometimes there was talk, when the number of pounds next to someone's name was smaller than what they knew they'd picked, but no one was going to challenge the accuracy of the white landowner or the white men managing the weigh station.

My wife Connie was the fifth of eight children. From the time she was about 12 until she was 15, she and her older siblings worked a huge tract called Lottie Bottoms. Lottie Road is now the road to the Conway airport, and back then those thousands of acres were planted in cotton. Connie's family was a little better off than most. They lived close by and had a car, so they could drive to the fields together and then go home each night.

Field work was still the main way Black people could earn money, but it wasn't easy or safe. Connie's parents cautioned her and her sisters to always pick a row that kept them between their brothers and their male cousins, and to stay with their group and never stray away. Connie usually worked between her older brother LaDell and her cousin, Claude, both good pickers who moved down their rows pretty fast. But Connie was small and slow and couldn't keep up with the boys. When she fell behind, LaDell or Claude would come over and help pick her row until they got her back up to where they could see her. She still remembers that whenever they helped her catch up, they always put that cotton in her bag, instead of theirs.

No one wanted to stay in the fields, and if you got a chance to get another job and get out, you took it. My father finally made his way out of the fields when he got a job working for the railroad company. I remember driving on the old highway to take him to catch the train to Oklahoma or Nebraska to lay track. He left on Sunday and came back Friday. That lasted for several years, and then he was able to get work locally at Morris Furniture Company in Conway. He worked there during the day, and then he worked for the Human Development Center all night. I don't know when he slept, but it can't have been much. At the furniture company he made deliveries, repaired damaged items, cleaned, dusted, and when business was slow, cut the owner's yard or raked his leaves.

I got out of the fields when I was 14 or 15, when Daddy got me a job at the furniture company helping out. Before I started, Daddy told me the rules about what we could and couldn't do. For example, we couldn't use the store's restroom. Instead, we had to go across the street to the animal feed store, which had a filthy bathroom in the back. Another rule was that if a customer came in, or if the furniture store owner's friends came in to shoot the breeze, we had to get out of sight – literally. That meant if I couldn't leave quickly, or get to another part of the store, I had to get myself into a dark corner and stand still so I wouldn't be noticed. And always, always, we had to say "Yes, ma'am" and "No, ma'am," and "Yes, sir" and "No, sir" to any white people.

These rules came from the owner, Mr. Morris, to my father, who passed them on to me. This is shocking today, but back then it was understood that this was how white businesses operated. And the truth is, if I had to categorize white male business owners at that time, Mr. Morris was a good man.

In my sophomore year in high school I was going to the prom. Mr. Morris called me and said, "Ronnie boy, do you have a suit?" I told him I did not. He said, "Go down to Ed Camps and tell them I said to let you have a suit and let you pay it off." So I did. I paid Ed Camps $5 a week until that suit was paid off. Of course, then I thought I had an account there, and I was pretty proud of that. A little while later I went back to buy a shirt the same way. That's when the owner told me, "You can't buy anything here on credit. The only reason we let you do that is because C.C. Morris called and told us to."

I think back on that and I feel the weight of what that kind of treatment did to us, especially to young people. I hated it, it was hurtful and humiliating. But I survived it. I told myself that one day, I'd be in a position to buy better clothes than Ed Camps could sell. Believe me, that didn't take away the sting, but it was how I dealt with the humiliation. For people of color, that kind of behavior was constant, and it took a toll. I understand what that treatment was like, and I know personally what it took to get to where we are now.

* * *

I worked at the furniture store all four years I went to East Side High School in Menifee. By the time I started high school, my sisters Emma and Verna were living in Kansas City, and Ernestine and Barbara were living in Detroit. Donna and I were the only ones at home. In ninth grade I'd gotten to be a pretty good basketball player, and at the end of that year I made the high school varsity team. I played on it through 12th grade, and that's how I met one of my dearest mentors, Coach Eddie Boone.

Coach Boone was my high school basketball coach. Other than my parents, he had the greatest impact on my life of any adult. East Side High was an all-Black high school, and Coach Boone was dedicated to making us great athletes and good men. He always told us, "You're the best at what you do," and he made sure we looked and acted like it. When we traveled, we wore sports jackets with "East Side High School" monogrammed on the jacket pocket. He drilled into us how important our presentation was, how it sent a message. Coach Boone wanted our opponents to see how good we were before we even stepped onto the court. He wanted our team and our high school to be taken seriously and to be respected. His lessons impacted my high school years, and well beyond.

Some things didn't change in the years after Marvin died. As a person of color, you were still limited as to where you could safely go. Mountain View Park in Conway was where we liked to go on Friday and Saturday nights. And if there was a DJ playing music, it was like an open-air party.

One Saturday evening toward the end of my sophomore year in high school, my friend Robert Coleman and I were hanging out at Mountain View Park, which was the "place of choice" for Black teens wanting to meet someone of the opposite sex. Robert and I were sitting on my car, a 1964 Dodge my father used as his work vehicle and the only family vehicle I was permitted to use on the weekends. We were on what we called a 'scouting mission,' hoping to meet girls. I was laying back on top of my car, listening to soul music on radio station KOKY, when Connie drove by with her sister Sandra and her cousin Cosetta in a four-door Bonneville. We made eye contact, and that was it for me.

I remember exactly how Connie looked that night. Her hair was parted in the middle, and both sides kind of curled forward. She was wearing white jeans, and when she got out of the car... wow! I remember thinking it looked like she'd been melted and poured into those jeans; they fit just right. As we used to say back then, Connie was "f-f-f-f-fine." When she looked at me again, I turned to my friend Robert and said, "I'm going to marry her."

Later that night there was another yard party some other friends and I went to, and Connie was there. It was dusk, and I asked her to dance. For the rest of the party we danced to the Temptations, Al Green, Aretha Franklin, The OJs, the Chilites, and so on, and we talked. At the end of the night, I asked if I could come see her. Her response was to invite me to BTU (Baptist Training Union) at her church the next night. My friend Raymond was at that party too, and he was smitten with Connie's sister, Sandra. We would have done anything those girls told us.

The next evening I took Raymond and another high school buddy, Elijah, with me to BTU at Connie's church. We slid into the very last pew and sat down, trying to be inconspicuous. Of course, it was clear to everybody that we weren't there for religion, we were there to see the girls. Our plan was that as soon as the service ended, we'd go over and talk to them.

So there we were sitting in the back of the church in casual clothes, hunched down, trying not to be noticed, and one of the deacons who knew my father spotted me. He knew exactly why we were there, and he looked to the back of the church, right at me.

"Young Williams," he said, "Can you come up here and open with a prayer for us."

This was not a question, mind you. My buddies and Connie and her sisters started laughing, and I walked up to the front of the church. For the life of me, I can't tell you what I said, but it must have been the shortest prayer they ever heard.

After the service, Raymond talked with Sandra, Connie's sister, and Elijah talked with her cousin. I talked to Connie. Since now we'd attended their church, we were invited to come to her house and meet her parents.

But meeting her parents and asking her father's permission to date his daughter were two different things. The first time I went to Connie's home to ask her father if I could take her out, he gave me a serious tongue lashing. He told me he didn't let his daughter go out with "just anybody," and he wanted us back by 11 p.m. or he'd see that I regretted it. Connie was furious with him, and I was so terrified of him I had her back by 9:30. I guess I passed that test, because after that she and I dated all through high school.

I graduated from high school with honors and was offered a four-year basketball scholarship to Hendrix College, in nearby Conway. During my first year at Hendrix, Connie and I got serious. Back then, if a young man wanted to get serious with a young lady, the first step was to give her a promise ring. So I asked my parents to go with me to Hagar's Jewelers in Conway, and help me pick out a ring. It was a simple band with a small (very small!) diamond on it. The next weekend I gave it to her and she was surprised, but in a good way. She'd known how she felt about me but didn't know if I felt the same.

But I knew exactly how I felt about her: She was the one. Connie was very attractive, kind of quiet, a little bashful, and we had chemistry – it just seemed like we belonged together. We had similar goals and similar thoughts about family and church. We were both one of eight children and even our names went together – Ronnie and Connie. But we also had something else in common.

When Connie was 17, she lost her oldest brother, Lee Andrew, Jr. He was working in a manufacturing plant when a machine blew up and his clothes caught on fire. He made it outside the building but was severely burned. Lee Andrew lingered for seven days at St. Vincent Hospital, suffering terribly, and then he died at the age of 21. The fact that Connie and I had both lost older brothers was a deep bond between us. We didn't talk about it much, but it was a shared sadness and pain we each understood.

Lots of people gave promise rings then, and it didn't necessarily mean you'd stay together or get married. But for us, it was serious. About a year later, at the end of my sophomore year in college, we were so much in love that I knew it was the right time. I purchased an engagement ring, and on our next date I asked Connie to marry me. She accepted, and we decided that night to get married in September, at Connie's church.

At that time, weddings were a lot easier to plan. Connie was working part-time at Sears, Roebuck, and her co-workers gave her a bridal shower. Her church's choir director and organ player, Miss Smith, was also the church wedding coordinator, so all the details were taken care of. Connie's mother made her wedding gown and all her bridesmaid's dresses. On our wedding day, Connie got dressed in the Sunday school classroom with her mother, and then her father walked her down the aisle. I was truly relieved to see he had a big smile on his face!

My pastor, Reverend Smith, married us, and our family members came from far and wide to be with us. We'd only invited family and close friends, but in families as big as ours that meant we had almost 350 guests! Since the church's Fellowship Hall was small, we had our reception at Connie's parent's home. Of course, we didn't have any money for a trip, so after the reception we headed to Little Rock for our honeymoon – and we stopped at the first motel we saw.

* * *

When I went to Hendrix I'd already decided to pursue education. My sisters were all educators, and Mother always said, "If you go into education, you'll make a lot of money." Of course, once we were all educators and earning a salary, we used to laugh about that. But education was prized in my family. My sister Barbara was Assistant Superintendent of Curriculum Instruction in the Kansas City Public Schools and was also an interim Superintendent of Schools there, the first Black woman to hold that position. Ernestine, Verna, and Carolyn became elementary school teachers. Being the youngest, I felt I had no choice but to follow suit.

Hendrix College was a small, private, religious institution. It was like a small community within the larger community of Conway. There were only about 25-30 African Americans on campus and living on campus was my first opportunity to be in an integrated environment.

I had some phenomenal instructors at Hendrix. Dr. Cecil McDermott was a math instructor who sometimes traveled with the basketball team, which was great for me because I loved basketball and math. Two of my favorite professors both taught English Literature: Dr. Blane Crowder and Dr. Walter Moffit. Dr. Crowder had a beautiful voice, his accent was unlike anything I'd ever heard. I loved to hear him read passages or poems in class. Dr. Moffitt pushed me to read more broadly than I ever had. In his class we read classics like Wuthering Heights, and my favorite, Jane Eyre. Dr. Moffit had a way of bringing those books to life, and you never dared skip your daily or weekly reading assignment, because he'd call on you every day.

After we married, Connie and I lived off campus in a small two-room trailer her family owned until I graduated as an education major. My first job was at West Junior High School, in West Memphis, Arkansas, where I coached basketball and taught social studies. That's where we were living when Connie told me she thought she might be pregnant. She'd already arranged to take a pregnancy test, which meant going to a lab with a urine sample and waiting while they tested it. But, like I mentioned, Connie was shy, and she wanted me to take her sample in. She said she couldn't get off work to do it, but I think she couldn't bring herself to walk into a lab and hand a stranger a sample of her urine!

Since there was no convincing her to go, I drove across town carrying this little jar and took it in to the lab. Needless to say, they didn't see many husbands bringing in samples. I handed it over and stayed in the waiting room, and in a little while they came out and told me it was positive. So instead of my wife calling to tell me the news, I called my wife and told her we were going to have a baby! We still laugh at that.

The pregnancy went well, but Connie missed being home with her family. The baby was due in October, and Connie checked with her doctor about going home for Labor Day weekend. He told her, "Oh sure, you can go home to Menifee. You've got another month before this baby comes." So we did, and after church that Sunday, we each went to our respective parent's home to stay the night and have a good visit.

Late that night, Connie called. She was having light pains and my first thought was that we had to jump into the car and drive back to West Memphis to see her doctor. She convinced both of us it would pass, but a few hours later her father and sister took her to the hospital. I met them there, and our son Torre was born on Labor Day, 1978.

Back in West Memphis with a baby, we lived on a shoestring. I took classes at night and on Saturdays to get my masters, and Connie took care of Torre. After I got my degree the next year, we moved home to Menifee. With a new position and salary, we were able to buy a beautiful acre of land from the Mitchells, the same family Daddy and Mother bought their land from years earlier.

Connie had found a house plan she liked but we needed to borrow money to build. We heard that First National Bank would be offering a special home financing program with a very good interest rate for residents of Conway and Menifee. Applicants would be accepted on a first-come, first-served basis only, so if you qualified financially all you had to do was get there before the money ran out.

The day before the applications were given out, I left work early and got to the bank at 2 p.m. I was the second or third person in line. All that evening and night, the line slowly grew behind me, but from what I could see I was the only person of color there. Connie brought me a lawn chair and something to eat, and I sat in that chair all night. The next morning I got our loan application, and since we already knew we qualified, we thought that would be it. Instead, after we submitted our application we were told we'd been disqualified because of a delinquent payment on a credit card we'd never owned. I called the bank and told them it was a mistake because we'd never had that credit card, but they said the decision was final. Nothing I said or did made any difference. So I filed a complaint with an Equal Opportunity organization in Little Rock. Soon after that, the bank called and told us we were reinstated. Once we had that loan, we started to build our home – the home we still live in today.

Four years after Torre was born, we were expecting our second child. By then I was employed at UCA and working toward my doctorate and Connie was working at the UCA library. Toward the end of the pregnancy, I'd go by the library and check on her on my way back from class. I went in so often her co-workers started to tease me saying, "Oh, she went into labor, Ronnie. She's already at the hospital!"

June 1ˢᵗ was Connie's birthday, and I knew her co-workers were planning a little party for her. She had a doctor's appointment that afternoon and I had a meeting on my doctorate at the same time, so she arranged for her younger brother Gary to take her to her appointment. Sure enough, when she got there her doctor told her she was in labor, and sent her straight to the hospital. Gary was so nervous that as soon as she got out of the car, he drove away, literally leaving her at the hospital door.

Meanwhile, I finished my meeting and went by the library to check on Connie, expecting her to be back from her appointment. As usual, her co-workers said, "Oh Ronnie, she's gone into labor already and she's at the hospital!" I thought they were joking, until finally they convinced me they weren't. I raced over to the hospital, and our son Gregory was born on Connie's birthday.

The next year, I left my job in Conway when I accepted a long-term position as an administrative supervisor with the Arkansas Department of Education in Little Rock. Connie and I had our two little boys, a new home, and I had a long-term position with a great future. We thought we knew exactly how our life would unfold.

Years earlier, back in Daddy's potato field, I'd vowed that if I could just have the chance at higher education, I'd seize it and never look back. I kept that vow. And in hindsight, the Lord safeguarded my path, and protected my livelihood by moving my place of employment out of the City of Conway into Little Rock… just before our case became public.

Because all that brought us to the summer of 1984.

CHAPTER 15

The Autopsy

By 1984, race relations in Arkansas weren't perfect, but our state had come a long way since 1960. Gone were the days when police officers could beat men and women of color for no apparent reason and receive promotions for it.

The governor in 1984 was Bill Clinton, considered a progressive in the Democratic Party. Clinton had a vision for Arkansas; he wanted to transform our state into a national leader in educational reform and economic development. As an educational administrative supervisor with the state Department of Education during the Clinton years, I had firsthand knowledge of his plan for reforms and changes and I saw those plans implemented on many levels. But I knew things had really changed when I saw the Governor doing everything he could to advance diversity and inclusion.

* * *

Not long after my parents got Charles Hackney's letter, I got a call from a reporter named Mike Masterson. It turned out Hackney had also sent a letter to the Arkansas Democrat, one of two daily statewide newspapers at the time and the paper where Mike worked. Mike wanted to follow the story, and he became an advisor to me and then a friend. Mike was a godsend, and from the start we got along as if we'd known each other our entire lives. He understood that a terrible injustice had occurred and, like me, he was determined to get to the bottom of it.

In our first conversation, Mike and I agreed we needed more forensic evidence. All we had was a letter from a white guy in prison. I told Mike I'd start with the Faulkner County Coroner's office, which was still housed at the McNutt Funeral Home.

A few days later, I stopped at McNutt's to see what information the Coroner's office had on file regarding Marvin's death. I asked the receptionist if there were copies of my brother's death certificate and autopsy reports, and she went in the backroom to speak with someone. When she returned, her demeanor had changed. She told me those documents had been sent to the office of George Hartje Jr., the 20th Judicial District Circuit Judge. Hartje's name meant nothing to me, but the person she'd spoken with now stood in the doorway, and she and he kept glancing at each other as she talked to me. I could tell they were uncomfortable with me being there. I didn't know why, or if anyone else had contacted them about our case, but nothing felt right. So I left McNutt's and went directly to Hartje's office to inquire about the documents.

At Hartje's office, I explained why I was there and the lady at the front directed me to go on back to his office. When I got there the office door was open so I walked in. There in front of me was the judge and what appeared to be two female assistants seated on each side of him, so close that their legs were touching his. Clearly, I'd interrupted something, and it took a few seconds for them to realize I was there. It was, to say the least, an awkward moment.

I decided to act oblivious to whatever was going on in front of me, and I told the judge I was there to get copies of two documents, the death certificate and the autopsy report for my brother, Marvin Williams.

As soon as I said Marvin's name, Judge Hartje's expression changed from slightly annoyed to what I can only call contempt. Very slowly and deliberately he dropped his glasses to the base of his nose, and with a look of utter disgust said to me, "I don't know what you're talking about. I haven't seen those documents. You need to look somewhere else."

Offended by his tone and response, I told him that I'd get a copy of those documents with or without him, and I left.

Now I knew I was getting the run-around, and I called Mike to tell him something wasn't right. He said, "You know, Ronnie, they're required by law to keep those documents on file. You may need an attorney to get what you need."

Before taking that step, I decided to give the McNutt Funeral Home one more try. So I drove back across town and went up to the receptionist and started telling her it was my understanding that they were required by law to keep the documents I'd requested on file. Before I could finish, an older gentlemen came out from the back with two documents, Marvin's death certificate and a one-page preliminary diagnosis of the autopsy findings. He handed them to me and said, with no other explanation, "They were misplaced."

After I left McNutt's I drove a ways to get out of the area, then pulled to the side of the road to skim the documents. The one-page report of findings contained a lot of medical jargon I didn't understand, but there was one finding I did understand: There was no ethanol in Marvin's system when he died. Marvin had not been drinking the night of his death.

I called Mike to let him know I had the documents. When I told him the autopsy report was a one-page summary, he said, "Where is the rest of it? They didn't give you the complete document."

That was the day I got my first inklings that a bigger game was being played.

* * *

The autopsy report came from the Department of Pathology, now housed in the Arkansas Crime Lab. A few days later, I dropped by that office and asked if they had additional information regarding Marvin's death. The person assisting me went back to check. When she returned she said, "We sure do. We have the summary of his autopsy and photos of his body taken prior to his autopsy."

"You have… photos of his body?" I stammered.

"We sure do," she said again.

I was speechless. Again, the feeling came to me that God had preserved this information for twenty-four years for me to find. I asked if there was anyone available who could explain the autopsy findings to me. After a brief wait, a distinguished looking gentleman walked out, greeted me, and introduced himself as Dr. Fahmy Malak, Chief Medical Examiner for the State of Arkansas. I told him what I needed and why. I also told him the only thing I knew about my brother's death was that he died from a blood clot which resulted from an accidental fall while entering the Faulkner County Courthouse.

Dr. Malak invited me back to his office where he read through the full autopsy summary. When he finished, he looked up and said, "Now tell me again, what did they tell you was the cause of your brother's death?" I told him it was from a blood clot which resulted from an accidental fall.

"Your brother did not die from a fall," he said quietly, looking directly at me. "He was struck multiple times in the back of his head. It was not accidental. Your brother was murdered."

I stared at him. This was confirmation of Hackney's letter. Immediately the image of Marvin being struck over the head multiple times filled my mind. Why? Who? Why would anyone do this?

Dr. Malak walked over to a full-size skeleton standing in a corner of his office, and I followed. Using the skeleton, he showed me where on Marvin's head the fracture occurred. He explained that it would have required 400 to 600 pounds of pressure per square inch to cause the four-inch fracture to Marvin's skull. The injuries to Marvin's forehead were distinct and were inconsistent with a fall. There was also bleeding from Marvin's kidneys, which he believed was due to some form of trauma in that area. Lastly, he said, "It is my professional opinion that your brother was murdered."

Dr. Malak made it clear that he could not be "absolutely certain without exhuming Marvin's remains and re-examining his skull." The problem with doing that was that our case was old, and he would need some type of directive from the governor before he could exhume the body.

Dr. Malak went on to explain what it had taken to do this kind of damage to Marvin's skull. The petrous bone, where the fracture occurred, is one of the hardest, densest bones in the entire body. It is so hard that it is extremely difficult to saw through this bone during an autopsy when necessary. In other words, he explained, one or two very hard blows would not have cracked it the way Marvin's was cracked. It had taken many more blows than that.

No one can prepare you for a moment like this. I remember being struck by how kind and patient Dr. Malak was, but I felt stunned. Dr. Malak probably sensed that I was having trouble taking it all in, and he said something like, "Let me put this layman's terms." He explained that to understand what 400 pounds of pressure means, imagine you have to drive a nail through a 2x4 with a hammer. One blow, even hitting as hard as you can, won't do it. It takes multiple blows. That's what happened here, he said, except that this bone was much, much harder than a 2x4.

That's when I got it. It took multiple, vicious blows to fracture this portion of Marvin's skull. There was nothing accidental about Marvin's death. He had been deliberately and brutally murdered by someone strong enough to administer repeated blows powerful enough to fracture an area of his skull that required 400-600 pounds of pressure per square inch to crack. This is not an accidental level of force. It's the kind of force used when the goal is to kill another human being. It seemed clear that my brother's arrest, incarceration, isolation, and bludgeoning were all deliberate.

CHAPTER 16

Mike and I team up

Shortly after receiving Harkney's letter, Mike Masterson started writing articles about our case in the Arkansas Democrat. The stories were usually on the front page, and soon the entire state became aware that a murder had taken place in the Faulkner County jail in 1960, and that key officials in the county might have been involved in its cover-up.

At the time Arkansas had two competing statewide newspapers. The Arkansas Gazette tended to be pro-establishment and pro-police and made little effort to pursue Marvin's story. Conversely, the Arkansas Democrat, with Mike Masterson as its lead investigative reporter, aggressively pursued every lead.

Suddenly, articles about our case were being written daily. Marvin's death investigation not only became the talk of the state, it started to receive national attention. Every day, Connie, my parents, and I would get up and steel ourselves for the day. It felt like we had to put on the full weight of what occurred and carry it every moment we were awake. Even though I was the point of contact for the family, all of us felt the burden.

One day Mike called to tell me there was a chance the TV news show 20/20 might be interested in covering our story. I was surprised and hopeful, and amazed the story had reached that level of interest. It was bittersweet – wonderful to think we might have the broader coverage, but sad at what it took to get it.

After my talk with Dr. Malak, it was clear we'd need to exhume Marvin's body. I decided to try to visit with Governor Clinton and get his support. My office was yards from the state capital building, but I couldn't just walk into the Governor's

Office. So I called one of his aides, gave him a quick overview of what was happening, and asked if he would arrange a time for me to meet with the governor. He replied with a list of reasons why he thought the governor would not get involved, the most important being the lapse of time. And then, without even asking the governor, this aide declined my request on the spot.

The next day, Mike called to say that 20/20 was coming to Arkansas to do a story about our case. I was elated! I couldn't contain myself, and called everybody in our family to let them know our case was about to get national coverage.

Armed with this development, I called another of Governor Clinton's aides whom I knew, Bobby Roberts. This time I started by saying that 20/20 was coming to Arkansas to cover our story and I wanted to be in a position to tell them we had the support of our governor. Bobby said he'd check with Governor Clinton and would have someone get back to me.

Within minutes, he called back and said, "The governor can see you now."

As quickly as I could, I walked up the hill to the state capital and into the governor's office. Governor Clinton met me with a smile and escorted me back to his private office. Clinton was very personable and approachable. He clearly understood that he was being pressured, but at the same time he asked many questions about the case. He said he wanted to know as much about it as he could, and his questions were serious and detailed. It seemed like he was sincerely trying to figure out what, if anything, he could do. So I told him everything I'd learned and when and how I'd learned it. After he heard the details, I could tell he was committed. Governor Clinton assured me the State of Arkansas would provide whatever resources necessary to have the case re-opened. "No rock will be left unturned," he said.

I left his office feeling encouraged, allowing myself to hope that perhaps justice was possible, even now. Although things had improved in the 25 years since Marvin's death, no Arkansas politician was going to win political points for helping a Black family determine if white officials were part of a murder and cover-up. If anything, the governor risked losing support by helping us. But 20/20 was coming to his state, and I believe Governor Clinton saw this as his opportunity to show the nation how far Arkansas had come in the area of race relations.

At this point, I felt good about the progress in our case. The gains we'd made, and the coverage Mike Masterson generated in the newspapers, were unheard of in Arkansas at that time. In the evenings, I was still debriefing my parents on each day's progress. I could tell they were pleased. Mother thanked the Lord for every win, however small, and for every new piece of information and every small step that brought us closer to justice for Marvin. They were so happy that progress was being made and that someone cared about Marvin.

The governor's support was essential, but he faced strong political headwinds. I worried that we needed more help, especially from the Black community. I didn't know if the efforts we'd made so far were enough to get results and allow the governor to intervene. But I did know it was an election year, and the more support we had from the Black community, the easier it would be for public officials to support us. So I contacted the Pulaski County Chapter of the NAACP, headed by the Rev. Robert Willingham, a well-respected leader in religious and political communities.

Rev. Willingham was amazing. He made it clear from the outset that he was there for us whenever and wherever we needed him, and we needed him a lot. After a series of meetings with Rev. Willingham, we decided the best way to maintain momentum was to conduct a petition drive. He felt this would engage the voters of our state and put additional pressure on key politicians who relied heavily on the African American vote.

There were chapters of the NAACP around the state, and Rev. Willingham helped me identify pastors and community leaders across Arkansas. Over the next few weeks, I visited all the black churches I could, particularly in Conway and Little Rock. I walked the streets of Conway with petitions, and went to black neighborhoods and spoke to families we knew. Across the state, volunteers were doing the same thing, handing out petitions and getting them signed and back to us. All of us knew that for a Black person, even signing a petition could be a difficult choice, and we respected that, so if someone hesitated, we didn't push them.

Even in 1984, it was inconceivable to the Black community across Arkansas that white police officers could be held accountable for a crime against a Black person, especially one that was 25 years old. You still had to walk gingerly, and there were many who were fearful and intimidated by what we were doing. More than a few Black businessmen said, "Hey, we're with you, but I have a little business here, and I can't put my name on that petition." We heard that a lot.

That fear was real; still very much alive and well. Sometimes it was a carryover from my parent's generation, but many of my generation had also endured intimidation, harassment, threats, bullying, and brutality. Until our case, there was little if any accountability for a white aggressor, and a whole lot of retaliation ready and waiting for a Black victim who spoke up.

Still others in the Black community were reassured by the strength of our case, and felt it might be a turning point. We had Charles Hackney as a witness to the beating of my brother, we had the autopsy report which included photos of my brother's body, we had the support of the NAACP, we had a lawyer, and we had front-page coverage across the state.

Equally important, we had the open support of the governor, who was willing to provide the essential state resources so our case could be reopened and thoroughly investigated. Governor Clinton was moved by the facts of the case and he knew our forensic evidence was solid. The fact that Marvin's murder happened a quarter century earlier could have given him an easy out, but he didn't take it. From the moment I sat down with him in his office and he made his decision, he never wavered in his support for our efforts. And at the end of our drive, we submitted 10,000 signatures to the governor's office in a press conference on the steps of the state capital.

While the petition drive was underway, I set up a meeting with Bill Brazil, Prosecuting Attorney of the district that included the City of Conway. Bill and his family were close friends of my family. My mother had cared for his wife, Suzanne, and her brother, Jack Roberts, when they were kids. She worked for the Roberts family for many years, dating back to when their father, Russell Roberts, was a circuit judge in the area. She often spoke fondly of Jack and Suzanne, and whenever they saw her in Conway they came up to her and gave her a hug. The support and friendship of this family meant a lot to us, so my parents encouraged me to meet with Suzanne's husband, Bill Brazil.

Bill and I met in his office, exchanged pleasantries, and I explained why I was there. I told him I had evidence that my brother was murdered while in the custody of police and that we wanted him to investigate and, if necessary, punish those responsible for Marvin's death. Bill said all the right things during our meeting, but I could tell he was uncomfortable with the conversation. As we talked, he appeared increasingly stressed, even a little agitated with my request. At the end of our visit, he asked if Marvin might not have been involved in an altercation in 1960, as if suggesting that this is what led to his injuries. I said, "A fight? With whom?" He said he didn't know but would look at the case and get back to me.

I left his office not knowing what any of that meant, but still believing Bill had our best interest at heart. My parents, especially my mother, were sure he would do the right thing.

By this time our case was in full motion. Everything we'd done to this point was done without the assistance of an attorney, but now it was time to take that step. We secured the services of John Wesley Hall, Jr., a Little Rock attorney with experience in civil rights litigation.

John's presence had an immediate impact on our case. He suggested a number of moves that were key in advancing the case, including recommending we ask the FBI to reopen their case.

Marvin was killed in 1960, which was an election year. Under the Federal Freedom of Information Act, Mike Masterson obtained documents that revealed that the day after Marvin died, an informant advised the FBI that information that the cause of his death might be suppressed to avoid unfavorable publicity. I never found out who this person was, but it had to have been someone on the inside, someone who knew what was being said by elected officials, several of whom were involved in the cover-up.

I wasn't surprised that nothing came of the informant's tip or the FBI investigation. In 1960, J. Edgar Hoover was head of the FBI, and every black person in America knew that he and his agency had a long history of ignoring cases like ours. Even so, just knowing there was an informant out there was encouraging. Someone had seen a wrong and tried to right it. Even though their efforts came to nothing, I thanked God for that person. I would give anything to have met that person and thanked them myself.

The FBI's response to our request was not what we had hoped. The head of the FBI in Arkansas, James Blasingame, said he would not reopen the case unless he was ordered to do so by the United States Attorney's Office in Little Rock or by the Justice Department. So we took our request directly to George Proctor, who was serving as United States Attorney, and we asked him to reopen our case. His response was, "The FBI has better things to do than investigate something we can't prosecute – just to satisfy someone's curiosity."

I was outraged. Since when is a desire for justice considered curiosity? His response was unprofessional and insulting to our family and to the larger community. After several negative editorials were written about him, he apologized, saying he regretted making those comments and that they were never intended to slight our family.

Our parents taught us that if you want to know what's in a person's heart, listen to what comes out of his mouth. I wasn't buying Proctor's apology, and I wasn't going to allow his inaction to prevent us from moving forward.

Since I hadn't heard back from Bill Brazil, I scheduled another appointment with him. During this second meeting, I showed him a copy of the autopsy report and pointed out the massive injuries documented in it. He acted surprised when he saw the report, as if it were his first time seeing it, and said, "Let me see that."

Bill studied the report and said, "Oh my, it looks like they beat him around the head." He asked me if he could have a copy, which I gladly gave him. His acknowledgement that a beating had occurred was key, but what was he going to do about it?

The answer came in the form of another document Mike obtained through a FOIA request. It was a letter Bill Brazil had already sent on June 1, 1984 to Ms. Sandra Johnson, a legal assistant in the U.S. Magistrate's office. In his letter Bill indicated that his office had investigated Marvin's death and found no grounds to proceed. More importantly, he said he'd seen the autopsy report almost two months prior to the date that he asked me to give him a copy of it. Finally, his letter stated that the statute of limitations had expired, thereby preventing him from pursuing criminal prosecution.

Finding that letter forever changed my relationship with Bill Brazil. I wasn't an attorney, but I knew there was no statute of limitations for first degree murder. I would never speak with Bill again.

In his letter, Bill referenced the transcript of the 1960 Coroner's Inquest. The jury at this inquest had ruled my brother's death an accident. I wanted to know how they came to that conclusion. Once again, Mike came through. He was relentless in his efforts to get to the bottom of what happened to Marvin.

Through a FOIA request, Mike got the transcript of the Coroner's Inquest. He and I spent days reading the document and comparing notes. Later I learned that the transcript was found in the office of the 20th Judicial District Circuit Judge, George Hartje, Jr., who, as Faulkner County Prosecuting Attorney in 1960, oversaw the inquest. This was same the man who rudely dismissed me from his office saying he had nothing related to the case. Brenda Graham, a case coordinator for the judge, had been looking for the transcript since the state reopened the case. She found it among some old files in Hartje's office.

In one of many conversations I had with God during those days, I remember thinking, "Lord, you have a strange sense of humor. You mean to tell me that you would allow one of the major figures in our case to keep the most important piece of evidence, which ultimately would bring into question his overall role in this case, for 24 years?" And what came into my mind, as if in response, was what the Lord tells us in Luke 20:43, "Till I make thine enemies thy footstool." Praise God!

All this time, there was growing interest in the case. Over the next seven months I did about 50 interviews. The coverage and interest was so strong that in its annual end-of-the-year news review, the Arkansas Democrat named Marvin's case the number one story in the state for 1984. His story held that spot for three consecutive years.

CHAPTER 17

The Summer of 1984

On the advice of our attorney, John Wesley Hall, our family filed a four million-dollar federal lawsuit against every person and entity that had a role in our brother's death and the cover-up that ensued. Those identified in our lawsuit were: Marvin Iberg, Bill Mullenax, Joe Martin, The City of Conway, Faulkner County, and the estate of Joe Castleberry, who was Faulkner County Sheriff at the time of Marvin's death.

Marvin's case changed everything in our lives. It changed how we were seen in the community, and how we went about our daily activities. My sisters, my parents, and my in-laws all feared for us, so Connie and I constantly had to give them an account of our whereabouts. When Connie took the boys to her parent's house to play with their cousins, she'd visit with her Mother like she always had. But now, each time she left, her father would come to her and say, "Baby, call us when you and the boys get home."

Neither of us was concerned about our wellbeing, but as a mother and wife, Connie was determined to maintain normalcy in our home. We got through those years by leaning on our faith, but it was still such a hard time. Our boys were too young to understand what was going on, but their teachers, coaches, and school administrators knew.

When she was asked later about those times, Connie said, "I truly didn't fear about our safety, because of my relationship with God; my prayer was that He would cover Ronnie and our family, and He did. I felt concern but not fear."

At that time Greg was 3 and Torre was 7. Connie wanted them to have a normal childhood, but it wasn't normal – it couldn't be with constant interviews and publicity, and the endless task of reviewing material every night. We never talked about the case in front of the boys, but we were both watchful, especially Connie. Every afternoon after school she'd question Torre and Greg about their day, listening to every detail to make sure no one was being ugly or mistreating them. "Eventually, I learned to live with the unrelenting pressure of the case," she says. "But it was hard. We're human, we couldn't help but think about what others were thinking, knowing we were viewed as someone trying to cause trouble, and worrying they might take it out on our children."

Most people we interacted with personally didn't bring it up, and that was fine with us. Connie was working in the library at Hendrix College at the time, and of course the librarians read everything on the case, but they never mentioned it to her. "I think it was their way of trying to protect me," she says. "They knew I needed someplace where I didn't have to think about it. And, in hindsight, I don't think people knew what to say. It was such a hard, sad thing to talk about."

Most of the time I was aware of what news was coming out and could share it with my family in advance. But there were some articles you couldn't prepare for. There was one article that contained new details about how Marvin was killed and testimony about what witnesses heard when he was being beaten. "That one really upset me," Connie recalls. "I couldn't stop thinking about how brutal the attack was, and that he was so alone. It made me even more determined to do what was right for Marvin."

My natural tendency is to think and reason things through, where Connie can get riled up a little quicker. But back then, we switched places. I was constantly in fighting mode. Some days I'd come home filled with frustration and anger, and Connie would sit for hours and talk everything through with me. Having her listen and understand my point of view made all the difference. She knew I was a hundred percent focused on the case, and her patience was amazing. Whenever I lost my temper because a news reporter misstated or misrepresented facts, she'd hear me out, allow me to vent and release that anger. Then she'd be that voice of reason, always bringing in something positive I could focus on, reminding me that it was all coming together and that God was in the plan. "We're all going to get through this together," she'd say, and then I could refocus. I could not have made it through the case without her.

* * *

As expected, the federal lawsuit brought about a certain public animus toward members of our family, particularly me. To put it simply, I was toxic. The people who really knew us, like my colleagues and my professors from Hendrix, were warm and kind. But others were the opposite. I was regularly the target of sneers and jeers from strangers when I was out in public in Conway, and people who resented our case found all sorts of ways to try to intimidate or punish us.

One day Connie called me from work, very upset. We'd been making monthly payments on a purchase at a local appliance store. Our payments were always on time and the bill was down to less than a hundred dollars, but out of the blue that day the owner called her and demanded that she "come pay this off now!"

This was a store Connie and I and our extended family had frequented for years. We'd literally spent tens of thousands of dollars there. I told Connie I'd handle it. Furious, I left my job, drove to the store, and went straight to the owner.

"How dare you call my wife at her job? You could have called me," I told him. "We're not behind on our payments and we've never been late." I added that I knew why he'd made that call, that it was about the case. "You're trying to put pressure on us and make us feel uncomfortable."

His response was, "I knew you'd bring that up."

Before he could go on, I pulled out my checkbook and paid our account in full. I reminded him of all the business our family had done with his store through the years and said we'd never do business with him again. That was the last time we stepped foot in that store.

That was just meanness and harassment from someone we barely knew, and there were many such interactions. We both experienced going into the grocery store and paying for something, only to have our change literally thrown back at us. Everyone knew who we were. You try not to dwell on those things, but other times it was more personal.

One evening I went to a basketball game. I got there a little late and saw Connie sitting at the other end of a row of seats. I didn't want to obstruct people's view by working my way down the row to reach her, so I slipped into an empty seat on the aisle next to Connie's former supervisor.

Connie and this woman had a great relationship, and she and I always visited comfortably. But this time was different. The woman was extremely nervous. She kept saying, "Connie's down at the end of the row, you should go on down there," and she was almost shaking as she said this. It was clear she didn't want me sitting next to her and didn't want anyone else in the stands to think we were friends.

During the 20/20 interview, Daddy talked about what it was like for him after Marvin was killed. He had seven other kids, he said. And back then, they could come back and do something to you.

That was my father's reality in 1960. But it wasn't my reality in 1984. Like Connie, I was also concerned for my parents, and for our children in the Conway public schools. But I wasn't concerned about my own safety. I think it was the sense of calling I had, of being called to pursue justice for my brother, that gave me confidence, because not once did I fear anything or anybody. Not even when Sheriff Castleberry tried to stare me down.

Connie and I were standing in a corridor at the Faulkner County Courthouse one afternoon when Sheriff Charles Castleberry walked out of his office and saw us. Charles Castleberry was the nephew of Joe Castleberry, the sheriff at the time of Marvin's death, who was named as a defendant in our lawsuit. When he saw us he stopped right in the middle of the corridor, turned to face me and gave me one of the most hateful stares a person could ever receive. It was more than a go-to-hell look. It was a "You need to be careful" look. His glare, his stance, his unmoving position in the hall – all of it was meant to frighten and intimidate us.

I knew exactly what he was doing and I stood there and stared right back. Minutes passed. Connie became really uncomfortable and wanted to leave, but I refused to succumb to his intimidation. I was sure it had worked for him many times in the past, but it wasn't going to work on me. Our eyes remained fixated on each other until he finally turned away and went back into his office.

In the fall of 1984, our oldest son, Torre, was a first grader at the Ellen Smith Elementary School in Conway. He'd been in pre-school for a couple of years and then in kindergarten at Ellen Smith, and he loved school. But suddenly, his behavior completely changed. I cannot erase from my memory the times I took him to school when he cried and clung to me, squeezing my leg, not wanting to go into his first-grade classroom.

As an educator, I knew this wasn't normal; either he was being bullied by kids in the classroom or he was being mistreated by his teacher, or both. I was determined to know what was going on, so I spoke with the principal, Mr. Ratliff, who was a friend. I explained the situation and asked if it was okay for me to observe this classroom, something I did regularly as an administrative supervisor with the Arkansas Department of Education. He agreed.

When I brought Torre to the classroom the next day, I met the teacher at the door and shared what was happening with our son. I explained that I would be sitting in the back of her classroom for the next few days. After one week of observing her classroom, something amazing happened; our son's behavior changed and he never cried or showed any fear or reluctance about entering her classroom again. I'm convinced that whatever he experienced in that classroom was a result of what was happening with our case.

Thankfully, there were also acts of kindness toward us, and some of these came from unexpected places.

Dr. William Roberts was a respected cardiologist in the City of Conway. I knew him as a big supporter of Hendrix, my alma mater. He and his family were regular attendees at Hendrix sports events and I used to see him in the stands when I was a basketball player there.

One evening Dr. Roberts and his wife, Betty, drove to our home in Menifee. Connie and I were outside working and were surprised to see them coming up the drive. We had no idea why they were there. I walked over to the car's passenger side to say hello, and Betty handed me a check for a substantial amount of money. They told me they wanted our family to know that they cared deeply for us, and that they wanted to do something tangible to support our case.

At that point, my sisters and I were scraping together whatever funds we could find to pay the attorney and legal costs. The Roberts' unexpected generosity not only helped us financially, it lifted all of us emotionally. These were genuinely good human beings who knew what we were up against and wanted to help us seek justice and truth.

With the help of the Little Rock NAACP and the support of Governor Clinton, we forced the local Prosecuting Attorney Bill Brazil and the Arkansas State Police to reopen the case. Bill's reluctance spoke volumes, and while he conducted a cursory investigation of our case, the Rev. Robert Willingham asked the governor for a grand jury investigation. Rev. Willingham also asked that the jury be empaneled outside of Faulkner County and that a special prosecutor be appointed, since many of the principals involved in the case lived in Conway and were closely connected to elected officials.

While Governor Clinton contemplated the NAACP's request, the Arkansas State Police concluded its investigation and turned the results over to prosecuting attorney Bill Brazil. After receiving the report, Bill was quoted in the Log Cabin Democrat, Conway's local newspaper, saying, "We are going to try to find something to charge someone with."

By this time, we knew Bill wasn't sincere. In a blatant show of bias, he'd already agreed to represent the former jailer, Joe Martin, and Faulkner County, two of the defendants named in our civil lawsuit. This was a real and substantial impropriety. In response to his unethical behavior, our attorney John Wesley Hall filed a motion in the U.S. District Court in Little Rock requesting that Bill Brazil be disqualified from representing these two defendants.

Days later Bill released his twenty-page report concluding that he did not have cause to bring criminal charges against anyone. Bill was entrenched in local politics and closely aligned with the very individuals we wanted him to prosecute. But what was new and disturbing was what I found in his investigatory summary. Reading his report felt like my family was being victimized all over again. This wasn't an investigation; it was Bill's attempt to discredit every piece of evidence that would support our case. As such, it was filled with inaccuracies.

On page four: "There is no doubt that Mr. Williams died of an injury to the left rear portion of his head. The transcript of the coroner's inquest clearly established that they also made that same determination."

Fact: The inquest did not make the same determination. It stated Marvin died of "a concussion to the brain" because crucial evidence was never presented and witnesses were intimidated. As a result, it concluded there was "no foul play."

On page 6: "The only indication or evidence of injury to his [Marvin's] head was a cut on his forehead and the injury that resulted in his death which was in the back portion of his head. There was evidence of an old scrape on his arm and some evidence of bleeding in his kidney, but nothing to indicate or point out any bruises or abrasions or anything that would naturally be the result of a beating as described by Hackney."

Fact: The wound on Marvin's forehead was not "a cut." It was so serious that it was still oozing hours later when Marvin's body arrived in Little Rock for the autopsy.

Bill had the photos of Marvin's body, which clearly show the unusual and distinctive shaped bruising around that wound, the bruising across his nose and a swollen area at his hairline…not to mention the cut to his upper lip. He also had the autopsy report which listed multiple injuries "that would naturally be the result of a beating."

Page 13, the most disappointing statement of all: "Whether he was or was not drinking was further complicated by the opinion we received from the current medical examiner's office. They advised us the injuries Williams received that resulted in his death could very well have given a layman the impression of drunkenness. That, of course, would also indicate that the injury to Williams was received prior to being arrested by the police… Looking back twenty-five years it is easy to see that those people who were with Williams prior his arrest, Flakes, Powell, Delph, and Oliver and others that might have been discovered at the time could have been questioned and investigated more thoroughly to get more specifics and details about the possibility of the injury being received prior to his arrest."

Fact: The toxicology report, which Bill had a copy of, found no alcohol in Marvin's blood. The Arkansas Chief Medical Examiner had publicly stated that the lethal fracture to the back of Marvin's head would have caused him to be in profound coma, unable to speak, and dying. So Marvin could not have received that fracture prior to incarceration. And, all of "those people who were with Williams prior to his arrest" were still alive during Brazil's investigation. If he'd believed what he was writing he could have interviewed any of them. But he did not.

There are other inaccuracies and false statements in Bill's report, and they all add up to one conclusion. Bill wanted to avoid re-opening this case, so he produced a hollow report that deflected attention away from the Conway Police Department.

Bill was part of the system that created and perpetuated the cover-up. He and the good old boys did not want this case re-opened, and he was willing to distort the truth to achieve that goal. My mother had believed in Bill Brazil. Never in a thousand years did she think he would impugn her son's integrity for political purposes. But that is what Bill did by twisting the facts to suggest that Marvin's injuries occurred prior to his arrest and implying his childhood friends were responsible for his death.

But Bill failed to consider that by the time his report came out, much of the information from the autopsy and toxicology reports would have been made public. He never understood how closely the public was following this case.

Bill's report was discredited almost as soon as it was released, and so was he.

CHAPTER 18

Run, Run, Run Around

In an attempt to add credibility to his findings, Bill solicited the services of Ron Fields, a prosecuting attorney from Fort Smith, to review the information he'd put together. According to Bill, Fields arrived at the same conclusion, that there "simply was not enough evidence to determine the time that the fatal injury was inflicted, nor the persons responsible for the injury." Bill stated that Fields determined Charles Hackney's credibility was poor for many reasons, but he only cited one: information obtained from an unnamed forensic pathologist who allegedly "felt that the injury occurred at the arrest site or before, and not after as Hackney had related."

Our attorney, John Wesley Hall, requested that Bill Brazil release to the public a copy of Ron Fields' report. Reporter Mike Masterson also requested this. Bill refused.

Years later, as I was writing this book, I had to know what was in Fields' report that Bill did not want the public to see. It didn't make sense for Bill not to release it if he'd quoted Fields accurately. In fact, releasing it would have bolstered Bill's credibility. There had to be more to this story, so I decided to try to find Ron Fields. I googled Fort Smith. found his number, and called and asked if he would meet with me at his office. He agreed. It had been three decades since his last involvement in our case.

At 8:30 on a Wednesday morning Connie and I met him at his office in Fort Smith. I explained that I was writing a book to unpack the circumstances surrounding my brother's death, including the cover-up that ensued. Since he was named as a collaborator in Bill Brazil's twenty-page investigatory summary, I wanted to know

145

if he agreed with the contents of that report. I told him I was not there to besmirch his character; I was there to get honest answers to specific questions.

To my disappointment, Ron Fields answered everything in broad generalities and hypotheticals, like "probably" or "that's possible." Unlike the other medical experts in the case, he simply was not going to give a yes or no or any clear opinion to any question. When I handed him my copy of Brazil's investigatory summary and asked if he was familiar with it, he scanned it and said with a smile, "they took excerpts from my report, but this is not my report. Do you not have a copy? I'm sure there are some floating around."

I told him, no, I did not have a copy of his report and that my family had made several attempts to get a copy from Bill Brazil but he refused to release it. I asked if he could find a copy of his original report and share it with us. He agreed to look, but said it was doubtful he'd kept a report like this, especially since he was now semi-retired and many years removed as a practicing prosecuting attorney.

It was clear that Ron Fields was surprised I knew as much about the case as I did. Again and again he wandered off topic, and each time I brought him back with specific questions. But he always answered vaguely.

Finally, after listening to him go on at length about the many cases he'd prosecuted in the Fort Smith area, I decided it was time for us to leave. As we were walking out of his office I think his conscience started to bother him. He stopped us and said, "What do you need from me?" I told him I needed answers to certain questions, preferably written responses. We agreed that if I would send him the list of questions, he would respond in writing.

When we left his office Connie looked at me and said, "Are you kidding me?" It summed up our visit perfectly.

The next day, I sent him these four questions:

1. Did you concur with Bill Brazil's written summary of his investigation into my brother's death?

2. Do you believe that my brother was struck with an object?

3. Do you think, based on the autopsy findings (bleeding from the kidneys, four-inch fracture to the back of Marvin's head, an open gash on his forehead, and bruises and abrasions that are visible above and beneath the open wound), that my brother was beaten?

4.   Lastly, do you think there was evidence to support a cover-up?

He responded with these words, "To start with number 3. I can answer many questions in the case but only with the words "probably or that's possible." I cannot answer very many with "absolutely" or "beyond a reasonable doubt."

That's it. That's all he said.

Initially, I thought this trip was a complete waste of our time. But the more I reflected on his response, the more I wondered if there was a subtle message there. The fact that he started with question number three about whether Marvin was beaten, and completely ignored questions one, two, and four, was as loud an answer as I'd get from him. Maybe he was telling me to read between the lines, as in, "I'm trying to tell you something I ought not to tell you."

I was disappointed that Ron Fields wasn't more forthcoming, but I recognized his position. He wasn't eager to destroy the character or reputation of one of his peers, Bill Brazil, but he also wasn't willing to lie for him.

Bill Brazil was shocked at how the public responded to his summary. It was not well received, particularly by Governor Clinton. The broader community knew justice had not been served and therefore needed further examination. Governor Clinton asked Bill Brazil to request that Circuit Judge George Hartje, Jr. call a special grand jury to review my brother's death. This was the same George Hartje, Jr. who bristled at me when I walked in on him with his two female assistants. This request made it very uncomfortable for Hartje, who was obviously implicated as a key figure in the cover-up.

Days after the release of Bill's report, the Governor sent him a hand-delivered written letter making it clear that Bill needed to step aside. One of the governor's assistants invited me to ride along with the courier so I would know it had been delivered. This was the governor's way of letting my family know that what happened to Marvin was bigger than politics; it was about doing what was right. I was a little uncomfortable sitting in that car outside Brazil's office but being there gave me some level of satisfaction. Bill had completely disqualified himself and could no longer be trusted with the criminal investigatory piece of our case.

While the public waited for Brazil to respond to the governor's request to step aside, U.S. District Judge G. Thomas Eisele decided to disqualify Brazil from defending Faulkner County and Joe Martin in our civil case. He wrote, "Brazil's position both as prosecuting attorney and the county's legal representative creates the appearance of impropriety that might diminish the public's confidence in the legal profession and in the fair and proper resolution of the issues."

Sadly, it took the governor of our state and a federal judge to convince Bill Brazil that he could not legally prosecute and represent the same people at the same time.

As pressure mounted on Brazil to remove himself and call a special grand jury investigation, Governor Clinton added to his woes by telling him that if he continued to stonewall and refused to empanel a grand jury, the governor would pursue legal options to let the state act instead. The governor was quoted saying, "my position is that if the government was involved in the wrongdoing and if the government was involved in the cover-up, then the government ought to be involved in finding out what the truth is...either through the grand jury or through some other mechanism." And the governor didn't stop there; he went on to say that the state would help pay for the special grand jury. "...since grand jury proceedings can be expensive, I would be willing to support your request for financial assistance." This was unprecedented, especially for a case that was twenty-five years old.

Governor Clinton had put Bill Brazil in a box. He had no other cards to play. Meanwhile, Clinton's public and very controversial stand did not win him political points or endear him to the good old boys. It was a courageous act, and my family will be forever grateful to Bill Clinton for his commitment to finding the truth and getting justice for our brother. If not for his determined support, our case would never have gotten off the ground.

Out of options and with no more political games to play, Bill Brazil did what he should have done months earlier – he exited the case, but not before asking his friend and political ally, George Hartje, to empanel a grand jury to investigate Marvin's death.

This was inviting the fox to sleep in the chicken house. As Prosecuting Attorney for Faulkner County in 1960, George Hartje oversaw the coroner's inquest, threatened Charles Hackney and other jailed witnesses, and told them to lie to the jury. During the inquest he belittled, intimidated, and threatened Black witnesses; failed to admit any forensic evidence; ignored evidence and testimony; and assured jurors there was no reason to wait for the autopsy report to reach a conclusion.

Citing concerns the State Supreme Court's judicial department would have with his appointment, Hartje reluctantly stepped aside and let the Judicial Affairs Department appoint a special judge.

* * *

Meanwhile, in the fall of 1984, the ABC/TV News Magazine, "20/20," was preparing to air a segment about Marvin's death. Geraldo Rivera, a nationally known investigative reporter at the time, had visited our state and interviewed several people, including my parents and me. His interview with Daddy took place in our den, where the crew set up lights for filming. When the interview was over, they realized that one of the lights had burned a hole in our ceiling. They felt terrible and offered to pay for it, but of course we said no. We were so grateful they were there, and my parents were proud that our case had finally received the attention it deserved. We were all looking forward to the show airing.

What we did not know was that the segment would include photos of Marvin's body taken prior to his autopsy. Until now, my sisters and I were the only family members who had seen those photos. We never wanted our parents to see them.

On the night the 20/20 episode about Marvin aired, Connie and I were watching it at our house with my parents. When the autopsy photos came on the screen, Mother cried out, "Oh, no!" and began to weep inconsolably, she was beside herself. My father put his hands over his face and cried silently.

These images were a complete shock to Mother and Daddy. Before seeing them, my mother only remembered Marvin as he had been: handsome and almost always smiling, with a beautiful complexion and not a scar or scratch on his face. To see him on television in his blood-stained white dinner jacket, a vicious wound on his forehead and bruises on his nose and face was too much for her. What began as an evening of hope and excitement ended with more grief and heartache.

A few days later, I watched the show again in private. That's when I realized the enormity of my brother's story receiving such attention. This young Black man, who'd been so maligned after his death by Conway city officials, had been seen in the homes of millions of people around the world who now knew his name and the truth surrounding his death. I'll never forget my dad's prophetic statement that aired in the segment: "Whatever is done in the dark will eventually come to the light. And I thank God I've lived long enough to know what happened to my son."

CHAPTER 19

Unexpected Support

Predictably, the 20/20 segment spurred letters of protest from locals, including two opportunistic young attorneys with ties to Bill Brazil's office. Both Brazil and Hartje had refused to be interviewed for the show, but now they criticized its accuracy and fairness. I did not dignify these letters with a response. The two young attorneys were rookies, I knew both of them and had been in college with one. Their primary motivation was to protect a self-perpetuating system they desperately wanted to join. Their letters were their way of showing the good old boys that they would protect the status quo.

As we waited to hear the names of the new prosecuting attorney and the judge who would oversee the grand jury investigation, something interesting happened. A woman by the name of Juanita Thomas, formerly of Greenbrier, Arkansas, was quoted by one of the state newspapers saying that former Conway Police Chief C.O. (Rod) Hensley and Bill Mullenax had come to her home around 4 a.m. one morning on or around the day Marvin was killed. Hensley was a drinking buddy of her husband's, and during this visit "Hensley told she and her husband that he had just hit a young boy, Mr. Williams from Menifee, and he had just died." She added that Hensley, who was now deceased, went on to tell them that "he guessed it would be the last time we ever seen him as chief of police because he had hit this boy over the head."

Family members of Mrs. Thomas quickly tried to discredit her account by saying that she was living in Texas at the time of my brother's death. Mrs. Thomas never denied having moved to Texas, but said that she and her husband also owned and maintained a home in Conway which they visited. Their home was only four or five blocks from the courthouse.

Even in the midst of attacks by her own relatives, Mrs. Thomas stood by her account of this pre-dawn visit by Chief Hensley and Bill Mullenax, stating "we may have come back up from Texas that week. I know my relatives are all up in arms about this. But I also know what Corby Hensley told me about hitting that man. I may be wrong about the date, but I'm not wrong about the man and what happened. I'm sure not lying. I got no reason to lie about something like this."

It was clear Juanita Thomas knew Chief Hensley by how she used his name. In fact, reading this quote was the first time I'd ever heard Chief Hensley's first name. He was known as Rod Hensley, or officially as C. O. Hensley. His first name was something only someone who knew him very well would use.

In the article, Mrs. Thomas talked at length about how long she and her husband had known Hensley and Mullenax. She'd worked with Mullenax at a local company, so there was no way she could have been mistaken as to who came to her home in May, 1960.

Ironically, Mrs. Thomas's account echoed the testimony of officer Marvin Iberg, who implicated Hensley in his 1960 inquest testimony. According to Iberg, Hensley accompanied him twice to Marvin's cell, around 2 a.m. and again around 3 a.m. the day Marvin died. I believe it was during these encounters that my brother received the blows that killed him.

For us, Mrs. Thomas was a messenger from God. She was courageous and unflinching. She did everything in her power to make sure that every news outlet and every official heard what she had to say. She even contacted Sheriff Charles Castleberry, the man who tried to have a staring contest with me.

Asked about his encounter with Mrs. Thomas, Charles Castleberry said, "I wasn't paying a lot of attention to her bullshit." True to his word, Castleberry ignored what Mrs. Thomas had to say, as did other local officials, who instead worked overtime to portray her as an unstable attention-seeker even though Iberg, one of their own, had corroborated Hensley's involvement years earlier.

Undeterred, Mrs. Thomas was quoted in the Arkansas Gazette saying she had "no doubt who was in her home and what was said the night Williams died. You don't forget anything like that."

We finally received word that a special judge and prosecutor had been appointed to empanel and oversee a grand jury proceeding to investigate Marvin's death. This was the moment I'd longed for, to move beyond the grips of the local good old boys. The judge chosen was John Lineberger of Fayetteville.

Judge Lineberger had previously assisted a former Faulkner County circuit judge in easing an overloaded docket, so he was no stranger to that county's judicial proceedings. He appointed Gary Isbell, a deputy prosecutor for Baxter and Marion Counties, to be the special prosecutor for the grand jury. Isbell, the judge said, was appointed "because of his experience, ability and the fact that Isbell would be able to spend the time needed to review the case, as well as the fact that he once served as an assistant attorney general."

My initial reaction to Isbell's appointment was one of concern. He lived and worked in a region of our state where there were few people of color. How could this man understand the Black perspective if he had little or no interaction with us? I would later come to learn just how wrong I was. Gary Isbell and John Lineberger were men of enormous integrity, resolute in their efforts to follow the law, unwilling to succumb to local political pressures and politics, and guided by a "higher calling" evident in their decisions.

The grand jury proceedings were about to get underway when our attorney, John Wesley Hall, told us that an exhumation of Marvin's body would be necessary due to the lack of certain medical records, particularly the x-rays which were never found. The thought of disturbing Marvin's remains was difficult, but the possibility that this second autopsy might help determine the type of instrument used to murder Marvin outweighed the emotions we felt.

After making that decision, we learned that we would be responsible for all costs associated with the exhumation. This was a complete surprise to us. My parents' social security checks were their only source of income, there was no way they could incur additional debt. Knowing we'd also need funds for the impending civil trial, my sisters and I agreed that I should pursue a loan at a local bank in Conway. We decided to use the 40 acres our family owned in Menifee as collateral.

I took the deed to our bank and met with a loan officer I'd worked with in the past. I explained that I needed to apply for a loan for approximately $40,000, and wanted to use our land as collateral. Since the land's value far exceeded the amount of the loan, this should not have been a problem.

As soon as I was finished, and without even asking me to complete a loan application or get an appraisal to determine the value of the property, the loan officer told me no. No explanation, no application, no consideration. Just "No."

Obviously, this wasn't the bank's usual procedure. In fact, no procedure was followed at all. His response had everything to do with our case, and it was clear we weren't going to get any money from a bank in Conway.

Since I worked in Little Rock, I decided to take a chance with one of the larger banks in the city, Twin City Bank in North Little Rock. I didn't know anyone in the bank or have an account there, but I just walked in one day and asked to speak with a loan officer. Instead of a loan officer, the president of the bank (I believe his last name was Wilson) came over and personally assisted me.

I was surprised to be talking to the bank president, but I explained my request and told him the amount my family needed and why. I also presented him with the deed to our property as collateral. Mr. Wilson looked at the deed, then handed it back to me and said, "I will not need your deed. I know who you are; I am familiar with your case. How much do you need and how soon do you need it?"

All I could say was "Thank you, Jesus!" Mr. Wilson not only approved everything, he had the check ready for me that afternoon. I didn't have to do an application, go through a credit check, nothing. All I did was sign the loan documents. Truly, God has a way of putting certain people in your path when you need them, and Mr. Wilson was one of those individuals. He was a kind, fair man who believed in justice and supported our case in an extraordinary way.

CHAPTER 20

Exhumation

Marvin's body was exhumed on Saturday, December 1, 1984 at approximately 10:30 am. My father and I were present during the exhumation. Dr. Fahmy Malak, Arkansas' State Medical Examiner, was on site and guided the entire process from start to finish. He told all the parties present, which included members of the media, state crime lab investigators, and attorneys for the City of Conway, Faulkner County, and our family's attorney John Wesley Hall, that he wanted complete silence as he prepared to remove Marvin's remains from his grave.

My father was a "kingdom man," a great man of faith. The only way he could get through this was to ask for God's strength and guidance. So, prior to the start of the digging (done at no cost by my cousin, Roger Black, a private contractor from Plumerville), we had a word of prayer.

Then Dr. Malak carried Marvin's remains from the grave site to the state crime laboratory in Little Rock. Marvin's metal coffin was left in the grave as his remains would be returned later in the day. Dr. Malak completed his findings around 1:30 that afternoon. He confirmed that Marvin's death was the result of a skull fracture located behind his left ear.

From a legal perspective, our attorney, John Wesley Hall, was ecstatic over this report. But my family and I could not rejoice. All we could think of was how much did Marvin suffer, and what were his last words?

My father and I were at the grave site when Marvin's remains were returned in a plastic bag and placed in his casket. Daddy did not want a ceremony during the re-burying of Marvin's body, it would have been too painful for him.

Watching as Marvin's casket was closed, and his grave was once again covered with dirt, I felt robbed. Robbed of the love and companionship of a brother I barely knew; robbed for my nephew, Ricky, and my niece, Sharon, who never got the chance to know and experience the love of their father; robbed for my brother who never got to realize his full potential in this world; robbed for my parents of the precious place and space he occupied in their life; and robbed by a judicial system that refused to acknowledge or recognize my brother's worth and value as a human being. As painful as it was to see my brother's body returned to earth, I used that pain to motivate me to get justice for Marvin.

While we waited for the start of the grand jury investigation, Mike Masterson discovered, through a FOIA request, a document sent to the FBI on May 7, 1960, the day after my brother was beaten to death in the Faulkner County Jail. The document included a message with the caption "URGENT INTRAOFFICE MESSAGE." The message was sent to the Director of the FBI in Washington D.C. According to the message, the caller told the FBI that a "Negro Male, last name Williams" was found dead in the Faulkner County Jail on May 6, 1960. The caller went on to say that the "sheriff" had called the local coroner, Robert McNutt, who initially declared Marvin's death due to heart attack. Although the informant's name was blacked out in the FBI document, it was clear this person knew that information regarding my brother's death was being suppressed. But the informant didn't stop there, he/she identified another person (whose name is also blacked out) "that has information concerning this matter." Apparently, this phone call prompted two very limited investigations by the FBI, both of which failed to hold anyone accountable for any wrongdoing.

In an article written by the Arkansas Democrat, a veteran FBI agent was quoted saying, "Based on the wording of the 1960 intraoffice message, the informant was likely to have been close to Conway area law enforcement officers and courthouse activities. It appears from the wording of the message that this informant was passing along information supplied primarily by another person, probably an officer."

I was pleased to read what this veteran FBI agent had to say and encouraged that there might have been someone in the city's law enforcement community who tried to do the right thing. At the same time, it saddened me that this person couldn't go against the status quo and make their statements public.

It's horrifying to think how close the police and city officials came to a successful cover-up. Here was the coroner, Robert McNutt, initially declaring the cause of Marvin's death a heart attack. How could he examine my brother's body and come to such a conclusion? His behavior was beyond unethical, it was evil. It was what a morally compromised person does when they have no conscience and no fear of the punishment God will inflict on them for committing such a heinous crime.

In the same stack of FBI documents were other pages with redacted names of people they'd interviewed. One name we were able to glean was the Morrilton mortician, Mr. Fred Thrower. Thrower Funeral Home was the largest black funeral home in the area. After the coroner's inquest, Mr. Thrower received and prepared Marvin's body for burial. In addition to the wounds and bruises documented in the autopsy, he also noted a bruise above Marvin's right ear and another on top of his right hand.

How could Fred Thrower and Robert McNutt, both experienced morticians, examine the same body and come to such vastly different conclusions? Because only Fred Thrower saw a human being with massive injuries to his body that were suspicious and worthy of documentation. Robert McNutt viewed the same body like it was 'road kill,' something to quickly dispose of before it starts to smell. The way to do that was to list a cause of death that wouldn't attract attention, then hurriedly embalm and bury the body, hoping no one would ever know the truth.

But that's not how God operates.

Robert McNutt died of a massive heart attack on October 26, 1963, three years after attempting to cover-up my brother's murder. I wish he and his co-conspirators were around today so I could remind them of a quote by William Cullen Bryant. The Reverend Dr. Martin Luther King was so inspired by this quote that he used it in several of his speeches: "Truth, crushed to the earth, shall rise again."

PART IV

The Grand Jury

CHAPTER 21

Motive

The selection of the grand jury to investigate my brother's death was scheduled to begin in February of 1985. Special Prosecutor Gary Isbell and I met several times before selection began. Any lingering reservations I had about Gary dissipated after these meetings. I was convinced he was a man of integrity and would do the right thing, even if the facts led us to a different conclusion than we originally thought. Not only had God assigned the right judge to replace George Hartje, He had given us the right prosecutor to replace Bill Brazil.

On February 12, a sixteen-member jury was selected to begin the grand jury investigative process. Not surprisingly, only one of the sixteen jurors was black, Mr. Willie Hinton.

In his preliminary comments to the grand jury, Judge Lineberger was quoted saying, "I will ask you to either indict or not indict. If you find criminal conduct, will you promise me you won't hesitate to indict? It is your duty to investigate. We don't want to leave a stone unturned. I don't want to hear of any leaks. That's one way to mess up a grand jury investigation. Everything you do may be undone. If there is a leak anywhere there will be harsh penalties."

As the grand jury prepared to hear from its first witness, the chambers where the hearing would be held had to be swept for listening and recording devices. Once the facility was cleared, the first two individuals sighted in the courthouse were the two arresting officers, Marvin Iberg and Bill Mullenax. When Iberg finished testifying he was so confident about the outcome that he was quoted by the Arkansas

Democrat saying, "I have nothing to be ashamed of. If there is justice, I don't have anything to worry about. It's an unfortunate situation that this whole thing came up."

Many of those who provided testimony to the grand jury had also testified at the coroner's inquest of 1960, including Iberg, Mullenax, Joe Martin (the jailer), George Hartje (prosecuting attorney in 1960), Robert Delph (Marvin's friend who drove Marvin's car to Conway), Lou Cogbill (also incarcerated in the Faulkner County Jail on the night of Marvin's death), Joe Flakes (who was arrested with Marvin), Robert Oliver (who was also in the car), and Charles Hackney, whose letter to my parents initiated our search for the truth. Hackney testified that he saw two officers enter Marvin's cell, take him out to the stair landing, and beat him.

There were also individuals who had not testified at the inquest but now testified to the grand jury, including Arkansas' State Chief Medical Examiner Dr. Fahmy Malak and John Ellis Green, my mother's nephew and the person who notified my parents of Marvin's death.

Then there were the names that were new to the case: Dr. Edward O. Fox, who performed Marvin's 1960 autopsy: Ora Macon, the wife of now deceased Harve Macon; Juanita Thomas, who said police chief C.O. Hensley came to her home and told her and her husband that he hit Marvin in the back of the head; Nora Martin, wife of jailer Joe Martin; Bobby Walton, who was sitting outside the Sunset Café and witnessed Marvin's arrest; and two women, Peggy Greene and her mother, Lavenia Martin, who lived near the Sunset Café and who were rumored to have had relationships with officers Iberg and Mullenax.

Since the grand jury proceedings were not open to the public, there were others who testified whose names were kept in confidence. However, some who testified before the grand jury did interviews with the media that were published. Of particular interest was that of Mrs. Ora Macon, the wife of Harve Macon, whose testimony raised questions about the cover story police had concocted.

The cover-up story maintained that on or about midnight Friday night, Harve Macon called and asked officers to come to his home and arrest his son, Curtis, because Curtis was drunk and out of control. The officers said they came, arrested Curtis, and then invited Harve to accompany them to take Curtis to jail, ostensibly so he could 'witness' his son's incarceration.

Afterwards, they drove Harve Macon back to his house. There, they said, Harve saw Marvin's car parked in front of his house and Harve asked the officers to check it out. That request was their excuse to approach the car in the first place.

The problems with this story are legion:

- Curtis Macon testified that he was arrested around 10:30 p.m. Iberg and Mullenax testified Curtis was arrested around 12:45 a.m. That two hour and 15 minute difference is significant. If Curtis was arrested at 10:30, the officer's cover story about being on Markham because they were taking Harve Macon home after Curtis' arrest is not true.

- The police logs from that night would have shown what time Curtis was arrested, but they could not be found and have never been found. These logs could have incriminated the officers. Someone disposed of them.

- Why would they invite Harve Macon to 'witness' his son's incarceration? And if Harve called police because he was afraid of his son, would the police then ask Harve to sit in the back seat of the cruiser next to his son?

- Harve lived next door to the Sunset Café and across the street from the Deluxe Café, two popular night-time gathering places for the Black community. He was used to lots of cars parked on his street. Why would he suddenly be bothered by Marvin's car?

- Harve Macon never testified that he was actually with the officers at any time that night. But he did use some of the same phrases and wording as the officers, as if he'd been coached from the same script.

- There was another, very different and much more plausible, explanation for why these two officers were already on Markham at 1:00 a.m.

Ora Macon's testimony also explained why, during the inquest two and half decades earlier, George Hartje had put a strange emphasis on making sure the jury heard that Ora did not see Marvin's arrest.

In an interview with Mark Carnopis, a writer with the Arkansas Democrat, Ora Macon said that two Conway Police officers came to her home on Friday, May 6, 1960, and talked to her husband in their police car for about 20 minutes. She said her husband told her the police kept telling him over and over that Williams was drunk.

Ora's testimony raised the question of why on the morning after Marvin is beaten to death, the two arresting officers would go back to Harve Macon's house? Why would they have him come out and sit in a police car where they could talk to him privately for about 20 minutes? Why would they tell Harve Macon, over and over again, that Marvin was drunk?

I believe this conversation was when the officers gave Harve Macon the "script" for what he and his son, Curtis, had to say at the coroner's inquest the next day. I also believe they made it clear to Harve what the consequences would be for him and his family if he deviated from that script, which Harve never did.

What Harve and every African American knew back then was that his life and the lives of his family would have been in jeopardy if he'd refused to cooperate with the police department and their allies. His son Curtis had just heard a Black man beaten to death in jail. Curtis had already told complete strangers about the beating, and no doubt he told his father, too. Knowing what white officials would do to hide the truth, Harve Macon must have felt he had no other option than to testify as they told him. Harve, too, was a victim.

Another key person to testify before the grand jury was Peggy Green, the African American woman who lived with her mother near Markham Street, one street over from the Sunset Café. By her own admission to the press, she had dated Marvin before his marriage. According to the testimony of others, Peggy was known in the Black community for having relationships with white men, especially police officers, but in her testimony she denied having relationships with either Iberg or Mullenax.

Our cousin John Ellis later told our family what he said to the grand jury, some of which involved this woman. He told them that against his advice, Marvin continued to have a friendly relationship with Peggy after his marriage. John Ellis firmly believed that in Marvin's eyes this relationship was only friendly, but that Peggy was still in love with him. John Ellis also told us that officer Marvin Iberg was having an affair with Peggy Green.

And there it was. Motive.

This was the bombshell information John Ellis and others testified to before the grand jury. This explained why Marvin had been stopped numerous times by

Iberg and Mullenax, a fact which also came out in the grand jury trial. It explained why they threatened him to stay out of Conway. Most of all, it explained why both Iberg and Mullenax were on Markham Street that night.

Iberg was involved with Peggy, but the other arresting officer, Bill Mullenax, was also known to visit the house, supposedly spending his time with her mother, Lavenia Martin. Other officers also visited the home, including Police chief C. O. Hensley, who accompanied Iberg to Marvin's cell twice on the night he was killed, and who told Juanita Thomas that he had "hit and killed a boy, Williams of Menifee."

But it was Marvin Iberg who was obsessed and enraged by Peggy's lingering feelings for my brother. John Ellis and others believed that Iberg's jealousy set the stage for what happened the night my brother was killed. John Ellis was not bashful about his views of these two women. He said he pleaded with Marvin not to speak with Peggy when he visited the Sunset Café or the Deluxe Diner, but Marvin did not heed his advice.

John Ellis also told the grand jury that in 1960 he worked at the Conway Movie Theater. Because the theater was segregated during that time, he had to enter and leave through the rear entrance of the building. This entrance led down a stairwell to the street where Peggy and her mother lived. His walks home from work between 11:30 pm and midnight took him directly past their house, and it was not unusual for him to see Iberg and Mullenax parked in Peggy's front yard at that hour. Sometimes he would see one of the officers sitting in the police car with a woman. The other officer, he assumed, was inside the home.

The more I thought about John Ellis' comments, the more I believed them. A few years ago I reached out to Peggy through a friend of hers and asked if she would be willing to talk to me about the case. I was surprised when she refused.

Why would she not speak with the brother of the man she once cared for? Six decades have passed, Marvin is gone, the officers are dead. I have no doubt that Peggy has a difficult story of her own and I have compassion for her. The power imbalance in relationships between white men, especially those in authority, and Black women is well-documented in American history. Beyond that, her home situation was clearly dysfunctional, to say the least. So I do not judge Peggy or hold her responsible. But I do believe there is information that only she knows that could shed light on the truth of what happened to Marvin. To me, her silence speaks volumes. And when a man has been murdered, silence is complicity.

Had these women been forthcoming they could have confirmed the one piece of evidence that eluded us – motive. Embarrassing as it might have been to admit to these relationships, it could have sealed the fate of these lying, murderous police officers and restored the honor and dignity my brother deserved.

CHAPTER 22

Indictment

The special grand jury began its final deliberations on Wednesday, March 6, 1985. At least 39 witnesses testified during the fourteen-day proceedings. The Arkansas Gazette reported that two witnesses, Iberg and Mullenax, were recalled by the grand jury, and they talked to each of them for about an hour and twenty minutes. We didn't know if this was a good sign or not. All we knew was that another chapter in Marvin's death was about to be written. This jury, from all indications, took their work seriously and did a thorough job.

As Judge Lineberger assembled the jurors in the courthouse to read them their instructions, we learned that their findings would be revealed on Friday, March 8, 1985, at 9 a.m. Until then, it would be secret.

On March 8, 1985, Marvin Iberg and Bill Mullenax were charged with the murder of my brother, Marvin Leonard Williams. The indictment read, "We the special grand jury of Faulkner County, in Conway, Arkansas, believe after our diligent investigation of the last 13 days (February 18 through March 6, 1985) that those in authority and responsible for convening of the coroner's inquest of May 7, 1960, into the death of Marvin Williams, did not do so in a manner necessary for the public to have been sufficiently involved. We believe the coroner's jury did not have adequate information, specifically:

- The failure to introduce the Conway Police Department logs;
- The failure to introduce the Conway Police Department Radio logs;
- The lack of a completed autopsy report;

- The lack of sufficient witnesses, testimony and evidence.

Therefore, we disagree with the results of the 1960 coroner's inquest into the death of Marvin Williams."

As the indictment was read aloud in the courtroom, I remember turning around in my seat, trying to make eye contact with my mother and father, my sisters, and Marvin's two children, Sharon and Ricky. Daddy was in disbelief, rubbing his head over and over, his eyes filled with tears. The faces of my loved ones in that moment will live with me forever. I was so thankful that God allowed them to live long enough to see some semblance of justice for their son, father, and brother.

It took twenty-five years to learn the truth, and that is a long time to wait. When I think about that, a message Martin Luther King gave during a commencement exercise at Wesleyan University comes to mind, "The arc of the moral universe is long, but it bends towards justice."

We had so much to be thankful for that day. I was grateful to the men and women who served on the grand jury. They'd shown tremendous courage and, in the words of Gary Isbell, "incredible integrity," especially at a time when the political establishment and other centers of influence and power within the City of Conway simply wanted our case to go away so that whatever sins their colleagues had committed would stay buried with my brother's remains.

My family and I were deeply grateful to Mike Masterson, the investigative reporter with the Arkansas Democrat, who literally risked his life and career as he worked tirelessly to keep our case in the public's eye. The national attention Marvin's case received was largely due to his work. Whenever my mother would speak of Mike, she would do so in a loving fashion. She was so fond of Mike that she collected and placed in a binder every article he wrote about Marvin's case. Mike Masterson is a rare breed of investigative reporter, and we praised God for bringing him into our lives.

I was also grateful to Governor Bill Clinton, who risked his political future by investing his time and the state's financial resources to reopen a 25-year-old suspicious death case involving a young Black man. Bill Clinton knew the credibility of the judicial system was at stake, and he still pursued justice. He saw a wrong and sought to right it.

Lastly, we were thankful for Gary Isbell and Judge John Lineberger. These men were incredible. I never asked them if they were men of faith, but I know beyond a shadow of doubt that God used these men to unearth that which had been hidden for so many years.

It was apparent from news accounts that the prosecutor Gary Isbell respected this jury. He was quoted by Lamar James of the Arkansas Gazette (Thursday, March 7, 1985), "I was really excited with this jury. These people have incredible integrity. They put their hearts, their minds and souls into the investigation, any decision they made people should be proud of."

The respect was mutual. Gary devoted countless hours to the case and when it was over the grand jury presented him with a wooden plaque for his work. The plaque read: "Indictment."

That was a tremendous day of celebration and thanksgiving for our family and friends. We all gathered at Mother and Daddy's house. Connie and my sisters Carolyn, Verna, and Donna were there, and so were Marvin's children Sharon and Ricky. We were excited and cautiously optimistic. Mother was praising the Lord, she and Daddy were so grateful. Over dinner we talked about how far we'd come, what it had taken to get to this point, and how it wasn't all in vain. Carolyn, who to this day is very emotional when she talks about Marvin, was elated that someone would finally have to give an account of what happened to him.

As happy as we were, we only shared our true feelings within our close family. My mother and father were very private individuals who weren't comfortable in the spotlight and preferred to be in the background. They were careful and selective in when and how they celebrated that one victory. A lot of that had to do with the era in which they came up. In their experience, to openly express relief that a white person might be punished for a crime could get them killed. So they only showed emotion in private with us, where they felt most comfortable and safe.

While the indictment was an essential first step, we knew it would take a miracle to convict these men. A grand jury is not a public proceeding, so it was protected from the public scrutiny and pressure such a sensitive trial would receive. We had no illusions that a public trial would be able to focus so completely on justice. Everything from this point forward would be an uphill challenge for us. Marvin Iberg and Bill Mullenax were not going down without a fight. Though no longer police officers with the Conway Police Department, they were well-entrenched and had the benefits and protections of a racist system that would support them no matter what.

In light of the indictments, our family decided to postpone our civil suit until the criminal charges against Iberg and Mullenax were resolved in state court. As we waited to see who would be appointed judge and prosecutor for the criminal trial, Helen Rice Grinder of Conway, who was both Marvin Iberg's niece and his defense attorney, filed two motions in the Faulkner County Court to set aside the charges of first-degree murder against Iberg.

Within eleven days of the issuance of the two indictments, current Conway Police Chief Vonnie Taylor and former Police Chief Ruben Goss, who at the time was serving as Faulkner County Clerk, wrote letters to the editor supporting the indicted men. The letters were published in the Log Cabin Democrat and stated that Iberg was a "fair, honest, and dedicated policeman and never used more force that was absolutely necessary in an arrest." It claimed that he called every woman "ma'am" and every man "sir." He and Mullenax "…were some of the most honest, upstanding people in the world… Their character is above reproach."

As the Log Cabin Democrat marketed this op-ed piece to its predominantly white readership, the same readership from which the criminal jury would be selected, the message these two elected officials were sending to their white base was obvious. They wanted every prospective juror to know that irrespective of the facts or medical science, these two officers were "good ole boys."

The truth was not so pretty, however. Marvin Iberg frequently used the word "Nigga" when speaking to or about Black men and women. He might have called every white man "sir" and every white woman "ma'am," but it's laughable to think he addressed Black people that way in 1960. Testimony before the grand jury made it clear that these officers were known to beat up Black men whenever they had the chance, and especially when the Black men were locked up in jail and powerless. It was the way they passed their time, it was a recreational activity. "Let's go down to Markham Street and harass the black folk," they were quoted as saying. One grand jury witness recalled Iberg saying, "We got some Niggers in the jail, let's go have some fun," before he and another officer terrorized and beat some Black inmates.

As for the two public officials lauding Iberg and Mullenax, I thought to myself, where were they the night these officers unlawfully removed my brother from his vehicle? Or when they sent officer Langford ahead of them with Joe Flakes while they kept Marvin behind? Or when they brought Marvin into the courthouse bleeding profusely from his forehead? And what about when Iberg and Chief Hensley returned twice to my brother's cell, supposedly to bring him his shoe?

Could they explain why these "honest men" lied about Marvin reeking of alcohol when the autopsy report said there was none in his system?

And finally, could they explain why, if these "fine men" would "go out of their way to help someone if they were black or white," would the Black community have feared them so much?

The letter was a dog whistle to the white community, meant to reach those who would be called to serve as jurors in the upcoming criminal trial.

The deck was already being stacked against us.

PART V

The Criminal Trial

CHAPTER 23

Mullenax

The long-awaited announcement as to who would preside over the first-degree murder cases of Iberg and Mullenax had finally come. Chief Justice Jack Holt Jr. selected Judge Don Langston, the 12th Judicial District Circuit and Chancery Judge from Fort Smith, Arkansas. In addition to presiding over the cases, Judge Langston would name the special prosecutor, and appointing Gary Isbell was first on his list. Judge Langston was quoted in article written by the Arkansas Gazette as saying, "I intend to ask Mr. Isbell to continue on the case. I believe it would be proper because he did secure the indictments. It would take him less time to prepare himself."

We prayed Gary Isbell would accept the judge's invitation to continue his role as special prosecutor, but Gary decided to decline. He'd been in the City of Conway and away from his family for weeks, and the weight of responsibility and the stress of this case was intense. I knew that as well as anyone and could not blame him for his decision.

On Tuesday, April 30, 1985, Judge Langston named Sam Heuer of Batesville, Arkansas, 16th Judicial District Prosecuting Attorney as special prosecutor.

As the criminal proceedings were about to get underway, I noticed something peculiar about the date set for Iberg and Mullenax's arraignment, May 13, 1985. It was one week after the 25th anniversary of Marvin's death. To me this was not a coincidence. God's hand had directed us and this case from day one, and now these officers were charged with first-degree murder. They would enter the same building and walk up the same stairwell they used to bring my innocent, bleeding brother to his cell. They never dreamed that someday they would have to account for what they did that night. But neither did I. It was one of those moments that forced me to stop and acknowledge the power and the goodness of God, as I watched Him weave together all the interconnecting pieces of the puzzle that would tell the story of my brother's final days.

On the 25th anniversary of Marvin's death, we held a small gathering of family and friends at the burial site. We placed wreaths and baskets of flowers near the small tombstone that marked Marvin's grave. The service started about 3 p.m. in the afternoon, the same time of day my parents were notified of Marvin's death. It lasted about 20 minutes. My mother could not attend; it was more than she could bear. The service concluded with words from my pastor, the Reverend Matthew Smith, and from Brother Brutus Moored of Harrison Street Church of Christ in Conway, where Marvin's children Ricky and Sharon attended.

As expected, Iberg and Mullenax plead innocent in the Faulkner County Circuit Court to first-degree murder charges in connection with Marvin's death. Both were allowed to remain free on $10,000 signature bonds. Judge Langston denied two motions filed by defense attorneys Helen Rice Grinder, the attorney for Iberg, and Bart Mullis, who represented Bill Mullenax, which argued that the statute of limitations had expired by the time the case was reopened. In denying the motion, Langston had to remind the two attorneys that there was no statute of limitations on first-degree murder charges.

Listening to the arguments of these two defense attorneys, I found it interesting that initially neither of them argued their clients were innocent. The position they took was 'Look, our clients may have done it, but it's too late to charge them with it.'

Then Bart Mullis, who represented Mullenax, filed another motion that was even more revealing: He asked the court not to consolidate the trials of his client and Iberg. To justify his request, Mullis claimed that "evidence in the case doesn't apply equally to both defendants. There would be issues presented at the trial which could allow the jury to reach a different conclusion on each defendant."

Wow, what a bombshell! Put simply, Mullenax's lawyer was acknowledging that there was evidence that Iberg was guilty of murder, while Mullenax was not. The only reason Mulllis would ask to separate the cases was because he knew it would benefit his client.

Left to his own devices, I think Mullis would have encouraged Mullenax to talk. The facts supporting the first-degree murder charge were solid and would be difficult to disprove. By talking, Mullenax might avoid or lighten a lesser charge.

At the time of the trial Iberg was 50 years old and Mullenax was 48. Iberg was now a truck driver and Mullenax was a Sargeant in the state police. They'd grown up together, worked on the Conway police force together, and were still keeping each other's secrets. Iberg struck me as the leader of the two and probably the initial aggressor, while I've always felt Mullenax was the weaker of the two and behaved like more of a follower. He did not accompany Iberg and Chief Hensley back to Marvin's cell the night of the murder, but he knew what happened and he participated in beating my brother in the parking lot. I believe Mullenax would have talked, but there were too many people still in positions of power who could have been implicated if he had. So, his former and current enablers convinced him that if he stuck with the cover story, he would again be exonerated. And that is what he did.

* * *

As the trial proceeded, you could see the swagger return in these officers. They were among friends who had allowed them to operate with impunity as officers with the Conway Police Department. They could rely on friendships with certain people in positions of power and decision making, and they could rely on history (especially in the south) as a reliable predictor of what the outcome would be for white officers accused of assaulting and murdering Black men. They were in good hands, and they knew it.

At the outset of the criminal trial, Faulkner County officials made clear their unwillingness to bear any costs associated with Marvin's death. It was as if they would dirty their hands by supporting efforts to find the truth. Faulkner County Judge Gerald Ward, at the urging of the Quorum Court, asked Governor Clinton for financial assistance to fund the trial. The Governor had already allocated $58,410 for the costs of the Special Grand Jury that indicted Iberg and Mullenax. But Clinton, keeping his commitment to have Marvin's case thoroughly investigated, responded in the affirmative, just as he did with the grand jury investigation.

Here's what the governor said in his response to Judge Ward's request:

"I do not believe that it is the responsibility of the governor to finance criminal proceedings. I do recognize, however, that without my...

offering of funds, the calling of a grand jury to look into the death of Marvin Williams would not have occurred. Given the unusual nature of this case, I am willing to provide assistance for actual costs incurred in the trial. The money remaining after the payment of costs incurred during the grand jury investigation will be made available to the special prosecutor for verified expenses directly related to the trial. If this amount is not sufficient to cover the expenses, I will consider making additional money available to Mr. Heuer, the special prosecutor."

Once again, this was not a politically popular position for Clinton to take, to say the least. After providing funds for the grand jury, no one would have faulted him if he declined to pay for what should have been a county expense. But I believe this case had become personal for him, too. His support of our family's search for truth and justice never wavered. If he hadn't opened the state's coffers to cover these expenses, I'm not sure what would have happened to our case. In 1960, Faulkner County officials made it crystal clear that Marvin's life meant very little to them. That was still the prevailing attitude in 1985, and these officials made sure none of their local tax dollars were used to resolve a murder that occurred in one of their own county facilities.

On Wednesday, July 3, 1985, jury selection began. Judge Langston drew the names of 180 potential jurors from the county's jury wheel. Prospective jurors were told to appear in the courtroom the following Monday, when they would be asked questions about any pre-existing biases or connections to the case, and the final jury would be chosen.

Monday morning, as we waited for the voir dire process to start, I learned that the key witness in our case, Charles Hackney, who saw and heard two officers beating my brother, had filed a motion in the Faulkner County Circuit Court asking to be excluded from testifying in the trial. In his motion to the court, he cited threats, including a personal threat against his wife, as the reason for his reluctance to testify. He also said an unnamed person had threatened his family with bodily harm if a conviction occurred as a result of his testimony.

This wasn't the first time Mr. Hackney was threatened. He was threatened in 1960 by then prosecuting attorney, George Hartje, Jr. A few hours after Marvin's death, jailer Joe Martin took Hackney to Hartje's office where Hartje told him, "If you want to get out of my jail, you better say you didn't see a G*d**n thing." The fear

Hackney felt for his family was one our community knew all too well. It was the same fear my father now felt for me and my family.

One day, Daddy asked me to stop by his job. He still worked as a day laborer for Morris Furniture Store in Conway, and I met him at the back of the store. Daddy told me that someone had told him there were threats on my life. I believed what he was telling me was true, because he was literally shaking as he spoke. I promised him I'd be careful.

Later that evening, I stopped by my parents' home to check on them as I always did. My mother pulled me into a separate room and told me that what my father said earlier was not true. She wanted me to know my dad was terrified by the attention our case had received and was worried someone might try to hurt me. I went to the back room where Daddy was sitting and asked him why on earth he would make up such a story? His response was so kind and loving that the disappointment I felt disappeared. With tears in his eyes, he said, "I lost one son, and I don't want to lose my last one."

So I understood Mr. Hackney's request. It was not made from cowardice, it was made from fear for his family and his own safety.

CHAPTER 24

Secret Testimony Comes Out

Two weeks before the trial, a 36-page report summarizing the secret testimonies of the witnesses who appeared before the grand jury was released to the public. The Arkansas Democrat published excerpts of the testimony of at least thirty witnesses. In this article, reporter Mark Carnopis identified by name those individuals whose testimony changed the trajectory of our case.

- Mrs. Ola Ward testified that she, her husband, and two friends were parked near the courthouse on May 6, 1960. They were there because the courthouse was used as a civil defense area for the City of Conway and there had been tornado warnings. She saw Iberg and Mullenax picking up a black male who was on his hands and knees in a parking lot close to the courthouse. She testified that she turned and saw them after someone in the car yelled, "They are going to kill him!"

- Joe Goss, a Faulkner County resident, testified he worked with Iberg at a trucking firm after Iberg left the Conway Police Dept. Goss said he overheard a discussion in the firm's office in which Iberg mentioned an investigation. Goss said Iberg appeared to be upset and said something like, "We thought he was already dead when we got him into the courthouse or jail." Goss said Iberg told him prior to his appearance before the grand jury that he should forget what he'd heard.

- Dr. Joseph Davis, the Chief Medical Examiner in Miami-Dade County, Florida for 28 years, also testified and explained his conclusions saying, "What is unequivocal is that there was force applied in the region of the left ear. The petrous ridge, which was fractured here, is one of the hardest bones in the body. It is phenomenally hard." Davis said the autopsy showed that blows had likely been applied to Williams' body from various directions. He said bleeding described in the left kidney is consistent with a blow. A cut on Williams' forehead in itself could have been caused by a fall on stairs, he said. But the two triangular shaped bruises surrounding that cut would not have been caused by such a fall unless there was a corresponding pattern on the stairs, which there was not.

- Dr. Charles S. Petty had been both the Chief Medical Examiner in Dallas, Texas and the Director of that city's Southwest Institute of Forensic Science for 16 years. He was a graduate of Harvard Medical School and had been chosen as a member of the forensic pathology panel for the U.S. House of Representatives Select Committee on Assassinations which investigated the death of President John F. Kennedy. Dr. Petty said he, too, had never seen or heard of a forehead injury causing such a fracture behind the left ear. "Oh, come on now, I can't go along with that," he said. "I don't think that (falling on the forehead) caused the injury at all. I think he was hit over the head in the left temporal area…The injury, itself, is the fracture of the skull. That's what killed him in association with the bleeding."

- Ms. Marie Bradford of North Little Rock, Arkansas, testified that a man who was in the jail that night told her that police beat a man to death that night. Ms. Bradford said the man (possibly the man Hackney referred to as "this other boy that slept right by me") told her, "They beat him coming up the stairs and they beat him until he quit hollering."

- Ms. Emogene Handley testified that Marvin Williams had been stopped by police and was told to leave Peggy Green alone. At Marvin's funeral, she observed Peggy become so upset she had to be taken out of the church.

- Wendell Green Jr., a friend of Marvin's, testified that Marvin told him a Conway Police Officer had followed him home once. Green also said Marvin was seeing Peggy even after he was married.

• Dr. Edward O. Fox, a 1957 graduate of Yale School of Medicine, was a resident clinical pathologist at the University of Arkansas for Medical Sciences at Little Rock in July of 1959 through July of 1961. He conducted the autopsy on Marvin. Dr. Fox identified a document as a copy of a report he prepared on the autopsy performed on Marvin Williams on May 6, 1960. Dr. Fox described a soft area of swelling which was palpable, superior to posterior to the left ear of the decedent. In describing this for the jury, the doctor remembered this area was about 3½ to 4 inches long and about 1½ inches wide and described it as a sausage shape. He further stated this palpable or swollen area was directly over the skull fracture. Dr. Fox stated the injury to the forehead could have possibly been caused by a fall, perhaps if the subject was manacled, but it looked more like the body was still and was hit by something that was moving. The doctor stated he did not find any external evidence with respect to the left shoulder or any kind of trauma that would have related to a fall. He further stated that the injury to the forehead was not associated with the death of Marvin Williams, but the fracture of the back of Williams' skull caused bleeding and the bleeding caused displacement of the brain. The displacement of the brain caused hemorrhage into the pons and this hemorrhage was ultimately fatal to the decedent.

As to the analysis of blood alcohol of the decedent, Dr. Fox testified that the Department of Pharmacology performed the analysis to determine the level of blood alcohol and his role was in getting the specimen and that he drew blood from the heart, placed it in a container, labeled it, and gave it to the Department of Pharmacology. Dr. Fox further testified about the dissipation of alcohol in one's blood level. Dr. Fox stated this matter was brought up again when Charlie Thomas, a producer for "20/20," called and asked him if he was ever a pathologist in Arkansas. Dr. Fox said he responded by saying yes, and that he knew what Charlie Thomas was calling about, that it was concerning the Black boy that was killed. Dr. Fox further stated that he did not recall discussing the case with Mr. McNutt on the day of the autopsy.

- Dr. Fahmy A. Peter Malak testified he was the chief medical examiner for the State of Arkansas and had been for more than six years. Dr. Malak stated that he came into contact with the case at the request of the prosecuting attorney of Faulkner County, Mr. Bill Brazil. At that time he reviewed the autopsy report and slides taken from the organs of Marvin Williams. In addition, he reviewed the photographs on file in the University and obtained duplicates of these. He identified photographs for the grand jury, and the photographs were intro- duced. Dr. Malak described the autopsy report concerning Marvin Williams as being a very good, thorough autopsy, and thereafter went into his observations of various portions of Dr. Fox's autopsy report with the grand jury. After a review of the autopsy and the slides, Dr. Malak concluded within reasonable medical certainty and accuracy that Marvin Williams was a healthy individual and had no pre-exist- ing diseases. He further concluded that Marvin Williams was not an alcoholic. He stated that 24 years after the autopsy, he exhumed the body and observed the same crack or fracture of the skull as was described in the original autopsy report of Dr. Fox. He informed the grand jury that, through experience on cadavers, studies show that it takes about 400-600 pounds of pressure per square inch to crack the skull in the manner that he had observed. Dr. Malak further stated that the method of determining blood alcohol as existed in 1960 was an acceptable and reliable method. Dr. Malak stated that within a reasonable degree of medical certainty, Marvin Williams died of a head injury as a result of the fracture in the rear of his head, which caused the damage to his brain and meningeal artery. He stated that the area of the skull in which the fracture existed was a hard area to crack. Dr. Malak described the laceration over Mr. Williams' right eye and the bleeding around Mr. Williams' kidney. He stated that he felt the fracture of the skull was caused by a blunt object applied to the skull along the area of the fracture line. He further stated that in his opinion, Marvin Williams died a minimum of six hours after he received the injury, but that it could be longer.

- Bill Langford was employed by the City of Conway as a police officer and radio operator from late 1958 until 1961. He stated that at that time he worked a 12-hour shift from 6 a.m. until 6 p.m. and probably spent 80% of his time inside as a radio operator, where he was responsible for keeping records in the office, the radio traffic, the telephone calls, and administrative duties. He stated that on May 5 he was called over the radio and asked to come outside and accompany two field officers to the courthouse to help lock up two subjects who had been arrested. As best he could remember, they came in the same car and unloaded the prisoners at the west door of the courthouse. He stated that one prisoner seemed capable of walking and did walk under his own power, and he was instructed to take that prisoner and go with him to the jail. He entered the courthouse while the other two officers were lifting the other prisoner from the back seat of the patrol car, and at that point he lost sight of their activity, going on up the courthouse steps and locking the prisoner up. He stated on the way back down he met the two officers with their prisoner and, as best he could remember this was the second landing, which was where a steel or wrought iron type door was located. He remembered it being extremely stormy and one of his primary duties during stormy weather was to obtain as much information as possible from the state civil defense, and that as best he could remember sometime prior to midnight they had put some watches or some warning out. Regarding the location of the prisoners in the police car, he recalled that one was sitting upright in the back seat and the other was laying over in the seat with his head and shoulders against the door on the back of the side of the car. Mr. Langford testified that as best as he could remember, when he met the officers with Mr. Williams on the steps as they were coming up and he was going down, the officers stated that Mr. Williams had fallen on the steps and cut his head. At that point, he recalls observing one officer on either side of Mr. Williams, with the officers having Mr. Williams by the arms but Mr. Williams appeared to be standing on his own will power. Mr. Langford further recalled Chief Hensley calling later that night and asking for someone to come by and pick him up. Mr. Langford felt like he had dispatched officer Iberg to pick up Chief Hensley due to the fact that officer Iberg would have been the senior officer on duty at that time. Mr. Langford further testified as to the weaponry and law enforcement equipment that was maintained by officers in May of 1960, which consisted of a night stick and "slappers."

• Joe S. Martin stated he started work for Sheriff Joe Castleberry as a deputy sheriff in June of 1956 and worked as chief deputy and jailer until 1975. He further testified as to the location in which certain prisoners were placed in the jail at that period of time. As to the night of May 5 or the morning of May 6, concerning Marvin Williams, Mr. Martin testified that Mr. Iberg and Mr. Mullenax brought a black subject upstairs and woke him up to tell him it was coming a storm, a tornado or something with bad winds, and then told him that "this boy," he fell outside, out there on the step. Mr. Martin stated that at that point he went back and laid down. Mr. Martin stated the officers were on each side of Mr. Williams at the time of the conversation and that Williams was moving one way or the other all the time they were standing there. A few minutes after they left, he heard the doors rattling up in the jail and got up and saw the subject standing up holding the bars to the door. Mr. Martin said he asked the subject to stop shaking the bars to the door, and the subject stated that he wanted to get out. The subject stated that he was picked up by the city, in response to [Mr. Martin's] question as to who had gotten him. The subject stated that he needed to go to work the next morning because he worked for Wards Body Shop. When he asked the subject what he did there, the subject said he painted. Mr. Martin asked if he knew Wade Howell and the subject responded that he worked for Wade Howell. Mr. Martin told Mr. Williams that the city would come over between 6:00 and 7:00 to get their prisoners out of jail and that he should just lay down and be quiet. Mr. Martin stated that Mr. Williams informed him the police had picked him up at Plumerville in his car. Mr. Martin stated that Mr. Williams then walked back over to his bunk and sat down. Mr. Martin stated he observed the cut on Mr. Williams head during the course of this conversation but did not notice any blood on Mr. Williams, and during this conversation Mr. Williams was crying when he was shaking the door. As Mr. Williams was crying he was wanting his father to get him out.

Of all the excerpts published in Mark Carnopis' article, Joe Martin's secret testimony bothered me the most. Twenty-five years later, he added one detail he did not mention in his extremely detailed testimony to the coroner's inquest the day after my brother's death.

The new detail was that "Williams was moving one way or the other all the time they were standing there."

This new observation was not mentioned in Joe Martin's original testimony, but conveniently, he recalls it 25 years later. The implication was that Marvin's unsteadiness was a sign of intoxication, and of course the cover story hinged on Marvin being intoxicated.

But Marvin had no alcohol in his system. So, if these observations were true, they were more evidence that my brother had been beaten in the parking lot and possibly also as he was being arrested on Markham Street.

It takes a special kind of evil, the highest level of evil, for a person to see and refuse to respond to the pain and suffering of another human being. Joe Martin watched my brother bleed and did not even try to honor his requests. His actions speak for themselves. Joe Martin knew drunk when he saw it, because he saw it all the time as the Faulkner County jailer. He was lying when he said Marvin was intoxicated, but lying to protect white officials came easy. It was pervasive within the city and county police departments, as well as among the judicial officers and elected officials who governed the City of Conway back then.

CHAPTER 25

A Certain Kind of Jury

One evening before jury selection for the criminal trial began, I received an unexpected phone call at 11:30 p.m. It was Sam Heuer, the special prosecuting attorney. The lateness of the hour and his tone told me this was not a casual call. Other than the first time Sam introduced himself to our family, this might have been the first time he and I spoke privately.

Bypassing all the pleasantries, Sam told me why he was calling. He said, and I quote, "You need to be careful in Conway. This is one of the most racist cities I've ever been in." He did not give me any specifics or share what he'd encountered – just the warning. Then he apologized for the lateness of the call, and we ended the conversation.

Sam had been spending a lot of time in Conway researching, gathering information, and speaking with numerous individuals as he prepared to prosecute the two officers indicted for killing my brother. At the same time there was a lot of press about the case, and I was in every interview. Sam never told me what prompted that call, but I suspect he'd heard something in his work or in his interviews for the case that convinced him I was at risk. I did not ask him for specifics and he never mentioned it again.

To say that I was unnerved by the call would be an understatement. What struck me most about Sam's warning was that it was so like the one my father had given me a couple of weeks earlier. For a moment, I wondered if it was worth it. Had we pushed the system beyond its capacity to deal with racially sensitive matters such as ours? I shared this information with Connie and she, too, was unnerved by Sam's warning to me. At that point, she became extremely fearful for my life. It was a moment of reflection for both of us, but then I encouraged myself by what the Apostle Paul told Timothy in 2 Timothy 1:7 – "For God hath not given us the spirit of fear; but power, and of love, and of a sound mind."

I would not succumb to fear by allowing it to win in this case. Fear can be paralyzing. The threats of a few "good ole boys" would not prevent us from taking Marvin's case to its completion. Marvin suffered too much for that to happen.

Finally, jury selection got underway. I sat through the entire process and you could feel the tension in the air. It was as if God had rolled back the hands of time to the 1950s and 60s, when someone of my hue was made to feel out of place and at risk in this setting.

There were several African Americans in the pool of prospective jurors, so our chances for having a jury that reflected the community it represented seemed good. It was extremely important to have someone on that jury who understood and could speak to a Black perspective. Only a Black person could understand the fears and experiences of our community. A white person could empathize, maybe even relate to a Black person's emotional experience, but that was as far as they could go. There were good and decent white people who lived in the Conway area, but they couldn't identify with the Black experience, and therefore could not understand the plight of Black Americans living in the south during the 1950s and 60s.

My optimism waned when I saw what the defense attorneys were doing. Their collective strategy was simple: they would use every one of their challenges to eliminate all prospective Black jurors as well as any professional, educated white juror. They not only wanted an all-white jury, they wanted a certain kind of all-white jury: one that was rural and non-professional, and that had little or no post-secondary education.

I learned a lot during that jury selection process, about myself and about the community. Some prominent people whom my family and I had looked up to and respected were interviewed as potential jurors. Their responses to questions exposed my naivete.

One potential juror Sam Heuer interviewed was the wife of a wealthy businessman who was quite successful in insurance and real estate. At the start of the interview, she told Sam she was pressed for time because she was on her way to an out-of-state church event or mission trip. As I listened, I thought she'd be an excellent juror. She was white, educated, successful, and was doing God's work. Maybe she could be a positive influence on this jury?

But when Sam pressed her about her thoughts regarding the Williams case, I was appalled by her response. She said, "These men, Iberg and Mullenax, are fighting for their lives and they are clients of ours, they have insurance with our company." Sam responded by asking, "What about Marvin Williams, are you not concerned about what happened to him?" To which she replied, as if it were an afterthought, "Yeah, yeah." And Sam said to her, "I think I'll let you go on your mission trip."

If someone of her stature would openly exhibit this level of insensitivity for a person who'd been bludgeoned to death, our case was in trouble. But she was merely a sample of what was to come.

The defense attorney's strategy worked. They got exactly what they were looking for. The jury was typified by juror Nola Harris of Conway, who was quoted by Lamar James in the Arkansas Gazette five days before the trial saying, "Naturally I want our hometown law enforcement to be found innocent, but added she wouldn't let that attitude get in the way of making a fair decision based on evidence."

Iberg and Mullenax were 19 and 20 years removed from their work as police officers with the City of Conway. But juror Nola Harris still saw them as "hometown law enforcement." She not only identified with them, she openly cheered for them as well. And she had no compunction about saying so before the trial even started.

* * *

Twelve white jurors and two alternates were selected for the criminal trial. Opening arguments started at 9:00 am. on August 19, 1985. The courtroom was so packed with onlookers that many stood along the wall and in the hallways. Television cameras were everywhere.

More than 15 members of our family were in attendance for the start of the trial, including my mother and father, Johnnie and D.V. Williams. We were seated together in a section reserved for us, but as I started to take my seat I noticed a white man embedded right in the middle of our section. I turned to get a better look and recognized Dr. Bland Crowder, my former English professor from Hendrix College. Dr. Crowder smiled at me warmly and gave me an encouraging thumbs up in support of our cause.

Years later I spoke at Dr. Crowder's Memorial Service, and I shared how eight years after I graduated he came to the trial and positioned himself right in the middle of our family. His respect and concern for us and for justice is something I will never forget.

In his opening argument, Sam Heuer gave a brief account of Marvin's actions the night he was murdered. He also gave an overview of what he thought the case was about. Though we all knew race was a motivating factor in Marvin's unlawful arrest, Sam tried to downplay this fact, thinking it would not be well received by this particular all-white jury.

Defense attorneys Helen Rice Grinder and Darrell Stayton, an assistant to Bart Mullis, delivered opening arguments for Marvin Iberg and Bill Mullenax. Both attorneys stuck with the original 1960 script.

In her opening argument, Grinder took a page right out of George Hartje's playbook by suggesting that Marvin's injuries, particularly the four-inch fracture that took his life, occurred prior to his arrest. She told the jurors "there were questions that needed to be answered about Williams' activities the night of his death. I want to know what happened from the time he was at Menifee awake and capable of navigating on his own power until he arrived at Conway incapable of navigating on his own power."

Her inference echoed the one made by George Hartje and Robert McNutt who argued to a jury of twelve white men in 1960 that Marvin in some way contributed to his own demise.

On the other hand, in his opening statement Darrell Stayton suggested that his client, Bill Mullenax, was innocent. He said, "If Iberg and Mullenax had intended to murder Williams, they would have taken pains to hide their actions, which they did not."

My mother was the first member of the family to testify in the state's case. In her testimony, she recounted the last time she saw Marvin, on the afternoon of May 5, 1960.

"He looked so good to me," she said, and when she repeated his last words to her, "I love you," she began to cry.

Several spectators, black and white, openly wept as they listened to my mother. Mother told the jury she didn't smell any alcohol on her son's breath and "she didn't raise him to drink." She told them that authorities never told her about her son's death, that she had to hear about it from her nephew, John Ellis Green.

My father was the next to testify. He told the jurors he never received a phone call or any notification of the coroner's inquest. Daddy said he heard about the inquest from one of his son's fellow workers. He shared that he had viewed his son's body and saw a gash on his forehead, a large "raised up" spot behind his left ear, and bruises on his son's left side and hand. He told the jury he did not recall what he said while testifying before the coroner's jury because his son was dead and a tornado had demolished his home the night before. "I lost everything I had, plus my son."

My father also said that he was told the FBI investigated Marvin's death in 1960, but he had no memory of being questioned by federal authorities, something the defense attorneys inferred had happened. He said he was not satisfied with the coroner's inquest investigation and had asked Guy Jones, a local attorney, to investigate his son's death. He said Jones later told him that he didn't find anything. Sam Heuer asked my father why he did not continue the investigation? My dad said, "Being Black in 1960, a Black man, it was difficult to get anything done."

Following my dad was Marvin's wife, Bonnie, who had remarried and was now living in San Francisco. Bonnie also said she had no memory of being interviewed by the FBI in 1960, and she believed the FBI could have made up the report of her interview. She shared that she and Marvin were happily married, and that she did not think it was unusual for Marvin to go to Conway that night. She hadn't wanted to go to the prom because she had one small child at home and was very pregnant with another.

The idea that my father and Marvin's wife would have forgotten being interviewed by the FBI is ludicrous. Can you imagine having no hope of justice and then the FBI shows up and gives you hope and wants information? Of course, they would have remembered that.

Two of my sisters, Verna Hammond and Carolyn Giles, both of whom attended the prom, testified that Marvin had not been drinking before or during the prom. William T. Keaton, who was Superintendent of the school district in Menifee, testified that nobody was drinking alcohol at the prom.

Also testifying that day was Maggie Powell, the wife of Allen Powell. After the prom, Marvin drove Maggie and Allen to Plumerville before he and three friends drove to Conway. Maggie testified that she danced the last dance with Marvin at the prom and there was no alcohol on his breath. She remembered the last song that was playing just before the prom was cancelled. It was the original version of "Goodnight Sweetheart, Goodnight" by The Overtones.

That night my family gathered at my parent's home. As we discussed the first day of testimony my dad was visibly upset because certain people in Conway whom he and Mother had worked for had failed to appear at the trail. He kept saying to us over and over again, as if he was trying to convince himself, that these people would surely come to the trial soon to support my parents out of respect for all my parents had done for them for so many years.

But those people never came.

My parents gave their best to these people, to their families, and to their companies. They cleaned their homes, washed their clothes, picked up their children from school, cut their grass, carried away their trash, painted their houses, worked in their businesses, and delivered their furniture. They were so loyal to those families. It was painful to watch Mother and Daddy agonize over the conspicuous absences of people they'd believed in and trusted, people they thought would surely stand with them in times of crisis. The least those people could have done was to call my parents, just once, during the five weeks of testimony. Or send a card saying, 'I can't make it but I want you to know I'm thinking about you.' But there was no call, no card, nothing.

What Mother and Daddy didn't understand was that these individuals had already taken a stand. They just didn't have the courage to let my parents know which side of this case they were on. As Martin Luther King once said, "The ultimate measure of a man is not where he stands in moments of comfort and convenience, but where he stands at times of challenge and controversy."

CHAPTER 26

More Testimony

A couple of witnesses testified that they were parked outside the Sunset Cafe and witnessed Marvin's unlawful arrest during the early morning hours of May 6, 1960. One was William Gault of Conway, who testified that he was sitting in his car near the cafe and "I saw the two officers taking Marvin out of the car." He couldn't recall if Marvin went under his own power or had to be helped. Gault further testified that sometime before that night, he saw these same two officers, Iberg and Mullenax, stop Williams' car in Conway and talk to him outside the car.

Leo Morgan was also sitting in a parked vehicle outside the Sunset Cafe. He testified that the officers had to help Joe Flakes into the car, but Marvin simply appeared reluctant. He described Marvin's reactions as "Why are you arresting me – what have I done?"

The testimonies of William Gault, Leo Morgan, and Wendell Green established a pattern of previous harassment of Marvin by Iberg and Mullenax. They revealed that these two officers knew exactly who Marvin was and most certainly recognized his unusual car, a 1953 Chevrolet Bel Air 2-door coupe with a white top and egg-shell body.

Emma Jean Handley of Menifee told the jury she danced with Marvin at the high school prom earlier that night and did not smell alcohol on his breath. Later, when the prom was stopped because of bad weather, she said Marvin and several persons decided to drive to Conway. She said Marvin drove up in his car, got out and said, "Whoever is going to Conway, you'd better come on."

Also testifying for the state was Ollie Willborg, who served as chief deputy for the Faulkner County Sheriff's Office. He brought with him an old sheriff's jail record book, which listed the names of people in custody at the jail in 1960. The court allowed this book to be admitted as evidence. Mr. Willborg told the jury the book contained the names of six people who were in jail the morning my brother was murdered, not just five as was stated at the 1960 inquest. Willborg also said an entry that Marvin was released was crossed out and "Died in Jail" was written above it.

Willborg's introduction of the county's jail record book was a key piece of evidence for the state. It proved that in addition to Marvin, five other men were incarcerated in that jail that night. But only four had testified at the 1960 coroner's inquest: Joe Flakes, Curtis Macon, Lou Cogbill, and Charles Hackney. Where and who was the sixth person?

I believe the missing person was Louie Smith, the inmate to whom Marie Bradford referred in her testimony who told her that police had beat a Black man to death. He's the person Charles Hackney said was "That other boy who was asleep next to me."

It was no accident the coroner's jury did not call Louie Smith to testify at the inquest in 1960. Charles Hackney and Lou Cogbill were out-of-towners. They had no ties to the community or the people in it. But Louie Smith was a local resident. He was a white man from our community, and he might have been less willing, or perhaps outright refused, to help cover up a murder in his own town. That's why George Hartje and Robert McNutt wanted the public to believe he did not exist, and it explains why they disposed of the police logs which would have recorded his presence in the jail. His non-appearance, his non-identification, and his non-testimony was a significant omission.

Unfortunately, by the time of the grand jury hearing, Louie Smith was dead.

Charles Hackney, the person who witnessed my brother being beaten to death in the Faulkner County Jail, appeared under subpoena, and testified reluctantly. Prior to the start of the trial, he received threats that his family would be in danger if he testified and a conviction resulted. Hackney was completely transparent about the threats and intimidation he was experiencing, so we weren't surprised that his testimony now contradicted his previous statements.

Hackney and his home-town friend, Lou Cogbill, were arrested on May 5, 1960 for stealing cash from the Town House Motel Café in Conway. They were put in the "white man's cell" in the Faulkner County Jail, directly opposite Marvin's cell.

As he'd previously testified, Hackney stated that he heard a racket outside the cell around 2 a.m. and looked through an opening and saw two men, both in uniform, with a Black man at the top of the stairs. He said the two men struck the Black man repeatedly with blackjacks and then let him fall to the floor. As Marvin moaned and groaned, Hackney heard one of the two officers say, "That should take care of that son of a bitch." Hackney further testified that the FBI later spoke with him about the beating and told him they would follow-up with him but they never did.

But Hackney made one major change from his previous testimony. He now said that the two men who beat Marvin were Sheriff Joe Castleberry, who was dead and therefore safe from prosecution, and Joe Martin, the former jailer. Hackney also testified that both men were wearing uniforms.

Beyond the known threats against Hackney if he testified against Iberg and Mullenax, there were clear problems with this new information. It was well known that as the jailer, Joe Martin did not wear a uniform. He wore a hat and jacket. And according to his original testimony, which no one refuted, after he spoke with my brother he received a call from Greenbriar and left the prison for the rest of the night. Finally, no one had ever testified that Sheriff Joe Castleberry had been in the jail the night Marvin died.

On the other hand, Officer Iberg himself testified that he and Chief Hensley returned to the jail and went to Marvin's cell to "check on him" at the same time Hackney said he saw a man being beaten by two policemen.

In spite of the obvious discrepancies, the defense attorneys openly gloated as they listened to Hackney change his story about who beat Marvin. There's no question that Hackney's new and altered testimony didn't help our case.

Hackney also testified that later that morning he was taken to an office in the courthouse where he met with George Hartje, prosecuting attorney at that time. Hackney said he told Hartje what he saw, and Hartje cursed and told him he would say as he was told.

During his testimony, Hackney was asked why he felt it necessary to contact the Williams family after twenty-five years. He said, "I just feel that his people have the right to know."

John Ellis Green, my mother's nephew, was the next to testify for the state. John Ellis and Marvin had been very close. As first cousins about the same age, they'd grown up together. It was John Ellis who tracked Marvin's body to McNutt's Funeral Home. On the stand he was clear, direct, and unintimidated, and his testimony was riveting. You could see the shock on the jurors' faces when John Ellis turned, looked directly at them and said sternly, "I'm telling this jury that they killed Marvin Williams because one of them was dating Peggy Green."

John Ellis told the court that Marvin dated Peggy before he married Bonnie. And he said that after his marriage, Marvin would occasionally see Peggy "only on a friendly basis." He testified that Marvin told him Iberg and Mullenax had warned him not to come to Conway. John Ellis said he warned Marvin to "leave her alone, because she's going to get you killed."

John Ellis went to great lengths that day explaining every detail of his actions, from the time he saw Marvin at the Menifee prom to the time he last saw Marvin's body in the McNutt Funeral Home, when he interrupted preparations for the hurried embalming. He said he went to the Menifee High School Prom that night because he was dating a young lady from that community. He saw Marvin there and the two agreed to meet later that night at the Sunset Café. When he arrived at the Sunset Café, he saw Marvin sitting in his car parked in front of the café. He tapped on Marvin's window to let him know he was about to go inside, and Marvin said, "I'll be on in."

When Marvin did not come in, John Ellis went outside to look for him. As he approached Marvin's car he saw a shoe on the ground outside it. He looked inside the car and saw the keys still in the ignition. He said he eventually went to the police station where Iberg informed him that he could come back the next day to bail Marvin out of jail for $20.

When Marvin did not return the next day to pick up his car, John Ellis knew something terrible had happened. He went back to the police station and was told by Mullenax that Marvin had an accident and his body was over at the McNutt Funeral Home. John said when he started to question Mullenax about what had happened, Iberg, who was standing nearby, unsnapped his gun belt and touched his gun. Feeling threatened, John left the police station and went directly to the McNutt Funeral Home.

When he arrived at the funeral home, he could recall the person with whom he spoke, and that person told him they had Marvin's body in the back room preparing to embalm it. That's when John went to the back, saw Marvin's body, and yelled at the men that the family was unaware of Marvin's death, and they had no right to embalm him. John then left Conway to go to Menifee to inform our family but found our home had been destroyed.

John Ellis' testimony was too much for my mother. She left the courtroom and did not return for the remainder of the trial.

In cross examination, the defense attorneys pounced on John Ellis. Mullenax's attorney questioned his ability to recall events leading up to Marvin's death. Mullis and his investigators had learned that John spent a short time as a patient in the Arkansas State Hospital in Little Rock in February 1970, ten years after Marvin was murdered. He used that to question John Ellis' mental health and his sanity. Helen Rice Grinder, Iberg's niece and attorney, tried without success to point out discrepancies in John's testimony compared to what he'd recently told the grand jury.

Like Marvin, John had served in the Army. When he got out he finished his degree and went on to do post-graduate work. He was articulate, confident, and not easily intimidated. In short, he was not what a racist wanted to see on the stand. Nothing Bart Mullis and Helen Rice Grinder did or said unnerved John Ellis. They knew his testimony provided a motive for Marvin's arrest, beating, and murder, and they tried everything in the book to trip him up, but nothing worked.

When Bill Langford, the former officer who took Joe Flakes into the courthouse, came to the stand, he said that after he put Joe Flakes in his cell he came down the stairs to the landing where he met Iberg and Mullenax and saw Marvin standing between the two officers with his head up. Although he saw the open wound on Marvin's head and blood on his clothing, he did not ask how it got there. He said the two officers told him Marvin had fallen on the steps outside the courthouse. I noted that Langford's description of Marvin's condition differed from Joe Martin's.

The most interesting part of Langford's testimony came when Sam Heuer asked Langford if blacks and whites were treated equally during the time of Marvin's arrest? Langford responded by saying, "Yes." An Arkansas Democrat reporter later wrote that when Langford said that, several black spectators shook their heads in disbelief.

At the time of his testimony, Bill Langford was serving as Executive Director of Conway Memorial Hospital. He acknowledged that even though the deep gash on Marvin's forehead could have bled considerably, neither he nor his fellow officers felt a need to address his injuries. Listening to his words, it was as if my brother was a sheep being led to slaughter.

Jailer Joe Martin stuck with his original story for the most part but appeared nervous and uncertain the entire time he was on the stand. It seemed Hackney's testimony incriminating him and Sheriff Joe Castleberry had unnerved him. He testified that he knew nothing about how Marvin sustained his massive injuries while incarcerated in his jail. Asked by Sam Heuer if he had anything to do with Marvin's death, he pounded his fist on the witness box and said, "I did not beat Marvin Williams. Sheriff Joe Castleberry did not beat Marvin Williams."

He did not say that no one else beat Marvin Williams.

When Sam Heuer asked why he invited Joe Flakes and Curtis Macon to view Marvin's body in his cell, he was uncertain. After thinking about it for a moment, he said Joe Flakes had asked if he could see the body. But Joe Flakes testified later that Joe Martin came into his cell and asked him to come and identify Marvin's body

Joe Martin also verified the model replica of the jail that had been built for the criminal trial. Using the model, he pointed out exactly where he'd put Charles Hackney and his friend, Lou Cogbill. Martin said he placed these men in separate cells, and put Cogbill across from Marvin, not Hackney. It was a weak attempt to undermine Hackney's eyewitness account, as both Hackney and Cogbill testified otherwise.

Although the Faulkner County Courthouse no longer houses any prisoners, the layout of the jail today is the same as it was in 1960. It has two small cells to the front separated by a metal door which was occasionally left open, and two large cells in the back. As you walk up the stairs to the cell block, Marvin was placed alone in the small cell on the left. Lou Cogbill and Charles Hackney, according to their own testimony, were placed in the small cell on the right. A short corridor about 8 feet wide separates these two cells. Whoever was across from my brother had to have heard and seen what occurred.

CHAPTER 27

Memories and Experts

A s I watched the trial, I also watched the courtroom. Each day there were more throwbacks to the 1960s. Black and white spectators self-segregated into different sides of the room. Our family and Black supporters were on the right. The defendants and white supporters were on the left. In addition to the local police, white state troopers were strategically stationed to be highly visible throughout the building, an obvious and familiar effort at intimidation. One reporter described a white man who walked through the courtroom wearing a belt inscribed, "The south shall rise again."

Most concerning of all was that somehow Sheriff Charles Castleberry had appointed himself bailiff for the court during the trial. Charles Castleberry's uncle was the late Joe Castleberry, who was sheriff in 1960. In his key position as bailiff, the younger Castleberry became the "keeper" of the all-white jury.

Any ethical law enforcement official would know that his presence in these proceedings and in that role was improper. But Charles Castleberry, like his uncle, knew how the system worked. His constituents were in that courtroom and on this jury. From the start of jury selection until the middle of the trial, Castleberry positioned himself close to the defense attorney's table, making it clear to everyone who he supported.

In one article about the trial, a reporter describes seeing Castleberry shaking his head negatively and making other dismissive gestures as witnesses testified for the state. Another time he shook hands with the jurors when they recessed at the end of the day. Finally, Judge Langston had enough and removed him as bailiff. But even then, Castleberry remained in the courtroom, visible to the jury, now sitting as a spectator and supporter just rows behind Iberg and Mullenax.

It would have made a huge difference, perhaps all the difference, if the judge had intervened in the jury selection during voire dire, or if he'd removed Castleberry as bailiff sooner. But I suspect the judge was walking a thin line. Powerful forces wanted an acquittal or to have the case thrown out. We all knew that Judge Langston's every action and word was scrutinized for anything they could use. Back then, it took almost nothing to trigger a white person's backlash.

The first medical expert to testify for the state was Dr. Fahmy Malak, the state's medical examiner. Dr. Malak performed the second autopsy on Marvin and determined the cause of death was due to the four-inch fracture located behind Marvin's left ear. He testified that neither the four-inch fracture, nor the deep cut on Marvin's forehead were the result of a fall. Dr. Malak said if Marvin had actually fallen forward on the steps, as the officers said he did, more injuries would have been visible on his face. Dr. Malak also testified that the fracture was caused by a blunt object with a force of at least 400-600 pounds per square inch, and that the same object could have caused both injuries.

In an attempt to undermine Dr. Malak's strong testimony, Helen Rice Grinder asked him during cross examination if he had told Faulkner County Prosecuting Attorney Bill Brazil that this case, the Williams case, was a weak case. Malak responded that Bill Brazil was the one who told him it was a weak case, not the other way around.

Following Dr. Malak, limited testimonies were given by Marie Bradford of North Little Rock and Ola Ward of Conway. Ms. Bradford's testimony was limited because the court determined what she had to say was hearsay. Though her statements to the grand jury had already appeared in most, if not all, of the print media, she was not permitted to tell this jury about the conversation she had with an inmate who told her he heard the officers beating Marvin "until he stopped hollering."

Ola Ward, the Conway resident, testified that she, her husband, and another couple were parked near the courthouse when the other man in the car told her husband, "They're going to kill that boy." She turned and saw a Black man on his knees in the parking lot with Iberg and Mullenax standing above him.

The second and final medical expert to testify for the state was Dr. Joseph Burton, who had performed more than 8,000 autopsies as Chief Medical Examiner in North Metropolitan Atlanta during the previous 11 years. He told the jury he had extensive experience in investigating deaths of persons in police custody, had performed nine autopsies in the Atlanta child slaying cases, and had testified in the highly publicized Ted Bundy murder trial in Florida.

If there was any doubt as to whether Marvin was murdered while in the custody of the Conway Police Department, it was put to rest by Dr. Burton. He had spent fifty hours investigating my brother's death and had complete command of the facts. As he delivered one of the most compelling testimonies I've ever witnessed in my life, he had complete command of the courtroom as well.

Here are excerpts from articles written by Lamar James with the Arkansas Gazette and Mark Carnopis with the Arkansas Democrat. Both men were in the courtroom during Dr. Burton's testimony.

"Using a projector, Dr. Burton described injuries to Williams' face. He used enlargements of photographs taken of Williams' face before an autopsy."

"Dr. Burton testified that the steps could not have caused the triangular-shaped, geometric patterns around the gash. He said a flat surface, such as a board with a raised geometric pattern, could have caused the gash."

"The skull fracture likely was caused by a round, smooth object, such as a baseball bat, a bottle, a police night stick or a slapper, which is a lead-filled, leather-covered bludgeon, he said."

"Dr. Burton described other apparent injuries to the head not mentioned in the 1960 autopsy, including what appeared to be bruises on the nose and near the hairline and abrasions on the mouth and nose. He said a close examination of the photograph also turned up what appeared to be another bump on Williams head, in addition to the bump over the skull fracture."

"He testified that the notion that the skull fracture could have been a "distant fracture," caused when the front of Williams head struck the courthouse steps, "exceeds medical probability.""

"The strongest part of the skull was fractured," Dr. Burton said. "However, the skull over the right eye, which is one of the weakest parts of the skull, was not injured by the alleged fall," he added."

"Dr. Burton described the force needed to crack the back of the skull as being similar to the force of a hammer driving a nail into a two-by-four board with a single blow."

"Dr. Burton said that if Williams had a conversation with Joe Martin, the county jailer, shortly after Williams' incarceration as Martin has testified, then the skull fracture would had to have been suffered later that morning."

"Dr. Burton said the skull fracture caused "exquisite pain" and Williams would have been unable to carry on a conversation if the fracture had occurred before the conversation. If Williams had been able to talk with a skull fracture, he would have been asking for medical help."

"It would be my opinion that Mullenax did not have the opportunity to cause the fatal injury if the testimony from witnesses so far is true."

One of the reporters noted that Iberg dropped his head when he heard that statement from Dr. Burton, and Mullenax turned and smiled at his wife. Dr. Burton's statement made it clear that Mullenax did not administer the fatal blow but said nothing about the beating Marvin received in the parking lot.

"Dr. Burton said the absence of blood in Williams' car or the police car indicated that he was not struck over the eye at that time. He reiterated that the skull fracture occurred after the conversation with Martin."

"Dr. Burton also questioned the lack of blood on Williams shirt or pants as shown in the photographs. He said the forehead wound was severe enough to cause copious bleeding. Spots of blood were seen on Williams shoulder and coat sleeves."

"Dr. Burton said that if Williams had fallen on the steps, there would have been blood on his face, shirt, and the area leading up to the jail unless something was held to his head."

Previous witnesses, such as Joe Martin, who said he saw "one drop of blood" testified they had not seen any blood in the courthouse and little or no blood on Marvin as he was taken into the jail. Burton said, "it was possible somebody cleaned Williams up before pictures of the body were taken before the autopsy."

"Dr. Burton testified that Williams' injuries were consistent with a beating. Burton said it was difficult to determine how long Williams lived after the fracture, but said he was probably dead within 4-8 hours. He said his decision was based on findings that Williams brain had not swollen much, the large amount of blood in a brain hemorrhage near the fracture and the lack of cellular reaction of the injury determined during a microscopic examination of a slide of Williams brain tissue."

"Because of the extensive fracture, Dr. Burton said Williams would have been conscious for a short period of time. Burton described the injury as one that becomes progressively worse. Dr. Burton further stated that he would have classified the manner of death as a homicide if he had performed Marvin's autopsy."

Dr. Burton's description of the savage beating of my brother was intensely painful for my family to hear. It was little comfort to me to know that Marvin survived the initial beating in the parking lot. The fact that he was lucid and fully cognizant of what awaited him bothered me more.

I've often wondered what was going through my brother's mind after Joe Martin refused to free him or call our dad to come and bail him out. What was he was thinking as he sat on his bunk? What did he do or say when he heard the footsteps coming up the stairwell to his cell? Marvin must have been a hell of a man for it to have taken two trips for those animals to take his life.

CHAPTER 28

Iberg

D r. Burton's testimony was so thorough and convincing that neither defense attorney cross examined him. At the end of the court session, however, Bart Mullis was quick to tell reporters that Burton's testimony regarding the conversation my brother had with Joe Martin should absolve his client from having anything to do with the skull fracture that caused Marvin's death. Following up on his perceived window of opportunity, Mullis, with Helen Rice Grinder tagging along, filed a motion for dismissal of the charges, arguing that special prosecuting attorney Heuer had failed to present enough evidence to convict their clients.

Judge Langston called for a recess to consider the motion. After a considerable amount of time, the judge called the attorneys (as well as the reporters) to his chamber where he announced that the state had, in fact, presented enough evidence for this jury to render a fact-based decision.

Peggy Green and Lavenia Martin also testified. This was the first time I'd ever seen these women. Peggy was visibly nervous and uncomfortable, and so was her mother. Neither ever made eye contact with my family. Peggy acknowledged having a relationship with Marvin prior to his marriage but denied having one afterwards. When asked about their relationships with Iberg and Mullenax, and possibly other officers including Chief Hensley, they denied that any such relationships existed. Clearly, neither of these women wanted to be seen as the motive for Marvin's death.

Mullenax was the first of the two arresting officers to testify and he stuck with the original script, the one in which Harve Macon was offered and accepted the chance to ride in the back seat of a police car with his "out of control" son so he could see him incarcerated.

As he had in 1960, Mullenax said that he and Iberg were returning Harve Macon to his home when they saw a Chevrolet parked on the East side of Markham Street near the Sunset Café. The car was facing South, which meant it was on the wrong side of the street. He stated there were feet sticking out of the window. In the car were Marvin Williams and Joe Flakes. Marvin was asleep in the front passenger seat, and Joe Flakes was sitting in the back seat.

About Marvin's fall at the courthouse, Mullenax said he and Iberg heard a "loud clap of thunder" and both of them let go of my brother at the exact same time. He denied he ever "hit, kicked, cursed, or abused Marvin."

Even if Mullenax's testimony about where Marvin's car was parked were true, then Marvin deserved a parking citation, not incarceration, especially since neither Marvin nor Joe was seated in the driver's seat.

Ora Macon, Harve's wife, was a rebuttal witness for the prosecution. Ora testified that "She and her husband, Harve, were looking out of the door to their home and saw Marvin Williams being arrested. She said she did not see what condition Williams was in because it was just too far away."

Ora Macon's testimony was a problem for the defense as it placed Harve inside his home, standing with his wife, when they witnessed my brother's arrest, and not with the officers who claimed they'd just brought him home. Nowhere in Harve's 1960 testimony at the coroner's inquest does he say or imply that he was ever with these officers that night.

The second problem was Mrs. Macon's assertion that "It was too far away" for them to determine what condition Marvin was in. The Macon's front porch was about 10 feet from the street, so if Marvin's car was parked in front of their home, the Macons should have seen, and possibly even heard, what was said during the arrest.

Hearing Iberg's testimony was of particular interest to me. Marvin Iberg was about 5'7" tall with an average build. To control and abuse my 6'4" brother he would have needed help from Mullenax. And to beat to death an accomplished boxer who was also a former U. S. Army Paratrooper, he would have needed his supervisor, Chief Hensley.

As I watched Iberg testify, I thought about my brother's height and physique, his good looks, his intellect (graduating from high school at the age of 15), his sporty car, his military service, and the handsome white dinner jacket he was wearing that night. I understood why a white male from the south in the 1960s, particularly someone like Iberg, would be obsessed with my brother, especially since Iberg's girlfriend still had feelings for my brother. I can understand why this would have driven Iberg insane.

This is why Iberg repeatedly stopped and harassed Marvin, why he followed my brother six miles to his home in Menifee on at least one occasion, and why he told my brother to stay out of Conway.

I am certain that Iberg and Mullenax returned to Markham Street that night after arresting Curtis Macon because, even though they were on duty, they were getting together with Peggy and possibly her mother, Lavenia, too. That's when they saw my brother's car.

If they watched Marvin's car come down Markham Street and park in front of the Sunset Café, and if they saw his friends get out, leaving Marvin in the car, they knew this was their opportunity to make real on their threats to Marvin to stay away from any place Iberg's girlfriend might possibly see him.

Before the trial, I attended Iberg's deposition. His attitude was unforgettable, he was cocky and sure of himself, and anything but respectful. But during the trial he assumed a completely different persona on the stand; he spoke with an oddly soft voice, completely different than how he spoke during his deposition. His behavior was meek, and he sprinkled his testimony with well-rehearsed phrases like "Yes sir, Mr. Special Prosecutor" and "I want to make sure I tell the truth here, Sir." Suddenly he was the friendly neighborhood police officer.

Several times, though, Sam got to him. And when that happened, Iberg's face went red and he became visibly angry. This was especially noticeable when Sam asked about Marvin's shoe, which Iberg said was the reason for him and Chief Hensley returning to Marvin's cell twice.

"So you felt he needed his shoe but didn't need a bandaid or medical attention?" Sam asked.

When Sam Heuer asked if he'd ever used a "slapper," a weapon that all police officers in the south used in the 1960s, Iberg's unlikely reply was that "he never owned one." Heuer asked him if he had access to one. He replied that he "didn't know."

Armed with information about a prior beating Iberg was involved in, Sam asked Iberg if he'd ever heard of the name William Doyle Staley, whom Iberg hit in the head while Staley was in jail in 1961. Iberg didn't deny striking the man, but said Staley once knocked him into a bunk at the jail.

Helen Rice Grinder, recognizing how damaging these statements were to Iberg in terms of his prior bad behavior, strongly objected to Heuer mentioning Staley's name. Judge Langston overruled the objection and said Heuer could ask the question. Heuer then asked Iberg if he'd ever used the word "Nigger." Iberg admitted he had.

It was really difficult to see and listen to this, because Iberg showed absolutely no remorse, he was hardcore. I was sickened by this man, so much that one reporter described me this way, "Ronnie Williams, brother of the deceased, grimaced several times, and at one point placed his necktie over his face."

Feeling comfortable in this environment and with the all-white jury, Iberg relaxed and began to over-embellish, adding a new twist to his story. He told the jury that when he and Mullenax brought Marvin inside the courthouse into a lighted area, they stopped and examined the injury to Marvin's forehead. He said the injury was not serious. Of course, then he couldn't explain why he felt it necessary to return to Marvin's cell twice that night to check on this "not serious" wound.

"Well, what did he [Marvin] do when you manipulated the wound?" he was asked.

"He was non-responsive," Iberg answered.

It was clear Iberg was lying about my brother being non-responsive because minutes later, according to Joe Martin, my brother had a lucid and detailed conversation with the jailer.

Once again, Marvin Iberg's own testimony placed him at the scene of the crime at the same hour Hackney said he saw two officers beating Marvin. In addition, the timing of Iberg's self-admitted presence in Marvin's cell was consistent with the time Dr. Burton said the fatal blow would have been administered.

I kept telling myself no fair-minded person will believe this guy. I knew our case had touched some racially sensitive nerves in this community, but I was cautiously optimistic that this jury, although all-white, would be fair and objective.

CHAPTER 29

Closing Arguments

The last two witnesses to testify for the defense were medical experts they brought in to blunt the stunning testimony of the state's medical experts, particularly Dr. Joseph Burton.

The first defense expert was Dr. Allen Jones, chief medical examiner for Pima County, Arizona. In his opening statement he noted that he authored a medical paper in which he cited eight cases that supported his "contrecoup" theory, which is that a contusion (or fracture) can result from the brain contacting the skull on the opposite side of the impact. This was the same theory George Hartje used in the 1960 coroner's inquest. During cross-examination Sam Heuer challenged Dr. Jones' theory, asking about the circumstances in which the eight cases of contrecoup fractures occurred. Jones acknowledged that most of them involved automobile accidents, and he did not know the speed the cars were traveling when these fractures occurred.

The most embarrassing part of Dr. Jones' testimony, and the thing that most exposed his incompetence, was when he told the jury that it was possible for Marvin to walk up four flights of stairs and not complain of pain while suffering from the cut to his forehead, bleeding from his kidneys, the four-inch skull fracture, and swelling of the brain. At this, the courthouse erupted in laughter.

The second medical expert to testify for the defense was Dr. Stevenson Flanigan, Chairman of the Neurology Department at the University of Arkansas for Medical Sciences. Dr. Flanigan said although the injury to Marvin's forehead was not severe, it could cause the skull to become twisted and bend, causing a fracture to the base of the skull. Once again, during cross-examination, Dr. Flanigan admitted that most of the cases in which he'd seen this occur involved automobile accidents. He said he did not know of a case involving a free fall from a standing position onto a concrete step, as the officers claimed Marvin had done.

During Sam Heuer's cross-examination, both experts admitted they were first contacted earlier in the year by Jeffrey Bell, the Assistant Attorney for the State of Arkansas. In spite of his position with the state, Bell had agreed to represent George Hartje, a defendant in our civil lawsuit, and he told the experts that was why he wanted to discuss Marvin's case with them. Bell then shared their information with the Iberg and Mullenax's defense attorneys ahead of the criminal trial. In other words, the assistant state's attorney had provided assistance to the very defendants the states' appointed prosecutor, Sam Heuer, was prosecuting for murder.

Bell's excuse was that since he was planning to represent Hartje in the civil trial, and would be sharing information with the defense attorneys eventually, he might as well go ahead and share that information for the criminal trial. Of course, this ignored the fact that the civil trial and the criminal trial were completely separate, and his actions were grossly unethical.

Jeffrey Bell's involvement on behalf of Iberg and Mullenax was a watershed moment in the trial. When the jury learned that the Assistant Attorney for the State of Arkansas had obtained medical experts for the defense, and was sharing information with them, it was a powerful message of support for Iberg and Mullenax. Jeffrey Bell reinforced that message by sitting on the defendant's side of the courtroom through the entire criminal trial, physically and visibly supporting them.

I knew we were in an uphill battle, but I wasn't prepared for that.

Final arguments in the murder trial of Marvin Iberg and Bill Mullenax were made on September 3, 1985. Bart Mullis, representing Mullenax, said the state's own case had cleared his client. But he said something else in his closing arguments, and even today I get chills thinking of it. Here is his exact quote:

"The state's evidence indicates that if Williams was struck, the [fatal] blow would had to have occurred after Williams was incarcerated. There has been no evidence or testimony given which has placed my client in the jail after Williams was incarcerated."

All the science-based evidence was on our side and Bart Mullis acknowledged this in his closing arguments. It was as if he was telling this jury that even though his client might have been involved in the initial abuse of Marvin, he did not participate in the beating that took my brother's life. Therefore, Mullenax, his client, was not guilty.

In her closing arguments, Helen Rice Grinder did not attempt to explain to the jury why Iberg and his supervisor, C.O. Hensley, returned twice to Marvin's cell that night. Nor did she offer an explanation as to why Iberg and Mullenax were seen at Harve Macon's home the morning after Marvin was murdered. Instead, she accused the state of not meeting the burden of proof beyond a reasonable doubt that her client, Marvin Iberg, murdered my brother. She said the state left too many questions unanswered.

Sam Heuer's closing comments lasted for about an hour. He spoke to the jury about the medical evidence, the circumstantial evidence, and the racial atmosphere as it existed in 1960. He explained to the jury that in 1960, officers were not required by law to read a suspect his or her rights when they were arrested. He told the jury that Marvin's arrest was unlawful, as the evidence proved he had not been drinking when he and his friend, Joe, were arrested at the Sunset Café. Sam said, "He was not drunk, and he had a right to live." Heuer disputed the ridiculous notion that Marvin fell on the courthouse steps. He pointed out to the jury that "common sense" should tell them that if Marvin had injured himself in a fall, he would have complained of pain. But no testimony had been presented of Marvin complaining of his injury.

Sam also reminded the jury of the incriminating testimony of Nora Martin, wife of jailer Joe Martin, who said she saw Iberg and Hensley going to Marvin's cell later in the night. He made clear to the jury that it was unlikely these officers were concerned with Marvin's condition when they returned twice that night to his cell, especially given his race and the severe weather threatening the City of Conway.

Finally, Heuer told the jury that Marvin's arrest was not a coincidence; it was intentional. Iberg and Mullenax had motive, and that motive was that Iberg was dating Marvin's former girlfriend. Although the woman denied on the stand that she had dated either officer, Heuer told the jury she could not be expected to admit anything like that on the witness stand because she would have been ridiculed in the Black community.

Judge Langston, in his final instructions to the jury, told them they should consider each defendant separately. He gave the jury considerable latitude as he provided details on the various offenses for which the officers could be found guilty. Here were the offenses and their specified limits:

- First degree murder – life imprisonment
- Second degree murder – 5-20 years in prison
- Voluntary manslaughter – 2-7 years in prison
- Involuntary manslaughter – up to 3 years in prison and fine of $100 to $1,000

After Bart Mullis' closing comments acknowledging that Marvin's fatal injury occurred after his incarceration, and especially after Judge Langston's wide range of sentencing options and his directive that each officer be considered separately, I was confident we had a conviction.

CHAPTER 30

The Verdict

The jury began deliberations at 2 pm on September 3, 1985. One of the two alternate jurors, Wayne Lovell of Conway, who was not allowed to deliberate with the jury, was quoted by the Log Cabin Democrat (Conway's local newspaper) as saying he would vote to acquit. He said the special prosecuting attorney, Sam Heuer, had not done enough to convince him that the two officers had murdered Marvin Williams. Regarding the testimony of Charles Hackney, Lovell said, "He had a plea-bargaining thing going, I'm sure." He further stated, "There is no evidence to convict Mullenax, since testimony indicated Mullenax did not return to the jail after Williams was incarcerated."

After reading the quotes which had been attributed to this guy, I did not know what to think. I wondered where he'd been the past four weeks. How on earth could he have arrived at this conclusion and from whom did he get his information? How could he say, on one hand, that he could not convict Mullenax because he did not return to Marvin's cell; and then, on the other hand, not convict Iberg because he did return, not once, but TWICE? And then to add to his list of unintelligible statements, Wayne Lovell tries (as so many other local officials had done) to discredit Charles Hackney by saying – "He was working on a plea-bargaining thing, I'm sure."

During the four weeks of testimony no one testified to anything about an alleged plea-bargain for Charles Hackney. Hackney was incarcerated in another jurisdiction in southern Arkansas, and had written to Bill Brazil asking for assistance with his current incarceration, not understanding that Bill Brazil had no jurisdiction outside of Faulkner County. Consequently, there was no plea deal, and no one ever testified to anything related to a plea-bargain for Hackney.

Hackney's testimony was merely the spark that started the investigation. He testified that at 2 a.m. he heard and saw officers in uniform beating my brother. Wayne Lovell and the jurors should have focused on one simple question: Does the evidence (Marvin's conversation with Joe Martin, the distinct injuries to Marvin's body, no alcohol in his bloodstream, the time of death, the forensic reports, etc.) add validity to what Hackney testified to? But the jurors did not seem to grasp this core question.

My mother and father were absent during the latter days of the trial and during the jury's deliberations. My father wasn't feeling well, so I took him to our family physician, who recommended further testing. Three days prior to the jury announcing its verdict, my dad was admitted to the hospital for a biopsy of his prostate. I wanted to be present when the urologist gave my dad the results, so I made daily trips from the courthouse to the hospital. At no time did either of my parents ask about the trial. It was as if they'd resigned themselves to the fact that nothing would happen to the men who took their son's life.

Finally, the urologist came. He informed us that Daddy had prostate cancer, and it had metastasized. I followed the doctor into the corridor and asked how long my father had to live. He said to me, very compassionately, "I think your dad has one to three years."

I was devastated. I couldn't return to Daddy's hospital room weeping, so I held it all in until I got to the parking lot. Then I broke down and sobbed.

The next day, after only eight hours of deliberation, the jury reached a decision. I entered the courtroom with my sisters, Marvin's children Sharon and Ricky, and a host of friends and supporters. As it had been from day one, the courtroom was packed.

After the jury was seated, Judge Langston entered the courtroom and asked the jury foreman if the jury had arrived at a verdict for both of the accused officers. The foreman said, "Yes," and handed the judge their decision.

Judge Langston looked at each verdict, then raised his head and stared at the jury. With a look of disgust, he read aloud their decision of "Not guilty" for each of the accused. A gasp echoed around the courtroom.

Our family and our supporters were in tears as we sat and watched the other side applaud, grin, hug, and pat each other on the back. I was completely numb as I watched the jury file one-by-one out of the jury box, walk through the middle aisle, and smile and shake hands with the defendants and their attorneys. All of them avoided any eye contact with our family.

Here are the names of the jurors who on Thursday, September 5, 1985, acquitted Marvin IBerg and Bill Mullenax:

Carla Bentley (Conway)

Debbie Lou Brantley (Vilonia)

Rebecca Jane Cox (Greenbrier)

Linda F. Favre (Conway)

Glenda Jean Hall (Conway)

Nola M. Harris (Conway)

Milton F. Jackson (Conway)

Monita B. Kelley (Vilonia)

Robert Gene Kelly Jr. (Conway)

Walter K. Mayfield (Mayflower)

Earl W. Roland (Conway)

Kathy Jo Smith (Conway)

CHAPTER 31

Heartbreak

Outside the courtroom, my family and I were bombarded with questions from reporters who wanted to know our thoughts regarding the verdict. We declined their requests. As my family prepared to leave the courthouse parking lot, I told my sisters I needed to be alone. I didn't want to see or talk to anybody. Our family had been betrayed again by a racist judicial system that had deceived us and the rest of the country into believing that justice was possible for a Black man.

I got in my car and started to drive. I drove and drove and swore at my steering wheel. I was angry with the justice system, and yes, I was angry with God. I could not accept that God would bring us this far, and then not punish the people who murdered and covered up the death of our loved one. Why, I asked God, was it necessary to put us through all this pain if all we would see from this experience was a bunch of racists high-fiving each other because the system had once again been manipulated in their favor?

My anger was at the boiling point. I felt as if we were reliving May, 1960 all over again, when my family lost Marvin to hate, lost our home to the tornado, and was denied justice by a coroner's jury. Only this time we'd lost a criminal trial and now faced losing my father to cancer. I questioned God as to why we were, once again, placed on the losing side of this equation? I felt like I was about to lose control. All kinds of crazy things went through my mind. I tried to imagine ways I could hurt the men who killed my brother without destroying my family, especially my two young sons. We'd worked so hard to get our case reopened and tried. I felt like I'd failed my parents, who continuously looked to me for guidance in every decision that needed to be made in our case. Driving in that car that night was at the lowest point of my life.

Then God spoke to me deep in my spirit. He said, "Ronnie, your perception of justice may never come. This trial was not for you; it was for them. It was intended to give those individuals, including those who willingly participated in the cover-up, an opportunity to acknowledge their wrongdoing."

Gradually, I felt God steady me as He broadened my perception of what Marvin's case was all about. I felt the Lord lift my anger off me.

Slowly, a feeling of resignation replaced my anger. Finally, I drove to Little Rock to check on my dad. Neither of my parents were aware of the verdict, and I dreaded having to break the news to them.

As I entered the hospital, two reporters were waiting at the front entrance. Rumors had started to circulate as to why my parents were absent for the reading of the verdict. Earlier I'd told these same reporters that I was not in the mood to talk with them. But given their persistence and respectful demeanor, I decided to give them my reaction. I said I was surprised by the verdict, and that I thought special prosecuting attorney Sam Heuer had done an excellent job in presenting all the evidence. I told them that the city and county political systems had once again protected these men.

Regarding the jury's decision, I said those twelve men and women would not only have to live with their conscience, but one day would have to account for their decision. I went on to say that justice eventually would be served because in the end there would be another courtroom over which God himself will preside. And in God's courtroom, there would be no politics, no "good-ole-boy" system, and, most importantly, no racism.

Sam Heuer, the special prosecuting attorney, was more direct in his reaction. He said the fact that Marvin Williams was Black and the defendants were white worked against him. He told the reporter that under the judge's instructions the jury easily could have found either man guilty of a lesser offense. He clearly felt racism was the motivating influence in the jury's verdict. Heuer further stated that "he resented the presence of Jeffrey Bell, an assistant attorney in the state attorney general's office." He said, "The fact that Bell sat on the defendant's side during the trial doesn't leave a good taste in my mouth."

Mark Carnopis with the Arkansas Democrat, reported that a source told his newspaper that "a tape recorder had been found during the trial behind a bookcase in the judge's chamber." The recorder was found by Karen Curley, who worked for the Prosecutor Coordinator's Division of the State Attorney General's office. Mr. Carnopis said several attempts were made by his newspaper to reach Ms. Curley, but she was never available for comment.

Secretly recording the judge's chamber was the kind of thing you saw in a movie, not in real life, but at this point nothing surprised me. I knew we were dealing with a corrupt system that was self-perpetuating. What I had not understood was the extent to which this system worked cooperatively and collaboratively with individuals from other state agencies, like Dr. Stevenson Flanigan from the University of Arkansas School of Medical Sciences, and Jeffrey Bell from the Arkansas Attorney General's office.

I finally got to my dad's hospital room and received the much-needed hugs and kisses I could always expect from my mother. There was never a time my parents were not eager to see one of their children, and this time was no exception, even though they were in a hospital not knowing how long my dad had to live. After spending some time loving on my parents, I finally mustered enough courage to tell them the dreadful news of the acquittal. There were several minutes of silence, then my mother started to cry. My dad showed little or no emotion. In his stoic fashion, he just looked at the wall and said nothing. My parents had seen this movie many times.

I didn't know what to say to console them, so I tried to encourage them by reminding them that we would take our case to the federal courts by pursuing the civil case that was pending. But nothing I said could help. They nodded their heads and said, "Son, we will do whatever you think we ought to do."

Weary from the weight of everything that happened that day, I drove home to see my wife and two young sons. It was around 10 p.m. when I got home, so our boys were already asleep. But Connie was waiting to see me, and to talk.

When I called Connie earlier to tell her the verdict, her first reaction was stunned disbelief. Then she started to cry. She kept saying, "Why? Why?"

Connie and I had only talked for a few minutes when the telephone rang. I couldn't imagine anyone calling our home on this night at this hour. I answered and to my surprise, it was Judge Don Langston, the special judge who presided over the criminal trial.

He said, and I quote, "I normally don't make these kinds of calls, but I wanted you and your family to know that justice was not served in your case today. I also want to commend you and your family for the way in which you responded to the verdict. You handled it with dignity and class." Judge Langston's words of consolation helped me get through that evening, and brought some solace on one of the most difficult days I've ever experienced.

Days later the Faulkner County Quorum Court added insult to our injury. In a vote of 10 to 1, it passed a resolution asking that Governor Bill Clinton pay Iberg and Mullenax's attorney fees. Even though Faulkner County had invested zero dollars in either the grand jury investigation or the criminal trial, both of which were funded from Governor Clinton's discretionary fund, and Bill Mullenax had not been a resident of Faulkner County for 18 years, Justice of the Peace Ann Harrell of Mayflower introduced the bill saying, "These men have probably spent every penny that they have ever made, or saved, or borrowed, or whatever." Her argument was that if it was okay for the governor to pay for the costs to prosecute, then it should be okay for him to pay for the defense.

For all the people who did things like that, though, there were many others who felt terrible about the verdict and found ways to let us know. When I wrote a letter to the editor in response to that article, a number of people reached out and let us know they liked it. Connie's director at the time went out of his way to stop by her desk and tell her he thought it was a good letter. It was his way of saying that he supported us and thought we'd been wronged. Small actions like this may not seem like much, but in those days any expression of support was a powerful statement for us.

A friend asked Connie how she got through it, and she replied that she had looked to Mother and Daddy, that it encouraged her to see how they were able to live and move on after losing Marvin, even though she knew they thought about him every day of their lives. She said, "I can only speak of an African American family going through hardships, but you take your cues from your parents. When I lost my brother in high school, my mother continued to get up every day and make breakfast for the rest of us and make sure our needs were met. I saw Mr. Williams and Miss Williams doing that, and it was an example for us. What they did for us, we tried to pass on to our boys.

"You don't ever really recover from a thing like that," she said. "You learn to manage the disappointment and grief in a way that allows you to continue to live your life. You learn to store those disappointments in a place where you can function and live and interact with other people, but you never really recover."

PART VI

The Civil Trial

CHAPTER 32

Ricky and Sharon

After recovering from the criminal trial, my family held lengthy discussions about how to proceed. My parents, my sisters Carolyn, Barbara, Verna, and Donna, and my niece Sharon and nephew Ricky, and Connie and I were in agreement. Our family decided to aggressively pursue our civil case.

We understood that the acquittal in the criminal trial could have an impact on our civil case, but we were committed to exhausting all means of getting some justice for Marvin, and we knew our case was strong. The driving force behind the acquittal was racism, that was obvious from the strategy to remove every prospective black juror, from the sheriff's behavior in the courtroom, and from the jury's comments in interviews. We prepared ourselves to face the same playbook.

We were also in agreement that if the verdict had been "guilty," we would not go forward with any more trials. We'd sacrificed and endured so much; it was too hard, too disruptive, too emotionally and physically exhausting. But when those officers got off, it put new motivation into our whole family, including my parents. We would not let them win so easily.

After the decision was made, Connie and I prayed like we always did, for God to give us strength to go through the next step. We prayed hard, and often. That is truly where our strength came from.

* * *

As we prepared for the next phase of ligation, we needed additional resources. With the help of others in the community, we held various fundraising events. The most profitable of these was selling hamburgers at the Menifee City Park. Town officials gave my father permission to set up a makeshift stand and the word spread that he'd be selling hamburgers to raise money for our case. Members of my family came from as far away as Detroit, Michigan and Kansas City, Missouri to show their support. Hundreds of people came that day to help our cause by purchasing a hamburger and a soda.

This event gave all of us, especially my mother and father, an opportunity to smile again, to see and be surrounded by people we loved who supported us. While our family was cooking hamburgers to raise money for our legal expenses, Bill Mullenax's legal fees were paid by the Arkansas Peace Officers Legal Defense Fund, a fund formed in direct response to Mullenax's indictment and his subsequent criminal trial. Board members included Col. Tommy Goodwin, Director of the State Police; Little Rock Police Chief Walter "Sonny" Simpson; Pulaski County Sheriff Carroll Gravett, and Little Rock attorney Sheffield Nelson, former head of the Arkansas Louisiana Gas Company. The powers that be were making it known who they supported. And in a state like Arkansas, that carried a lot of weight.

After Iberg and Mullenax were acquitted of murdering my brother, our family experienced a series of setbacks in our civil case. The last domino to fall was a decision by U.S. Attorney George Proctor, who closed the federal investigation into Marvin's death. He cited the results of the 17-day trial of Iberg and Mullenax as the basis for his decision. The Arkansas Democrat quoted him as saying, "We (in Little Rock) and they (in Washington) were looking at the case to determine whether or not there was any evidence of conspiracy within the five-year statute of limitation. That's the federal requirement for jurisdiction in any case."

The second setback literally destroyed our civil case. The defense made a motion which argued that our lawsuit should be dismissed because the statute of limitations had expired. In his ruling on that motion, Federal Judge G. Thomas Eisele decided to release Marvin Iberg and Bill Mullenax and the City of Conway from our $4 million lawsuit. In the same ruling, Eisele initiated an appeal to the 8th U.S. Circuit Court of Appeals in St. Louis, which automatically opened the door for John Wesley Hall, our attorney, to challenge his decision.

His ruling did not preclude us from proceeding with our lawsuit against the remaining four defendants, Faulkner County; former jailer Joe Martin; The Estate of the late Sheriff Joe Castleberry; and Circuit Judge George F. Hartje Jr., but it prevented us from punishing the real culprits in my brother's death. Testimony that came out in the criminal trial and the facts of the case made it clear the remaining defendants had a role in the cover-up, but they were always secondary rather than primary targets of the suit.

There was never a doubt in my mind as to whether our family would challenge Eisele's decision, so we instructed our attorney to immediately file an appeal with the court of appeals in St. Louis. If we were destined to lose this civil case, we would do so only after exhausting every available possibility. The proposed damage award, $4 million, was never the goal for us; we knew we'd never be awarded such a sum in Arkansas. The amount was intended to be a "mark" that would speak to Marvin's dignity as a human being and address the terrible loss his wife, children, parents, and family had endured.

As preparations continued for our civil trial, my father was deposed by Robert Henry, who was representing one of the four remaining defendants in our civil case. Incredibly, this was the same Robert Henry who participated in the 1960 coroner's inquest as attorney for the City of Conway.

By this time we were confident that Marvin had defended himself before he died, and had probably injured police chief C.O. Hensley when he fought back. This was why Hensley did not attend the inquest, and it was something Robert Henry, the city's attorney, would almost certainly have been aware of. Henry was the city's attorney, and I found it incredibly suspicious that he had not inquired about Hensley's whereabouts during the inquest.

I took my father to his deposition and was in the room when Robert Henry posed his first question to my dad: "Can you read?"

With a slight smile, my dad said, "Yes, I can read." My father stayed calm at this question, but I was incensed. It was an open insult, meant to degrade and demean. I was not going to allow him to get away with it.

As soon as my father's deposition was over, I met Robert Henry in the corridor, and in words I won't repeat in this book, made clear to him that my parents had earned the right to be treated with dignity and respect, and that I was not going to allow them to be reduced to some stereotypical figment of his racist imagination. I also told him that illiteracy exists in all races, particularly his.

Our appeal to the 8th Circuit Court of Appeals was heard by a three-judge panel, which refused to consider whether the three-year statute of limitations had expired in our civil lawsuit. The three-judge panel gave no reason for turning down our appeal, which surprised all of us, including our attorney, John Wesley Hall. On the advice of our attorney, we filed a rehearing request with the full court. And to our surprise, the court granted our petition to consider whether the statute of limitations had expired in our wrongful death case. Though deeply weary from all the legal wrangling, we were glad our case was still alive.

* * *

We were waiting on the 8th Circuit Court of Appeal to rule on our most recent petition when tragedy struck our family again. My nephew Ricky Williams, the oldest of Marvin's two children, drowned in a Faulkner County creek near his home in Conway.

Ricky was quiet and easy-going, with a kind of 'old man' presence in his mannerisms and the way he walked that always made him seem older than his age. He wasn't as tall as Marvin, but he and Sharon both resembled their father. Occasionally, Connie and I would see him out around Conway with his girlfriend, but they never married.

Ricky and Sharon were inseparable, seldom would I see one without the other. They were a year apart in age and did everything together. As they'd gotten older and began to have lives of their own, their visits to our home were less frequent, but they still drove up on occasion to be with my parents.

Both pursued their education and received post-secondary degrees, Ricky completed his associate degree from the University of Arkansas Community College in Morrilton, and Sharon got her bachelor's degree from the University of Central Arkansas. Continuing the family tradition, Ricky loved the game of baseball and was an excellent pitcher in the city league.

Like me, Ricky and Sharon were not aware that their father had been murdered until Hackney's letter showed up. As the case developed, I shared all the information I was getting with them, including the heart-breaking details of Marvin's final hours. They were both always very stoic when we spoke about these things. If I was able to meet with them in person, I could sometimes see that Sharon was upset, you could see the anger, but it was always controlled. Ricky, though, was even less expressive. Somehow he was able to handle or hide his emotions so well that he was hard to read. In hindsight, I dearly wish I had called more often to see if they were okay.

One day when Ricky was about 18, my father took him to a job interview at the Human Development Center and asked me to drive them. Connie went with me, and while we were there, just before the interview, Ricky had a seizure and collapsed on the floor. It was the first seizure we were aware of, but it was not the last. He was diagnosed with epilepsy, and was put on medication to control it which he took regularly. In fact, one of our best visits happened a few years later when he was in Little Rock getting his medication at his doctor's office. We arranged to meet there after his appointment, and had a good, long conversation and caught up.

Like his father and grandfather, Ricky loved the outdoors and was an avid fisherman. He was fishing on a creek near his home when he apparently had a seizure, fell into the water, and drowned.

Sharon was devastated when she learned of Ricky's death. Following in her father's footsteps, she enlisted in the Army and was away completing basic training when Ricky died, but she was able to come home for his funeral. Later, she went on to serve one tour in Iraq, and eventually retired from the military after thirty-two years of service. Through the years she and I have become very close, and I had the great honor of conferring her degree at her graduation.

There were no obvious reasons for us to suspect foul play in Ricky's death, we all felt that his epilepsy might have caused or led to his death. However, given the circumstances of his father's case and the threats and venom that were constantly directed toward our family during these years, an autopsy was performed by Dr. Fahmy Malak, our state's medical examiner. Dr. Malak had guided me through the first truthful explanation of Marvin's death and now, three years later, he had to determine what caused the death of Marvin's son. His autopsy concluded that the cause of Ricky's death was indeed accidental drowning. He cited bite marks on Ricky's tongue, supporting our theory that Ricky probably had a seizure prior to falling into the water.

On March 28, 1987, our family celebrated Ricky's 28 years of life. Like his father, Ricky died very young. He never had a chance to realize his potential, have a family, or be an uncle to Sharon's three children: Darius, Robin, and Ricky, his namesake.

CHAPTER 33

Protecting the Corrupt

We received the federal appeals court's ruling on Friday, August 28, 1987. In a stunning decision, the three-judge panel of the 8th Circuit Court of Appeals ruled that George Hartje Jr. could not be sued for damages for his role in thwarting the investigation of Marvin's death. In summary, the judges said, "The actions of a prosecutor are protected even if they are patently improper."

The judges had all the testimony and the inquest transcript. They were aware of the actions Hartje took to conceal the facts, including threatening witnesses and coercing them to give false testimony, yet they gave the former Circuit Judge absolute immunity.

It's worth noting that at the time of this ruling, Hartje was no longer circuit judge. He'd been voted out of office. Apparently, there were enough fair-minded voters in his district who felt he was unfit to make formal judgements in a court of law.

The appellate court's ruling was not a surprise to our attorney John Wesley Hall, who was aware of this long-standing federal precedent. But it shocked the hell out of the rest of us. We couldn't understand how someone in Hartje's position could be absolved of civil liability when the court had testimony, on the record, of his criminal wrongdoing. We were in disbelief that in spite of everything, Hartje got a pass.

I didn't care about precedent. Corrupt prosecutors should not be allowed to hide behind a judicial shield that protects them from civil suits, nor should they be permitted to threaten and coerce witnesses or openly disregard criminal justice, which is exactly what Hartje did. The saddest part, to me, was that the wording of the appeals court ruling made it clear that the court knew Hartje was guilty of the things we accused him of doing. But even though his actions "were patently improper," it ruled that he was "protected." No matter what he did, Hartje was untouchable. It was another example of the injustice my family experienced at the hands of a criminal justice system for which I had lost all respect.

After the appeal court's ruling, the only defendants left in our civil suit were Faulkner County, the estate of Joe Castleberry, and the former jailor, Joe Martin.

Our quest for justice for Marvin had taken its toll on me. It had been exactly three years and four months from the day my father handed me Charles Hackney's letter. I was physically and mentally exhausted, not to mention the toll that it took on my wife Connie, who was my rock and my "voice of reason" throughout the case. It had been an uphill battle from day one, and by this point many days it felt like we were just going through the motions to get through the day. There were days when I'd say, "I've had it, I'm sick of this," and Connie would encourage me to continue. Just often enough, one or both of us would get a second wind.

Many times during this part of the case I thought about Coach Eddie Boone, my high school basketball coach, and how hard he made us train for the final quarter of the game. When we'd run, Coach Boone would drive behind us in the car, pushing us to keep it up, to be ready, telling us it was the last quarter and we could not give up, that we had to be strong enough to push through.

"In the fourth quarter you're going to be in much better condition than your opponents," he'd say. "And that's what will make the difference."

As exhausted as Connie and I were, we decided we couldn't quit in the fourth quarter. When we prayed, it felt like God was doing what Coach Boone did for me all those years ago. He was beside us, urging us on, telling us not to quit now.

This was the first time I'd contemplated quitting, something that was not in my DNA. I knew that what the "system" had done to my family, my wife, and to me was exactly what it has done to families of color for centuries, and to poor white families as well. It demeans, it devalues, and it depletes. It's designed to make you give up, and it's rigged with built-in hurdles that make fighting back so difficult you want to quit.

That is where we were.

* * *

After spending time alone, I realized quitting was not the answer. We'd come too far to allow the forces of hate and evil to win this case. Marvin suffered too much for us to quit. The least we could do for him was see his case to its completion.

Our attorneys advised that they thought it would be futile for us to seek a rehearing of the 8th U.S. Circuit Court of Appeals decision which dismissed four defendants from our case. Since our suit had already been subjected to a number of pretrial appeals and delays, we accepted the advice of our attorneys and Judge Eisele tentatively set the trial for July of 1988.

As we waited for the start of this trial, the defense attorneys orchestrated a number of political ploys. One was to make our family appear to be only interested in money. This strategy was revealed by the Log Cabin Democrat, the local newspaper for the City of Conway, which falsely reported that our family had made an offer to settle our case for $50,000, which was an absolute lie. I called several news outlets to let them know that what the Log Cabin had reported was false, and that no one in my family had ever initiated a settlement offer. I made it clear the only thing we ever wanted from this case was justice for our loved one.

Apparently, the Log Cabin gleaned its information from a Faulkner County Quorum Court meeting, where William Adkisson, the attorney who represented Faulkner County and former jailor, Joe Martin, talked about the possibility of a settlement. Rather than accurately stating that possibility of a settlement started with a defense attorney, the newspaper's headline of July 13, 1988 read, "Plaintiffs in Williams case offer to settle case for $50,000." Two days later the Log Cabin ran another article with the headline "Settlement offer never presented."

The jury selection process in our civil trial started and ended just as it did in criminal trial. Once again, we were forced to watch as the defense attorney eliminated every black prospective juror and got the all-white jury they so desperately wanted.

Robert Henry, who represented the estate of Joe Castleberry, understood how effective this strategy could be. It had worked in 1960, it worked in 1985, and it was his strategy of choice in 1988. He and his friends, George Hartje and Robert McNutt, were the creators and keepers of the original cover story, and they'd successfully peddled it for decades because racism, if played correctly, has always been a winning strategy in America.

John Wesley Hall and Larry Vault did an excellent job presenting the facts of our case. Many witnesses who testified for the state in the criminal trial also testified in our civil case. Among those was Dr. Joseph Burton, the noted medical examiner from Atlanta, Georgia. Just as he had done in the criminal trial, Dr. Burton was thorough and convincing. He again made clear to the jury that Marvin could not have died from injuries received in a fall, but that he was the victim of a vicious beating.

On the other hand, the defense attorney had their same group testify as well. Among them were Marvin Iberg, Joe Martin, George Hartje, Jr., and Dr. Stevenson Flanigan, the Little Rock neurosurgeon who was paid to say anything which was opposite to Dr. Burton's testimony. They even found Homer Jones, the juror in the 1960 Coroner's Inquest who had openly demeaned my brother and whose only goal was to find out which Black man was telling the truth about Marvin's death so he could stop what he called "the rumors." For us, his presence at this trial was a painful reminder of that jury's indifference to the circumstances surrounding my brother's death.

After receiving instructions from Judge Eisele, the jury began its deliberations. This time I was mentally prepared for what I knew would come. I'd seen how sophisticated racism can be. It can lull you into believing that there truly is justice and freedom for all, words my brother repeated many times as he stood in allegiance to our flag in two different branches of the U.S. Military. In reality these words were nothing more than a slogan; they did not apply to men and women of color. This case taught me a lot about racism, and a lot about the human psyche. I was prepared for and expecting a decision made solely on the basis of race, rather than facts.

The all-white jury deliberated for about four hours and then, as predicted, rendered a decision which cleared all the remaining officials of any wrongdoing in Marvin's death. No negligence; no malfeasance; no nothing!

This jury chose to believe that even though Marvin was housed in a county facility and had a lengthy conversation with a county employee who refused him medical attention, that none of the remaining defendants should be held accountable for his safety and wellbeing.

Judge Thomas Eisele, after reading the verdict, said, "The lawsuit was a very, very sad case for all involved." He then dismissed our case.

Our attorney, John Wesley Hall, immediately asked Judge Eisele to grant us a new trial, citing the systematic striking of all black jurors as the basis for his request. John also cited a recent ruling by the 8th Circuit, which granted a new trial for a black attorney in Eastern Arkansas when the prosecutor failed to give a good reason for striking six black jurors.

The day after the all-white jury was seated, John had requested a mistrial, and Judge Eisele denied the request. Later, we learned what Judge Eisele told the attorneys during a hearing in his chambers. According to John, the judge was not happy that no Blacks were on the jury, but he would allow the trial to proceed. When he asked the defense attorneys why they had stricken those Black individuals, they said, "She (referring to one of the Black jurors) could not be expected to understand the medical testimony."

If that doesn't meet the definition of racism, then nothing does. Excluding Black people from the jury panel was deliberate and should be challenged. I told our attorneys that our family wanted them to file an appeal with the court of appeals in St. Louis. We had not been particularly successful with this appellate court, but we wanted one last chance at getting justice for Marvin. Our attorneys did as we requested and the 8th circuit agreed to hear our appeal. My wife, Connie, my sisters Carolyn, Verna, Barbara, and I made the trip to St. Louis for the hearing. The judicial system in our state had failed us, so we could not miss this hearing. We were going to use every ounce of our being to fight for our brother.

The three-judge panel of the 8th circuit heard our case and decided to uphold the decision of the lower court. The only option left was to appeal the three-judge decision to the full 8th circuit court, which is comprised of eleven judges.

I told our attorney John Hall that we would take some time before deciding whether we would exercise our last option. At this point, I desperately needed some space. I'd fallen back into so much anger that I was messed up, ready to take on anything or anybody that looked like it wanted to discriminate against me. All I needed was for the right person to come along and push my buttons.

PART VII

Going Home

CHAPTER 34

Mother's Words

My mother was a Godly woman and very perceptive. During the case, when I visited my parents, she'd have me sit down so she could talk to me. She'd give me one of those deep, soul-searching stares that only a mother can give, and then she'd say, "Baby, are you okay?" My reply was always, "Yes, Mother, I'm okay." But she knew I was conflicted. She could see right through me.

I believe God gives good parents, godly parents, an extra something; an instinctive awareness that alerts them when their child is about to do something incredibly stupid, which is exactly where I was during that time. My mother could tell I was not in a good place. She could see my dysfunction.

What Mother said to me that day has forever altered the way I handle disappointment. She said, "Baby, you have enough of me in you to not do anything wrong." In essence, she was reminding me of everything she had poured into my siblings and me. She wanted me to remember that what she had deposited in me would prevent me from making poor choices when life slapped me in the face. She was betting that the way she had trained her children would help them outlive and outlast the injuries, psychological and physical, that each of us would suffer when we encountered racism in our society.

My mother's words, spoken at a time when my soul was teetering on the edge of anger and destruction, literally saved my life. I don't know where I'd be today if she hadn't forced me to sit down and listen to her, because I was a train wreck waiting to happen. Making me hear her words of wisdom while she looked at me with love and understanding in her eyes, opened my heart, and allowed God to speak to my innermost being, to my soul. It was during this time that God began to substitute my desire for violence with a desire for ministry.

Even after the intensity of my anger passed, and I was no longer interested in fighting with anyone, I still couldn't get over my disillusionment. I'd become disgusted with my surroundings. I needed to get away from both the City of Conway and the State of Arkansas. At the same time, I was reluctant to leave my parents, especially my father, whose health had started to decline. Finally, I spoke with them about my desire to leave the state. Being the supportive parents they'd always been, they did not discourage me.

I applied for and was offered a position with State Farm Insurance as an agent in Kansas City, Missouri. I was excited about this position because there were no limits on how much I could make and because it gave me an opportunity to leave Arkansas. It also put me close to four of my siblings, who for many years had all lived in the Kansas City area and were eager to assist me as I worked to build my clientele. My wife and two sons stayed in Arkansas while I made multiple trips to Kansas City to complete the licensure process, and then we rented a home just blocks from where two of my sisters lived.

As we loaded our things in the large U-Haul for the trip to Kansas City, my parents came to see us off. We exchanged hugs, smiles, and kisses, but I could see the disappointment in their eyes. They were happy for my family and me but sad for themselves. I was still stopping by my parents' home to check on them every morning and evening, and my departure would be a major adjustment for them. To fill that void, I asked my sister Donna, who lived forty miles away in Little Rock, to come weekly to check on them. She agreed, and we were off to K.C.

Life was good in Kansas City. My agency flourished, my wife was happy with her new job with the Kansas City School District, and our kids loved their new school. It was everything we imagined it would be. In Kansas City no one knew our story, so we got a break from all that anger, emotion, and sorrow that had followed us for four years. We didn't have to brace ourselves each time we went into a store or passed someone on the street. It was a healthy time of healing, recovery, and hope for us. It was a fresh start, and we got a chance to be ourselves again.

Meanwhile, my dad's cancer progressed and I traveled back home once a month to check on him. Whenever I came home, my parents put on their best faces, pretending everything was okay. But each trip, I could see changes in my father's physical appearance. It bothered me so much I told my parents I wanted to relocate them to Kansas City as soon as my agency could support them. In response, they said they wanted to spend their final days in their home. How could I argue? They'd earned the right to live out their lives wherever they wanted. So my wife and I continued our monthly commutes.

We'd been in Kansas City for about a year when we made a monthly trip to Arkansas and were taken aback at the change in my father. He'd lost a significant amount of weight and looked frail, and he was much more sedentary than usual. It was during this visit that Daddy called me aside and asked if I would move back home to take care of him. He told me he needed forty treatments of chemotherapy, and he didn't know how they'd make the daily trips to and from Little Rock, where the treatment facility was located. I took all this in and told him I'd speak with Connie and we would work it out.

I couldn't give my father a direct answer in that moment because I didn't know what to say. I loved my parents dearly, but I did not want to come back and be forced to raise our two sons in an environment which had approved and sanctioned morally offensive behavior. I couldn't see myself ever again living in a place which had protected those who murdered and covered up the death of my brother. I just couldn't do it.

That drive back to Kansas City was a long one. My dad's request weighed heavily on my mind, and Connie could tell something was bothering me. Reluctantly, I shared what Daddy had asked. We talked it over and agreed to pray about it and see where the Lord would take us.

My wife and I had sacrificed everything to make the move to Kansas City. Our home was on the market to be sold, we'd given up our jobs, and we'd withdrawn money from our retirement accounts to invest in the agency we started in Missouri. Even if we decided to return to Arkansas, where would we work? I was already labeled as this "angry black guy." No one would want to hire me; I was still toxic.

But I couldn't get my dad's request out of my mind. He needed those forty treatments. My sister Donna and her husband lived in Little Rock and had just one vehicle. It would be impossible for her to drive forty miles west to Menifee, pick up my parents, take them to Little Rock for his treatments, bring them back to their home in Menifee afterwards, then drive back to Little Rock all in the same day. My sisters and their families were long-time residents of Kansas City. Connie and I were the transients. And our home in Menifee had not yet sold. If anybody was in a position to go back home to care for my father, it had to be us.

Connie wasn't ready to come back, and it wasn't what I wanted, either. We dreaded facing the anger, the small retaliations, the pettiness that we'd encountered all during and after the case. We didn't know where we'd find work, or if I even could. We weren't sure how our boys would be treated. But we also knew how much my parents relied on me, for everything from decision-making to daily care and companionship. Knowing how much they loved and needed me was something neither of us could put aside. We only have our parents for a season, and I realized I wouldn't be able to live with myself if I did not honor my father's request. So we prayed about it, and asked for God's guidance.

Not long after we got home from that trip, Connie came to the same conclusion. "I will support you in this in any way," she told me. "Yes, we will go back."

* * *

Returning to Arkansas was not what I'd call a joyful move, but we were determined to make the best of it. I knew we were doing the right thing, but I was disappointed and disillusioned by Arkansas and I had a lot of concerns about how I could support my family. With no source of income, we needed to find jobs as quickly as possible. Fortunately, Connie got a job with a state agency in Morrilton that provided the basic income and benefits our family needed. I, on the other hand, had a much harder time securing employment.

Initially, I wanted to stay in the insurance business. I'd trained and licensed with State Farm Insurance, so that was the first company I contacted. I had numerous visits with one of the company's hiring managers, but apparently he wasn't satisfied with the reasons under which I'd left my agency in Kansas City.

As I was preparing to reach out to another company, I received a call from a former colleague, Larry Robinson, with the Department of Education. He heard I was back in the state and wanted me to know there was an opening in my old department, the secondary education department. Not only was it the same department, it was the same position I'd vacated when I resigned to move to Kansas City. I badly needed a job, so I applied for my old position, expecting to be a shoe-in because my former supervisor was still there. He knew I had well-established (six years to be exact), successful working relationships with the administrators in the school districts over which I would be assigned. He also knew the quality of my work and had always given me excellent performance evaluations.

To my surprise, however, this supervisor notified me that I ranked fourth on his list of candidates. He would only be interviewing the top three candidates for this job, so that meant I did not make the cut. On the call, his tone was strange. When I hung up the phone, I knew exactly why he did not want me back on his staff. He was from Conway, and this was "payback" for what our case had done to the image of his hometown. I had no desire to challenge his decision, I just needed to move on.

A couple of days later, I received a phone call from Dr. Ruth Steele, Director of the Department of Education for the State of Arkansas. Dr. Steele was a well-respected educator in our state and was familiar with my work at the department. She said she'd seen my name on a list of applicants for the job opening in my old department and was surprised that I was not recommended to fill it. She wanted to know if I was available to come to by her office to talk about it.

When I arrived, I was shocked to see my former supervisor sitting in the reception area as well. Dr. Steele came out and invited the two of us to her office, where she immediately turned to my former supervisor and ask him to explain his reason for not recommending me to fill my old position. I was not prepared for his response. I never thought he would stoop so low as to lie about my past job performance when he had given me high rankings on all my annual evaluations. He had the audacity to tell Dr. Steele, in my presence, that I had lied on one of my travel itineraries by failing to visit a school district that was on my itinerary. I told Dr. Steele that he was lying and encouraged her to call any or all of my former district superintendents and ask them if I had done what my former supervisor was accusing me of doing. She told me that would not be necessary. Then she turned to my former supervisor and said, "I don't think I can ever again believe a word you say." She turned back to me and said, "You can have your old job back." Later, I called Dr. Steele to thank her for believing in me, and for allowing me to return to my old job at the department of education.

On my first day back with the department of education I was warmly received. Many of my old colleagues were happy to see me return to the cubicle where I'd sat for many years. Not long after I sat down that first day, my former supervisor asked to see me in his office. I was reluctant, but knew I had to work with this guy even though he tried to destroy my reputation. I walked into his office and he said to me, without apologizing for what he'd done, "I hope we can work together, and there are no hard feelings." I told him I was there to do my job, not to be his friend. Then I left his office and returned to my work station.

Even though we'd only been in Kansas City for little more than a year, it was a reset for me. It allowed time to pass and let people think about other things. When we came back to Arkansas, people who had only known me during the case saw another side of me. Being back at the department of education was a blessing from God. I enjoyed the work and needed the income, and the location allowed me to transport my father to Carti (the cancer treatment facility), in Little Rock. This was the only place in central Arkansas that could administer the chemotherapy treatments he so desperately needed. As God would have it, the treatment facility was a few blocks from my office. This meant I could drop my parents off on my way to work, then pick them up at noon during my lunch break and take them to my sister's home. They waited there until I picked them up at the end of the day and took them home. It was as if God had made the arrangements for how we would care for my dad in his time of need.

Approximately one year later, I received a call from John Ward, an administrator with the University of Central Arkansas in Conway. I knew John and his wife, Betty, as she and I had worked together previously. John told me about a new program the university was about to start. He said his president, Dr. Winfred Thompson, was concerned about the retention and graduation rates of their African American students and wanted to hire someone who could address that issue. He told me he thought I'd be a good fit for the job, and strongly recommended I apply. I thanked John for his call and told him I'd think about it. But in my heart, I knew there was no way I was going to work in Conway. It was still too much of a risk.

I did not apply for the position and it was offered to a person from another state. For reasons unknown to me, that person did not stay in the job very long. Within a couple of months, the position was being advertised again.

By this time, my dad had taken all the chemotherapy and radiation his body could tolerate. His oncologist told me we'd reached the point where the only thing they could do for him was give him morphine to control his pain. Because of my dad's condition, I had to spend lots of time taking care of him, including attending to his personal hygiene. My mother tried to assist him, but my father wasn't having it. My dad had always been a strong, independent kind of man. The thought of a woman, even his wife, washing his private parts wasn't something he'd tolerate.

Taking care of my father while meeting the demands of my job, which required lots of travel to the western part of our state, was becoming unmanageable. About this time, John Ward called to tell me that the position with the university was open again. He told me he would be in Little Rock for a luncheon with Mahlon Martin, the former head of the Rockefeller Foundation, and a mutual friend of ours. He invited me to have lunch with them, so he could give me additional details about the job. After that lunch, John, being the salesperson that he was, convinced me to apply.

I did and to my surprise was notified that I was a finalist and that an on-campus interview would be forthcoming. The interview process culminated in a meeting with Dr. John Smith, who served as Vice President for Student Services, and was the person to whom this position would report. The meeting with Dr. Smith went extremely well. There was a certain "presence" about John Smith that appealed to me. He struck me as a man of enormous honesty and integrity. I think there was a mutual bonding that took place between the two of us the first time we met.

John offered and I accepted the position as the University of Central Arkansas' first Director of Minority Affairs. I started in January of 1990 and immediately fell in love with the position, the university, and my colleagues in the Division of Student Services. It was a perfect fit for me. I loved working in higher education, and I loved the fact that I was given full reign on how I wanted to develop the program. There were very few limitations on what I could do, as long as I addressed the graduation and retention rates of students of color. Since African-American males had the lowest retention rates on campus, they were to be my main focus.

At that time, there were very few men of color in mid-level management positions on campus. There may have been three of us in all. I knew this was a real opportunity for upward mobility for me and for the students I was there to support. Not only was it important for them to see Black men in management roles, I also was confident that through my work I could truly make a difference in their lives.

There was a popular saying at the time that I felt deeply: "If you want to be me, you have to see me." If we were going to get our students to focus on realizing their full potential, we needed to bring them in contact with successful professional Black men and women so they could see role models. That conviction led to one of my first initiatives, the Minority Mentoring Program. I set about asking nearly a hundred individuals that I'd come into contact with – pastors, lawyers, doctors, business owners, administrators, entrepreneurs – to volunteer their time to mentor our students. Person after person said yes.

As I settled into my new role, an unexpected benefit became evident. My old position had sometimes required me to spend hours on the road each week visiting school districts in western Arkansas. Now, I could occasionally drop off my kids for school and if necessary, respond quickly to the health concerns of my father. It was exactly where I needed to be during his final months.

The last time I took my dad to visit his oncologist he needed wheelchair assistance. As he and Mother and I were leaving the building for the parking lot, he looked up at me and said softly, "Son, I'm so glad you came back. You're doing a good job taking care of me."

My father was a man of few words and quiet dignity. Until his illness he'd always been remarkably strong and fit. Daddy believed his God-given role was to set a good example for his children and to be a good provider for his family. We all knew without a doubt that he loved us, but he was raised in a time when being manly meant you did not express affection. I was well into my adult years before I remember him telling me, "I love you." That day, those few loving words of appreciation and gratitude from him meant more to me than anything I'd lost by moving back to Arkansas. I could never have forgiven myself had I not sacrificed for the man and woman who had given me their best.

That was one of the last coherent conversations I had with Daddy. Without ever receiving justice for his son, my father went to be with the Lord on October 15, 1990. Connie and I had the comfort of knowing that when he left this earth, we had done everything we could for my father. We have no regrets, and there is nothing but peace in our hearts about the decision we made.

CHAPTER 35

An Angel Named Bullet

After Daddy passed, my sisters wanted our mother to come live in Kansas City. But Mother didn't want to leave her home, her garden, or anything that reminded her of Daddy. She wanted to stay in the house they'd shared. Unable to convince her otherwise, we decided to support her choice for the time being, and I continued going twice a day to check on her.

One evening a couple of weeks after Daddy died, I pulled up to Mother's house and was confronted by a very aggressive dog barking and lunging at my car. It was a border collie I'd never seen before. While I was trying to figure out how to get out of the car without this dog attacking me, my mother came around from behind her home. As soon as the dog saw her, he stopped barking and started wagging his tail. My mother smiled and went right to him.

I couldn't believe what I was seeing – my mother was hugging and kissing this dog as if she'd raised it from a pup. When I asked her where on earth it came from, she said she had no idea. She'd come outside to work in her yard that day, and there was this dog sitting underneath the carport, as if he were waiting for her. With a huge smile on her face, she told me, "Baby, I've already named him. His name is Bullet."

Bullet was our pet dog that was killed by the tornado the night Marvin died.

It took a couple of weeks for Bullet to reluctantly accept me as an auxiliary member of his newly adopted family of one, which was my mother. He was utterly devoted to her and became her constant companion. Whenever Mother worked in her yard, Bullet was right there behind her, following in her every footstep.

When Mother first decided to continue living in Arkansas, Connie and I expected her to spend the nights at our house and the days at her home. We didn't like the idea of her staying by herself at night, and we were confident that in time she would agree with us. Of course, Mother wanted nothing to do with that plan, no matter how we tried to convince her. And once Bullet showed up, the argument was closed. No one could have trained a dog to protect Mother better than he did. If someone came by the house, they had to stay in their car until Mother came out and held Bullet by the collar so they could get out. When Mother went inside for the night, Bullet waited until the door closed behind her, then went up on the porch and curled up right in front of the door. He'd guard the house all night, and in the morning he'd be in that same spot waiting for her. It gave us peace of mind to know he was there.

Over the next few years, Bullet became known throughout the community as my mother's fierce protector. Anyone driving past her house out on the road was fine. But once you turned into Mother's driveway, you were on Bullet's turf, and he let you know it. For the first few months, that included Connie and the kids, who had to wait until Mother came out and held Bullet so they could get out of the car. That procedure had to be repeated when they left her house to come home. Eventually, he accepted all of us, but when we went to Mother's we still waited until Bullet stopped barking and started wagging his tail before we got out of the car.

We never did learn where Bullet came from, but his devotion to my Mother was unlike anything I've ever seen. In later years, he sometimes even slept on a pad next to her bed, and that seemed to comfort her. My sisters and I have often said that dog was an angel, sent by God to be the companion and protector my mother needed and deserved.

* * *

Finding my place at UCA and working up through the administration allowed me to have a different kind of exposure to the community. After what my family and I had been through, my perspective on what was worth getting worked up about was a little different than other people's. I found it easy to stay calm and be objective in certain situations. It's my nature to think things through, and people who got to know me knew that I would be fair and honest. Slowly, I became someone to whom colleagues and students came for advice.

In October 1991, Governor Bill Clinton announced his campaign for president of the United States. After he leaned into our case the way he did, I was determined to support him any way I could. He'd taken a huge political risk to do what he believed was right by our family, and it cost him significant political support, especially in Faulkner County. To top it off, following his acquittal, Marvin Iberg had formed a group that he called, "Anyone but Clinton." It never amounted to much, but it got Iberg some attention and it was a way to distract from Clinton's achievements.

By this time, Governor Clinton knew Connie and me on a first name basis. When we happened to see each other, we'd visit and he'd always ask about Connie. He even invited us to a few events at the Governor's Mansion, including one notable evening with Bob Hope.

Shortly after Clinton announced, some of his supporters started a group called the Arkansas Travelers, as a way for Arkansans who believed in Clinton to support his campaign. I knew firsthand what he'd done for our state, especially in the area of education, and I wanted the rest of the country to see what we saw, so I volunteered. Sheila Gilbraith Bronfman was the head person and organizer for the Travelers, and she did an amazing job. Sometimes literally hundreds of people would show up at a Traveler's meeting. Sheila would blow her whistle, get our attention, and tell us what they needed volunteers for. Then we'd sign up for whatever we thought we could do well. It could be anything from flying to Milwaukee to doing a local radio interview. And whatever we did, we did on our own dime; we paid all our own expenses.

One time a group of us flew into Minneapolis to canvass for Clinton. We had our Arkansas Travelers caps and T-shirts on, and our Clinton buttons, and we fanned out across the city and state. We went to the Mall of America and passed out flyers from store to store. We drove to neighborhoods and went door-to-door, introducing ourselves, and talking to people about Clinton. People were amazed at our dedication, and they listened and asked questions when we told them what Clinton had done for Arkansas. We did radio and TV spots and held group discussions in small towns. One day we headed way up north to Duluth, and believe me, that was an experience. There weren't many people of color up there, that's for sure.

No matter where we went, people were friendly and we were well-received. It was a big deal that this group of Clinton supporters from Arkansas were traveling around the country at our own expense, and if we knocked on their door they wanted to know all about us. No other candidate had anything like it that I saw. If they did, they certainly were not as well-organized as the Arkansas Travelers.

Several times I was interviewed on TV and radio. Whenever I had the chance, I talked about my brother's case and Clinton's role in it. People were always moved, and I think some minds were opened and some hearts were changed. More than once, the thought came to me that 32 years after his death, Marvin was still helping people.

I also shared my experience working in education, and what I'd seen Clinton do for Arkansas. I talked about how he brought a more balanced curriculum to our 324 school districts, so that no matter where in the state students lived they had access to the same improved curriculum. I talked about how he raised teacher salaries, funded pre-school education, and made system-wide changes that could take years to show results, but would change lives when they did – something most politicians were afraid to do.

In addition to Minnesota, I went to Wisconsin, Iowa, and twice to New York. On one of the New York trips, a small group of us went over to Brooklyn and were handing out flyers. A group of black guys came up to us and said, "We're not happy with Clinton, he's the guy that refused to let those students into that high school." I told them "No, you've got the wrong governor, that was Orville Faubus and it happened in 1957." Here it was 1992, but that's still what a lot of people remembered about Arkansas. We had our work cut out for us.

The Democratic National Convention was held in July that year, at Madison Square Garden, and I was selected as a delegate. Connie and I decided to take the boys and make it a family vacation. Torre was 14, and Greg was 10, and we flew into Washington, D.C. and stayed in the One Washington hotel. Connie and I were so confident Clinton would win that we went ahead and reserved rooms for the Inauguration the following January – at $75 a night. From DC, we took a train into New York's Penn Station. When we walked out of the station and saw Times Square – well, let's just say the boys had never seen anything like it.

At the end of the Democratic National Convention, the Arkansas delegation came on stage. Back at home, our family and friends, including my mother and sisters, were all watching. Later they told me the camera repeatedly panned across our delegation and several times they were able to see me on TV. My mother was so proud of that.

After Clinton won, Connie and I were invited to the Inauguration. Of course, hotel rooms were now going for $500 or $600 a night – if you could even find one. The One Washington hotel called and tried to get us to pay the higher rate, but we already had our room confirmation and they eventually honored the original rate. The hotel was right on Pennsylvania Avenue, and the morning of the inauguration we took a taxi as far as we could, then walked the rest of the way, greeting friends and people we'd gotten to know during the campaign all along the way.

It was a sunny and beautiful day, very cold but not a cloud in the sky, and people were there from all over the world. Connie and I stood together watching Clinton be sworn in. We listened as Maya Angelou read her poem. It was thrilling to think that someone from Arkansas was now president of the United States.

That was a once in a lifetime trip for us, and we decided to celebrate it in style. For the Inaugural Ball, my wife ordered a custom dress. It had a long black velvet skirt and a black satin top, and she looked absolutely beautiful in it. Attending the Arkansas Inaugural Ball felt like a dream. Being in that moment, around so many dignitaries and actors and celebrities, and then having the President and First Lady come and speak, it was thrilling. It was such a historic celebration, and there we were, this little couple from Menifee, Arkansas, right in the middle of it.

After Clinton was elected, I would occasionally receive invitations to White House events. One of these was a small reception with President Clinton when we met with him privately, and he expressed his thanks and appreciation of our work. Another time, I was escorting a group of Indonesian deans to the White House and the President was on his way to board Marine One to go to Camp David. He saw us and came over and greeted me warmly and met the deans. Needless to say, it was the highlight of their trip.

* * *

One of my goals as Director of the Office of Minority Affairs was to give our students of color some insight into their history, particularly as it related to slavery and the experiences of their ancestors. The director of international student programs and I worked together to organize a series of trips to Africa, so students could see firsthand what their ancestors experienced before making that journey across the Atlantic. In 1993, our plans came to fruition, and several colleagues and I took the first group of 14 students from UCA to six West African countries: Senegal, The

Gambia, Ivory Coast (Cote D'Ivoire), Ghana, Togo, and Benin. We eventually made it an annual program, at least for several years.

We also designed the trip to address common misconceptions about Africa. Invariably, before the trip, a few students always asked how they would manage to sleep in the bush and whether they'd be safe. We made sure to give them an opportunity to see Africa's bustling modern cities as well as the traditional villages they expected. The most powerful day of the trip was in Dakar, the capital of Senegal and the westernmost point in Africa, where we visited Goree Island, a UNESCO Historical Site. We saw where slaves had been held in holding pens, and in dark, cramped cells with ceilings so low they could not stand up. We saw where slaves were herded down a ramp like a cattle chute, past the "Point of No Return," to be loaded onto ships and carried naked across the sea. Standing in that place, seeing the conditions under which our ancestors were held before they even made the trip, hearing how they suffered and the sacrifices it took to make it across the Atlantic, was intensely emotional. For the students, and for me, the impact of the trip was life-changing.

We often talked to the students during those trips about what it meant to be a person of excellence. The university felt the program was so successful and impactful that we were eventually able to start another study abroad program in East Africa, in which students spent five weeks in Dar es-Salaam, Tanzania.

After a year and half as the University's Director of Minority Affairs, I was invited to lunch by the president of the university, Dr. Winfred Thompson. During our meeting he told me he was quite pleased with the visibility the institution had received from our Minority Mentorship Program. He then said that Dr. H.B. Hardy, who served as his assistant, was retiring. He wanted to know if I would be interested in replacing him. Even though I was very happy in my current position, I didn't feel I was in a position to tell the president of the university no. So, I told him, yes, I would accept the position.

At that time I knew nothing about Higher Education Administration at the executive level, so I didn't know what I'd gotten myself into. I'd only been in my current position for a year and a half. I still don't know what President Thompson saw in me that would cause him to take such a risk on me, but I kept telling myself, go in there, work as hard as you can, and let the chips fall where they may.

I served as President Thompson's assistant from 1992 to 1996 and found myself being mentored by one of the brightest minds in the higher education profession. Win Thompson is an absolutely brilliant man. While there were those on campus who were not particularly pleased with his leadership style, I admired him and I liked his direct manner. You always knew where you stood with Win Thompson – good or bad. And if he told you he'd do something, you could count on him keeping his word. He allowed me the independence to rise and fall on my own, and whenever I would fall, he offered the kind of constructive criticism he knew would help me become a better administrator. During those years I learned so much about higher education administration. I would not be where I am today were it not for Winfred Thompson.

* * *

During all the years the boys were growing up, we continued our tradition of Saturday morning breakfast talks. We knew education would open doors for our sons, and we stressed that point until they were tired of hearing it. We talked a lot about how they should present themselves and how to speak. Greg still laughs remembering me saying, "I better not hear you say, 'You know what I'm saying?' when you're talking to an adult."

When they were younger, Connie would leave work every day and pick them up from school, and then take them back with her to the library. She made sure they did homework or had after-school tutoring if they needed it. We encouraged them to start foreign languages early, and made sure they always took higher math classes, which were a level up from their grades. Both boys had the grades to take advanced classes, but more than once we had to insist they be put in them. Most of the time, they would be the only Black students in that class.

We also taught our sons to stand up for themselves respectfully. One time, during Black History Month, Greg realized his class was the only fifth grade class that was not participating in the Black History Month curriculum. This primarily consisted of a short lesson each day, things like reading a Langston Hughes poem or a story about Jackie Robinson, and each class was planning an end-of-the-month skit related to Black History to perform for the other classes. So Greg raised his hand and asked his fifth grade teacher why they weren't learning what the other fifth grade classes were learning.

His teacher answered that they would not be taking part in the curriculum because Black people's place in American history was as slaves, and that this was their Biblically-ordained role. Greg came home and told me what she'd said, and, as you can imagine, I called the principal. The next day, and from then on, his class had the same curriculum the other classes had.

Since Connie and I both worked in education, we understood what to look for, what to watch out for, what to advocate for, and how to intervene. Whenever she could, Connie volunteered as a room mother or as a parent chaperone on field trips, and she made it her mission to see that all the students were included, not just our boys. Most of all, we made sure our sons always knew we were both in their corner, and that education came first. Six of my parent's surviving seven children graduated from college, and we made it clear to the boys that this is what we expected of them as well.

One of the greatest blessings of those times was knowing that Torre and Greg were growing up as part of a big family – really big. Eventually, there were twenty-three grandchildren in all. Torre and Greg and the other six oldest cousins called themselves "The Original Eight," because they were the first eight grandchildren on both sides. At Connie's parents' they rode horses and helped with the cattle and played around the farm. At my parent's house, Daddy took them fishing and hunting, and when Torre fell in love with baseball, Daddy spent hours teaching him different pitches. All the things he'd taught Marvin, and then me, my father now taught my sons. When Daddy's friends stopped by for haircuts, which he'd provide out under the carport, the boys would sit and listen to the men talk. Then Daddy would come inside and sit in his big green chair and let Greg comb his white hair and pretend to cut it.

The boys always knew they had an uncle Marvin who had died, just as they knew about Connie's brother, Lee Andrew. Mother kept Marvin's Army photo on a shelf in her living room and they knew he'd served his country with pride. Mother, who called all the grandchildren "Baby," would often comment how much Torre looked like Marvin. We never hid the fact that Marvin had been killed, but we didn't discuss the details in front of them until they were much older.

Growing up in a family of girls, I had always missed Marvin so much. I used to wish he was there so we could do things together, and so I could have an older brother I could talk to about things. Now that I had two sons, it was important to me that they grew up close. Connie and I wanted to make sure they had the memories Marvin and I never had the chance to have. So if Torre went somewhere, our rule was he had to take Greg. Torre wasn't always happy about that, especially as he got older. He didn't understand why he had to "drag around" his little brother, when none of his friends did. I tried to explain, but it wasn't until years later when he had children of his own that he told me he finally understood.

We were open with the boys about racism from a young age. We had to be – it was always there and they needed a framework to understand it. As they got older, those Saturday morning conversations included more and more of what we knew they'd face as young black men. They got tired of that conversation, but like my father before me, I knew they needed to be prepared for how they could be treated, especially when it came to racial profiling.

Among other things, we drilled into them what to do if they were ever stopped by the police. First thing, turn on the overhead light to make sure the police can see every move you make. Then put your hands on the dashboard so they can be seen. When the officer tells you to do something, like hand him your driver's license, say, "Yessir," and repeat his request, as in "I'm going to reach over with my right hand and get my driver's license now" before you actually do it. Don't hesitate, but don't move fast either. Most importantly, just comply and stay safe. Even if you feel you've been singled out for your race, stay calm and we'll deal with that the next day. This was no easier for them to hear twenty years ago than it is today. And it's no easier to write it today, either, because while many things have changed since 1960, many things have not.

Those were busy years for our family. Both boys were excellent students. Torre played baseball, basketball, and football, while Greg focused on basketball. We made it a priority to be at all their games, no matter where they were held. That was part of our commitment to them, but those games were also a lot of fun for us. At home, it was our determination to always be a united front when it came to decisions. To be honest, Connie and I didn't often disagree. But when we did, we did our best to keep it to ourselves and resolve it when we were alone.

* * *

After four years, Dr. Thompson decided to do a complete realignment of his Executive Staff. During this reorganization he appointed me Vice President for Student Services. It was the first time in the history of the university that a person of color had been elevated to the position of Vice President.

Mother was so proud of my new appointment. She told everybody she saw, especially her friends at the Senior Citizen's Building, that her son was a Vice President at a predominantly white institution. She even laminated the article about my appointment so she could carry it in her purse for others to read (which always embarrassed the heck out of me).

In 2000, Greg graduated from high school and Torre was finishing his final term in college. Connie and I were empty nesters now, and she was able to join me on a trip to Africa. During this time, the University was growing its study abroad program, and we finalized arrangements for a UCA campus in the historic city of Maastricht, The Netherlands. President Thompson, several board members, and a few others, including me, traveled to see the campus and the areas our students would visit. One of the student trips would be to nearby Germany, and I was part of that tour. I was keenly aware that Marvin had been stationed in Germany, and I made it a point to visit a nearby U.S. military base where some of our soldiers were buried and where I thought Marvin might have trained. Just being there gave me a sense of that part of Marvin's life, and that brief visit to Germany was spiritually therapeutic for me. Years later, when CR talked about his and Marvin's experiences there, I could see some of those places in my mind's eye.

As Vice President, I also had the honor of conferring the degrees of Marvin's daughter, Sharon, and two of his grandchildren. It meant a great deal to us both when I gave Sharon her degree. Years later, as I was giving her children Robin and Ricky their degrees, it dawned on me that if he had lived, Marvin would have been there with us. He would have been sitting there watching his grandchildren's graduation. The feeling of his presence at that moment was so strong, it felt as if he was saying, "Thanks, little brother, I'm here with you and my family." I had rarely felt Marvin's presence so clearly as I did that day, and I was so overcome with emotion that it was a struggle to make it back to my seat on the platform.

* * *

When the boys were younger and Daddy was feeling up to it, he and Mother loved attending their grandchildren's games or events. Mother continued to do that after Daddy was gone. She kept up with everything that was happening in her children's and grandchildren's lives. When she could no longer go to their baseball, football, and basketball games, she had me turn her radio to the correct station so she could listen to the games while resting in bed. She kept scrapbooks of everything her family did, and she especially loved Christmas and holidays when as many of us as possible would get together. In short, she loved her family – that's the essence of who my mother was. She celebrated all her children's accomplishments and she beamed with love and pride when she talked about them.

But Mother had lost family, too. In addition to losing her oldest son, her husband, and her grandson Ricky, she also lost her firstborn when our sister Emogene died in 1994. Four years later, our sister Ernestine passed away from lung cancer. Mother had now outlived her three oldest children, and I can't imagine how hard that was for her.

One day Mother wasn't feeling well. I'd taken her to the doctor and when we got home, out of the blue she started asking me when she could visit her mother and grandmother, both of whom had been dead for many years. I thought maybe she had a fever, or that it was a side effect of the illness. But it wasn't. Not long after that, Mother was diagnosed with Alzheimers.

At first, Connie and I took care of her ourselves. As she grew worse, to avoid institutionalizing her, we started a rotation with my sisters. Mother spent three months in Arkansas, and then went to Kansas City for two or three months, moving from one of my sister's homes to the next. While she was here in Arkansas, she stayed in her own home and we took care of her there. Sometimes Greg and Torre would sit or stay with her, too.

From the beginning of our marriage, Mother and Connie were close. Through the years they grew to love each other dearly, and Mother treated Connie like a daughter. Connie always called my parents Mr. Williams and Miss Williams because that's how you showed respect to your in-laws in those days. She still talks about how Mother carried herself with such pride and strength through every challenge, and about how she watched Mother in the courtroom, and listened to her on the stand, testifying about the last time she saw her son. She says she learned a lot about family from Mother.

So when Mother began to need more personal care, it was Connie who assisted her, bearing the brunt of taking care of Mother's needs and personal hygiene. As Mother got worse, this got harder on Connie, physically and emotionally. And of course, the whole time she was still working. Then, during a visit to Kansas City, Mother fractured her hip and was unable to ever return home to Arkansas.

Our mother succumbed to this dreadful disease on March 4, 2005. We celebrated her life in Arkansas and laid her to rest between the tombstones of my father and Marvin. It was so hard to say goodbye to the matriarch of our family.

CHAPTER 36

A Time for Everything

I stayed at the University of Central Arkansas as Vice President for the Division of Student Services for twenty-five years, serving seven different presidents. During these years, something remarkable happened to me. I can't tell you when or how it happened, but I slowly developed a real fondness for the City of Conway, the city I once despised. It was not just the passage of time that helped me heal. The City of Conway had changed. It was no longer the city that it was in 1960, nor in 1985.

Connie noticed the change in me and in how the city saw me. Over time, fewer people remembered the case, and many more knew nothing about it. My work was deeply rewarding; and each year I could see the difference I was making in young people's lives. As the success of the initial retention and mentoring programs became clear, we were able to expand beyond our original mandate of supporting the retention of male African-American students. Today our division provides support services and mentoring programs that stimulate, enhance, and extend student learning to all students.

Meanwhile, the City of Conway was becoming a more progressive city that saw its diversity as a strength rather than a weakness. I'd grown to embrace the new Conway and, in many circles, the city had grown to accept me and my family as well. One of the most touching experiences I've ever had in my life occurred when the city's current mayor, Bart Castleberry, a relative of Joe Castleberry, the Faulkner County Sheriff when my brother was murdered, approached me with tears in his eyes and said, "I think someone in my family may have done something to hurt a member of your family. If so, I want to say I'm sorry."

It was the first time anyone in a position of authority with the city or the county had ever apologized to any member of our family for what happened to Marvin. I was moved beyond words by Bart Castleberry's sincere apology, and it went a long way to heal the wounds of the past.

Now and then, over the years, people have remembered the case and made the connection to me. A few still avoid me as part of the guilt they carry. Others want us to know that they followed the case and supported us, then and now. Several years ago, right about the time I was starting to write this book, a man came up to me in a parking lot. He said, "You don't know who I am, but I followed the case. I want you to know that justice was not served, your family wasn't treated right. I just wanted to meet you and say hello and tell you that."

He did not introduce himself, and I have no idea who he was. Moments like that have happened a lot through the years.

My time at the university gave me opportunities to engage students from every walk of life, and I developed relationships with young people that continued well beyond their time as students at the University. One of those is Brad Lacy, who was president of the Student Body during his time at UCA. Some years after he graduated, Brad returned to Conway as CEO for the Conway Area Chamber of Commerce and asked me to serve as a member of the Chamber's Board of Directors. A few years later, I became Chairman of the Board (2011), a position no other African American had held during the chamber's 120-year existence.

After finishing that term, I was appointed to the Conway Development Corporation (CDC) Board, again the first time a person of color served as a member, and later Arkansas Governor Mike Beebe appointed me to serve as a commissioner with the Arkansas Educational Television Network (now PBS of Arkansas) and the Arkansas Community Foundation Board. In 2010, I was appointed to the Arkansas Supreme Court Committee on Professional Conduct.

I share this information because I want you to see how God has prospered me in the place of my greatest pain. Many times Connie and I have marveled at the arc of our lives in this place, amazed at how this story has unfolded. I've come to realize that all along, God's plan was for me to be here. He needed for me to chronicle the events of the life and tragic death of my brother, Marvin Leonard Williams. Writing this book was never a desire of mine; it was an assignment divinely given by our Creator, written over five years and four months. In fact, it was not until all of those who were directly and indirectly involved in my brother's death and the cover-up of his murder were dead that He gave me the inspiration to write this book. In this way, He could have my complete attention and could protect me from any anger and bitterness that might rise up in my life if I were to see these individuals during this process.

My parents taught me to always judge a person based on your personal interaction with them. If my parents, and others like them, could weather the racist storms of the 1960s, then there's nothing we can't handle today. Progress is a journey, and that journey continues. Today, both of our sons are now in the corporate sector; people paid a price for that to happen. We are well aware that none of what has happened in my life, or in my son's lives, has happened due to our efforts alone.

Several years ago, our son Torre was driving home from work and was stopped behind several other cars when his car was rear-ended. The driver was an older white man, who never took his foot off the accelerator. Even after this man had pushed Torre's car as far as it could go, he kept his foot on the pedal. Fortunately, there were witnesses and the other driver was clearly in the wrong, but Torre's heart was racing as the police pulled up. He immediately thought about Marvin's death, and went through a mental list of what *he* could do to avoid putting himself at risk, of how *he* needed to convince the police he was not any kind of threat, of how *he* should act and speak to make sure he got home safely to his sons and daughter. Here he was, well-educated, a good job, a family man, a devout man, saying a prayer that *he* would not be perceived as the problem.

Our son Greg is as tall as Marvin was, and has the build of a former athlete. He always dresses well for work or even casual events, but one hot Saturday afternoon he was taking his car to the car wash, planning to wash it himself in one of the bays. So he threw on gym shorts and a muscle shirt. With his hat on backwards, he was driving along listening to music and having a great day, until he heard the siren.

He pulled over and a white police officer got out of the cruiser. Instead of approaching cautiously from the driver's side, the officer went around to the passenger side of the car keeping his hand on his gun. This was not the first time Greg had been stopped for no apparent reason, but it was the first time he'd seen an officer approach in this manner. Immediately, Greg was conscious of how he was dressed, and how he might be perceived because of it.

Greg kept his hands high on the steering wheel, completely visible. Other cars in front of and behind him had been going the same speed he was, but the officer told him he'd been driving five miles over the speed limit and asked for his license and registration. Greg complied, narrating his movements, "Officer, I'm about to take my right hand off the steering wheel and reach for my license and registration." Then, "I'm about to reach my right hand up to the window and give you my license and registration," and so on. The whole time, anxious and frustrated, he was thinking about what happened to Marvin.

At some point, the officer realized he'd put my son in a box – the same box so many men and women are put in every single day simply because of the color of their skin. Somewhat sheepishly, he thanked Greg for his cooperation, did not give him a ticket, and drove away. But my son was left sitting there, with his heart racing, his weekend ruined, and the inescapable awareness of how easily that traffic stop could have ended very differently.

These are not the only stories of this kind my sons could tell. I have similar stories of my own. It never ends. It's not just law enforcement, it's all around us. It is exhausting to know that everything you do, even what you wear, may be used against you.

A few years ago, we were having dinner with a former student, a white man, who'd just learned about the case. At one point during dinner, he became somewhat emotional. He looked at me and said, "Ronnie, I can't believe you don't hate white people."

"Hate is too heavy a burden to carry," I told him. "It's all consuming."

All you have to do is look at what happened on January 6, 2021, to see what hate does to people. That is not the way forward. My mother and father taught their children to believe there is value and worth in every human being, and good and bad in all races. I do not believe that every white law enforcement official is a racist. However, there's no doubt that racism and police brutality took my brother's life and were the motivating forces behind the cover-up that ensued. As I write this, it's been sixty years since my brother was murdered, and I am disheartened by the fact that we as people of color continue to suffer because of the effects of systemic racism, which exists even today in every segment of our society.

As I conclude this book, I do so with the understanding that we have many good and dedicated men and women from every racial and ethnic group working in our law enforcement profession. They treat those whom they are sworn to serve and protect with dignity and respect. And I understand that we all have hidden biases that can catch us by surprise from time to time, and that includes law enforcement officers.

But I am also painfully aware that there is a small minority of police officers and others in power who see people of color as subhuman, who abuse us by putting their knees on our necks until the breath has left our bodies. They apply choke holds and use illegal devices to inflict as much pain as possible. They barge into our homes or stand on our bodies after they've taken our lives. They execute us for doing things that white men and women do with impunity. These individuals should be removed from the law enforcement profession, and those who commit crimes should be prosecuted to the fullest extent of the law.

Sixty years after my brother was killed, my wife and I marched in the Black Lives Matter protest in Conway in the summer of 2020. We carried a poster with three names on it: Breonna Taylor, George Floyd, and Marvin Williams.

George Floyd's death seared the conscience of so many people, but to Black people this brutality is not new. While we see the rising tide of awareness with hope, we also can't help but think, "This has been going on for so long, did you really have to watch a video to understand that it's been happening?"

I've learned to live with the outcome of what those individuals and others did to our family in 1960, in 1985, and 1988, but I can never forget how my brother suffered on the night of his death. Every May 5, our family feels that pain. Seldom does a month pass that I don't drive along Markham Street, and park in that place where my brother was unlawfully taken from his vehicle, or stop in the parking lot west of the Faulkner County Courthouse where the initial abuse took place. I do these things as my private memorial to my brother.

About two years ago, I ran into an old friend, a woman I'd known for more than three decades but hadn't seen for a while. As I walked toward her, she greeted me, saying, "Hi Marvin."

Immediately she put her hand on her mouth and looked aghast. She apologized sincerely and profusely, and I reassured her that it was OK, that it didn't bother me, and that it had happened many times, which is true. But the fact is, even after all these years, for many people this is how I am perceived. I am a reminder of something that has never been fully processed, that is still unfinished. I am a reminder that we still have a lot of work to do.

My brother's killers were indicted. His case made the newspapers and the television. His murder moved hearts and minds and changed perceptions and understanding across the country. In my lifetime, I have seen change beyond anything my parents dreamed of. My hope is that my sons and my grandchildren will live to see even more. My wish for them is to have a world so transformed by love and justice that I would not believe it.

As I close this book, I want you to know that I have been wonderfully sustained through all these years and events by the teachings of my parents, Johnnie and D.V. Williams. Because of what they poured into me, I have a relationship with our Lord and Savior Jesus Christ that sustains me, guides me, and leads me through dark times. A few weeks before I finished this manuscript, I was at home writing when I felt a familiar stillness enter my heart and soul. I sensed a voice from God saying, "Here's how I want you to end this book: With a different state of mind than you have had in the past. I want you to end it with a mind that aspires to forgiveness."

I wasn't sure what to do with this. At first I thought I had to find a way to fully forgive everyone involved, and if I couldn't then I would fail to complete the task God entrusted to me all those years ago. But as I prayed and worked through the final stages of editing and finalizing this book, an understanding grew in me that God doesn't expect me to achieve an over-arching, perfect, unconditional love in this lifetime. He is simply asking me to aspire to it, and work towards it.

Forgiveness is a slow walk. I am far past where I was in 1984, when the rawness and shock of my brother's brutal death and the blatant injustice of the courts left me struggling with an almost uncontrollable anger. I moved on from that state a long time ago.

But where I am today is difficult to articulate. No one can give me back my brother. I can never have the closeness with him that I longed for my whole life. I can never forget how horribly he suffered alone in that cell. Or the aching sorrow his death brought to lives of so many who loved him.

At the same time, my faith is crystal clear: God wants me to move toward a love capable of genuine forgiveness. I observed this forgiveness level in Nelson Mandela when he was asked if he had forgiven those who imprisoned and abused him for twenty-seven years. His response moved me: "They have had me for twenty-seven years. If I keep hating them, they still have me. They have taken everything from me except my mind and my heart. Those they cannot have without my without my permission. I want to be free, so I let it go.".

I, too, have chosen to be free. Hate and unforgiveness are too heavy of a burden to carry for a lifetime. And since God has given us his prescription for how we are to deal with hate and unforgiveness, I've decided to follow his plan. It is found in the gospel of John, 13th chapter, verses 34 and 35. It says – "A new commandment I give unto you, that ye love one another; as I have loved you, that ye also love one another. (35) By this shall all men know that ye are my disciples, if ye have love one to another."

As I end this book, I pray for the strength to continue on this journey, a journey I will stay on for the rest of my life.

Epilogue

Not long before I finished this book, at a community gathering in Conway, a good friend of ours, Lori Case, came over and said she wanted to share something with me. I could tell this was something personal, as she seemed almost hesitant to speak. When she did, I understood why.

Lori is a respected banker in the City of Conway, and decades ago she worked with Marvin's daughter, Sharon, at a local bank. She told me that one day while she and Sharon were both working, a customer, a white man, suffered a heart attack in the bank's lobby. Without hesitation, Sharon rushed over to him and was the first person to administer CPR.

Sharon did not know this man, Lori said, she only knew that someone needed help. It didn't matter to Sharon if he was black or white. Later, they heard that he had survived, and Sharon never thought any more about it. She never sought recognition of any kind. She never even mentioned to our family that she'd saved a stranger's life at work one day.

In spite of all the tragedy in her life, my niece's care and concern for others is immense. That is what is in Sharon's heart. The heartfelt instinct to help other people that she displayed that day in the bank was the same instinct her father displayed during his life, including the last night he was alive. Sharon helped that white man who collapsed just as she would have helped any stranger, regardless of their skin color, and she would do it again today.

Sharon did not know the name of the man whose life she saved, but Lori did. When she told me who it was, I was shocked to my core. In that moment, I felt God's mighty hand moving all of us to a higher purpose, with a wisdom and love that passes human understanding. For only He could orchestrate such an event.

The man Sharon saved that day was Marvin Iberg.

Appendix A – The Autopsy

Here is the summary of Marvin's autopsy findings (which is date May 5, 1960) – "Final Summary: This 21-year-old Negro Male was found to have a fracture of the base of his skull, with laceration of the middle meningeal artery, formation of an epidural hematoma, subarachnoid hemorrhage, and hemorrhage into the cerebral cortex in the left temporal area. Contusions and laceration were found over the right eye. The presence of ethanol was NOT detected in postmortem blood. Pulmonary edema was present."

External Appearance: "The body when first seen was fully clothed. Blood stains which appeared to be caused drops of blood were noted on the shoulder and right arm on a soiled linen jacket which the patient was wearing. These were pink in color and appeared to have been made by a mixture of fluid, possibly water and blood rather than pure blood. A wound was evident in the right supraorbital area of the patient. The wound dressed 1 ½ cm in length and had a width of 0.8 cm. Its long axis was transverse, parallel to the eyebrow, and approximately 1 ½ cm above supraorbital ridge. On manipulating the skin, it appears that this wound was circular in outline. The instrument of trauma seems to have entered LATERALLY since the wound penetrates medially. The skull here is intact. There is a minimal amount of blood staining on the forehead in the area of the wound. Above the wound is a discolored bruise, Triangular in shape, with the apex of the triangle medially. Around the previously noted laceration is a bruised and discolored area, also triangular in shape. The body was disrobed and examined.

There were no other areas of trauma noted on the body. There are no surgical incisions. There was dry, scaly dermatitis noted over the lower legs, bilaterally. There was no clubbing, edema or cyanosis. The breasts were those of a normal. The hair was of normal male distribution. The patient had a mustache and a small beard. A tattoo was present on the right forearm. This was of a parachute with "US Paratrooper" at its border. The head is abnormal and a large, soft area of swelling is palpable superior to and posterior to the left ear. Blood which had dried is noted in the left external auditory canal. The pupils are constricted bilaterally, round and equal. There is no deviation of gaze. The sclera is clear and non-icteric. The nose is filled with foul-smelling liquid material. The mouth reveals teeth in good repair without any abnormality of the gingiva of mucous membranes. Rigor mortis is present in the jaw. There is no livor mortis present. The body is warm, however"

Thoracic Cavity and Pleura: "The thoracic cavities bilaterally contained no excess fluids. The surfaces are smooth and shiny without adhesions. The organs occupy the usual anatomic positions. The pericardium is thin, pliable and translucent. The pericardial sac contains no access fluid, there are no adhesions noted. Hilar lymph nodes are unremarkable. There is one small node at the right which contains caseous material in its center. There is an enlarged node located in the left supraclavicular area. It is fleshy, non-fixed and yellow in color. This is saved for sectioning. The larynx and trachea contain yellow, frothy material. The mucous is not edematous, injected or hyperemic. The thyroid is of normal size and shape; however, the isthmus appears slightly larger than normal. The gland cuts with normal resistance to reveal normal red – brown thyroid parenchyma. Three parathyroid glands are identified; they are of normal size and shape."

Abdominal Cavity: "On opening through well-developed abdominal musculature, the abdominal organs are noted to occupy the usual anatomic positions. There are no excess fluid adhesions present in the abdominal cavity."

Heart and Major Blood Vessels: "The heart weights 330 gm. There is no dilatation nor abnormality noted of any chamber. The pericardial surface is smooth and shiny. The ventricular musculature is normal without fibrosis. The right ventricular muscle measures 0.2 cm, the left 1.4 cm at the base of the papillary muscle. The endocardial surface is normal. All valves are thin, pliable and translucent. The chordae tendinous are thin and normal. The valve measurements are: tricuspid 12.3 cm, pulmonic 6.3 cm, mitral 10.1 cm, aortic 5.4 cm. The foramen ovale anatomically closed. The coronary arteries are normal, with normal ostia and are free of atheromatous change. The aorta add other great vessels are normal, however a few very small areas of atheromatous change are noted in the wall of the aorta. The inferior and superior vena cavae are normal."

Lungs: "The right lung weighs 680 gm, the left lung 690 gm. The pleural surface of both is normal. Both lungs feel very heavy and have deceased crepitance. On sectioning the lungs, the parenchyma is noted to be uniformly wet, without any granularity. The lungs retain their shape and do not collapse on sectioning. Sanguineous fluid drips from the cut surface of the lungs. The bronchi are traced and contain material similar to that seen in the larynx which is yellow and frothy. The pulmonary artery if normal bilaterally. "

Liver and Gall Bladder: "The live weighs 1620 grams. Its capsular surface is smooth and without adhesions. It cuts with normal resistance to reveal slightly accentuated lobular pattern with what appears to be slightly sunken central veins without hyperemia or congestion. There is no fibrosis noted. The liver parenchyma has a slightly greasy feel to palpation. It is normally friable. The gall bladder is of normal size: its wall appears normal, the mucosa is thin and velvety. It contains normal bile which can be expressed into the duodenum through the ampulla of vater. The ductal system is traced and is normal throughout."

Gastro-Intestinal Tract: "The esophagus is normal without hyperemia, laceration of ulceration. The stomach is also normal. It contains approximately 350cc of clear yellow fluid without recognizable odor. There are scattered areas of punctate hyperemia noted in the stomach. There is no ulceration present. The duodenum is normal as is jejunum, ileum and colon. The appendix is in place. The rectum is normal."

*Spleen: "The spleen weighs 130 grams. Its capsular surface is normal. Its anatomy is normal. It cuts with normal resistance to reveal firm, spleen tissue with prominence of the germinal center."

*Pancreas: "The pancreas weighs 110 grams. It has a normal anatomy and normal dimensions. It cuts with normal resistance to reveal light tan pancreatic tissue. The duct is traced and is normal throughout."

*Kidney: "In the area of the left kidney there is seen HEMORRHAGE and DISCOLORATION in the perineal tissue. There is no evidence of trauma on the surface of the body, nor any fracture of the ribs. The capsule strips with ease from both kidneys to reveal the presence of fetal lobulation. The capsular surface is smooth and shiny. On section-ing the kidney, the cortex appears normal, is normally demarcated from the normal – appearing medulla. The cayycaal system and pelvis are normal. The ureters are normal. The ureters enter the bladder nor-mally. The bladder is distended with approximately 800cc of clear urine. The trabecular pattern has obliterated. The mucosa is normal and the wall is thin. The urethra is normal. The right kidney weights 190 gm., the left kidney 190 gm."

Musculo-Skeletal System: "The musculature is very well developed. It is symmetrical. The skeletal system is remarkable in that after reflect-ing the scalp, hematoma was noted in the body of the temporal muscle. On removing the skull an epidural hematoma was noted. It measured 7cm in its greatest diameter and was 75ml. volume. There was some clotting present in this blood and it was approximately the consistency of jelly. At the base of the skull, in the region of the middle meningeal artery, is a fracture line with surrounding hematomata that extends through the parietal bone and in the temporal bone. The fracture extends through the whole substance of the petrous portion of the temporal bone and runs anteriorly and medially, crossing the internal opening. Clotted blood is found in the external auditory canal. The line of fracture extends anteriorly and medially and the line of cleavage extends inferiorly and posteriorly into the auditory canal and long the roots of the acoustic nerve ending in the foramen magnum. No other factors are noted."

Adrenals: "Both adrenals together weigh 13 grams. They appear slightly decreased size but of normal anatomy. On sectioning, a very thin rim of normal cortical tissue is seen which is well demarcated with preservation of the brown zone from the normal appearing medulla."

Internal and External Genitalia: "The penis is that of a normal, uncircumcised male. There are no scares noted. The testes are normal bilaterally undesiring with ease. The epididymis, vas deferens and seminal vesicles appear normal. The prostate is of normal size. There are no areas of softening or change in consistency. There is no nodularity noted. It is symmetrical."

Brain and Pituitary: "The brain weights 1380 grams. It appears displaced a previously noted hematoma which is epidural. The pituitary is of small size, is symmetrical and appears normal."

Brain after Fixation: "External examination of the brain reveals a subarachnoid hemorrhage measuring approximately 3 cm in length, involving the anterior temporal gyrus as well as part of the middle temporal gyrus on the left side. Otherwise, the gyro and the sulci are essentially normal and the vascular pattern is also normal. Multiple cut sections through the cerebral hemisphere reveal the gray matter involvement under the previously described subarachnoid space to take in the gray matter in full thickness in a small area about the center of the lesion. Multiple sections in the coronal fashion through the cerebellum and brainstem reveal these structures to be normal."

Registration District No._____

Primary Registration District No._____

ARKANSAS STATE BOARD OF HEALTH
Bureau of Vital Statistics
CERTIFICATE OF DEATH

1. PLACE OF DEATH
a. COUNTY Faulkner

b. CITY, TOWN, OR LOCATION Conway   c. Length of Stay in 1b Life

d. NAME OF HOSPITAL OR INSTITUTION (If not in hospital, give street address) —

e. IS PLACE OF DEATH INSIDE CITY LIMITS? YES ☐ NO ☒

2. USUAL RESIDENCE (Where deceased lived. If institution: residence before admission)
a. STATE Ark   b. COUNTY Conway

c. CITY, TOWN, OR LOCATION Menifee

d. STREET ADDRESS

e. IS RESIDENCE INSIDE CITY LIMITS? YES ☐ NO ☐

f. IS RESIDENCE ON A FARM? YES ☒ NO ☐

3. NAME OF DECEASED (Type or print) First Marvin L. Middle Last Williams

4. DATE OF DEATH Month 5 Day 6 Year 196_

5. SEX Male   6. COLOR OR RACE Col.   7. Married ☒ Never Married ☐ Widowed ☐ Divorced ☐

8. DATE OF BIRTH 7-5-1939   9. AGE (In years last birthday) 20   If Under 1 Year Months Days   If Under 24 H Hours Min

10a. Usual Occupation (Give kind of work done during most of working life, even if retired) —   10b. Kind of Business or Industry Busboy at   11. BIRTHPLACE (State or foreign country) Menifee Ark. U. S.   12. CITIZEN OF WHAT COUNTRY

13. FATHER'S NAME Delawah Williams   14. MOTHER'S MAIDEN NAME Johnnie Williamson

15. WAS DECEASED EVER IN U.S. ARMED FORCES? (Yes, no, or unknown) No   16. SOCIAL SECURITY No. 42-2972-11   17. INFORMANT Delawah Williams   Address Menifee, Ark

18. CAUSE OF DEATH (Enter only one cause per line for (a), (b), and (c).)

PART I. DEATH WAS CAUSED BY:
IMMEDIATE CAUSE (a) Skull fracture   INTERVAL BETWEEN ONSET AND DEATH app. 12 hrs

Conditions, if any, which gave rise to above cause (a), stating the underlying cause last. DUE TO (b) not known

DUE TO (c)

PART II. OTHER SIGNIFICANT CONDITIONS Contributing to Death but Not Related to the Terminal Disease Condition Given in Part I(a) Epidural Hematoma 75cc. Concussion of Brain

19. WAS AUTOPSY PERFORMED? YES ☒ NO ☐

20a. ACCIDENT ☐ SUICIDE ☐ HOMICIDE ☐

20b. DESCRIBE HOW INJURY OCCURRED. (Enter nature of injury in Part I or Part II of Item 18.)

20c. TIME OF INJURY Hour a.m. p.m. Month, Day, Year

20d. INJURY OCCURRED WHILE AT WORK ☐ NOT WHILE AT WORK ☒

20e. PLACE OF INJURY (e.g. in or about home, farm, factory, street, office bldg., etc.)

20f. CITY, TOWN, OR LOCATION   COUNTY   STATE

21. I attended the deceased from _____ to _____ and last saw ___ alive on _____

Death occurred at 1:36 A.M. on the date stated above; and to the best of my knowledge, from the causes stated.

22a. SIGNATURE   (Degree or title) Coroner   22b. ADDRESS Conway Ark   22c. DATE SIGNED 5-9-60

23a. Burial, Cremation, Removal (Specify) Burial   23b. DATE 5-11-60   23c. NAME OF CEMETERY OR CREMATORY Community   23d. LOCATION (City, town, or county) Menifee Ark.

24. FUNERAL DIRECTOR COSMOPOLITAN FUNERAL HOME   ADDRESS

25. DATE RECD. by LOCAL REG.   26. REGISTRAR'S SIGNATURE

Appendix B – The Death Certificate

Coroner McNutt made gross omissions and errors on Marvin's Death Certificate, including the following:

- He doesn't list the manner of Marvin's death, and the spaces where he would check homicide, suicide, or accident are left blank.

- He wrongly lists the time between the onset of Marvin's death at 12 hours, rather than the 6 hours he stated in his letter to the state crime lab.

- He wrongly lists the approximate time of Marvin's death at 11:30 am.

- He wrongly noted that Marvin had not served in the military when he had served with distinction in both the Navy and the Army.

- He wrongly listed the date of Marvin's death as May 5, 1960. Marvin died during the predawn hours of Friday, May 6th, which McNutt acknowledges in his May 6th letter.

Appendix C – Excerpts from the Coroner's Inquest and Related Documents

Letter from Coroner Robert McNutt to the Arkansas State Medical Examiner

"Dear sir, the above captioned, Marvin Williams, died in the Faulkner County Jail, prisoner of the City of Conway, Arkansas. He was committed about 1 am today. His home is in Menifee, Ar., where the storm struck at about the same time that he was arrested. His baby was hospitalized by the storm. [*This was a mistake. I was hospitalized. Marvin's son Ricky was fine.*] It is not believed that this man was in the storm. He was arrested for drunkenness. He had to be supported to walk. The injury on his forehead was caused by a fall at the foot of the courthouse steps on the way to the jail which is on the top floor of the courthouse. Please determine the cause of his death by autopsy and notify me as soon as possible the results of your findings so that I can file the death certificate for record." Yours truly, R.A. McNutt, Coroner of Faulkner County."

Coroner's Inquest: The Opening Testimony of Officer Bill Mullenax

Mullenax: "Well, it was Thursday night I received a call from Patrolman Iberg in the car to come to the station, he would like me to assist in locking up a party and I came to the police station, got in the patrol car with him and we went over to the jail and locked up a Macon boy, Curtis Macon, for drunk and we left the jail and proceeded to carry Harve Macon home, the boy's daddy which was in the car and we went up to Markham Street where Harve Macon lived. When he got out of the car

I noticed a, uh uh Chevrolet parked on the left, parked on the East side of Markham street just about in front of Harve Macon's house and seen somebody's feet I thought, sticking up at the time, so Patrolman Iberg got out of the car and walked up to the car and I came walking up behind him and it was this Williams boy sitting in the front seat passed out and another colored subject laying down in the back seat. At that time we couldn't wake the Williams boy, we tried to but couldn't, so we carried him to the patrol car and placed him in the back seat and we did get this other party awake enough that he went to the car on his own. He didn't have to have no help. Uh, then we got over to the courthouse, uh – just before we went though, we called in and asked for Patrolman Langford to assist us over there and, which he did. We came over to the police station and picked him up and went over to the courthouse and opened, let's see – I was driving – opened the back door and this other colored boy that was in there, got him out and Patrolman Langford started on up with him and this Williams boy we, uh – got him out there and was holding him up, seemed liked when the wind and rain hit him he came to, he was standing there just on his own and there was a clap of thunder or something back in the west and we looked back there and when I looked back around he was falling and I think Patrolman Iberg and I both grabbed for him about the same time, but we was unable to grab him. He fell and hit his head on the second step. We helped him get up and he got up and stood him up on his own and we assisted him on up to the jail, uh, his head didn't look cut very bad, it was just a little blood. That's about all I know that happened."

Appendix D – Photos Prior to Autopsy

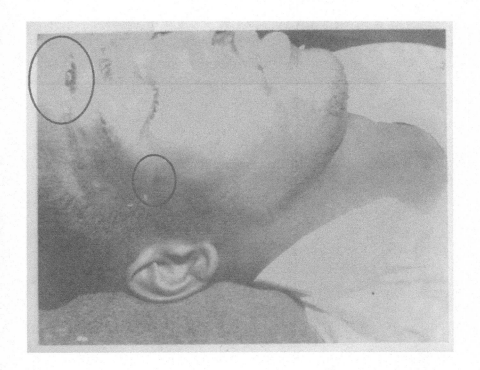

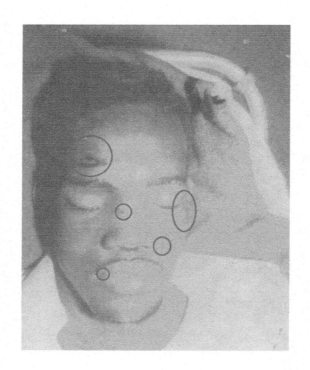

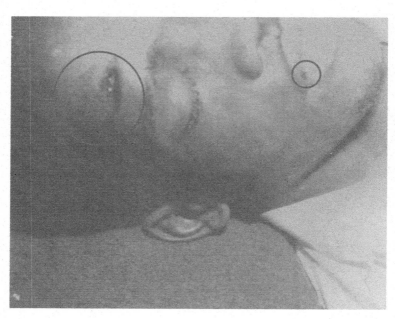

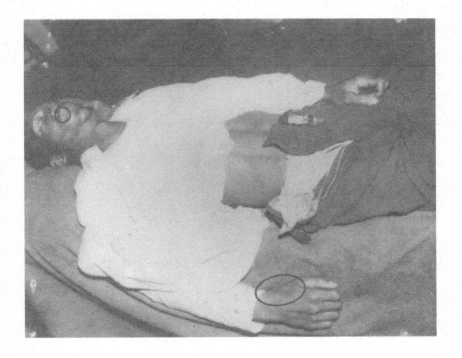

Photo Gallery

Marvin with sisters, Carolyn, Verna, and Barbara

SCHOOL DAYS 1948-49
CONWAY

Marvin preparing to jump during a training session in Germany

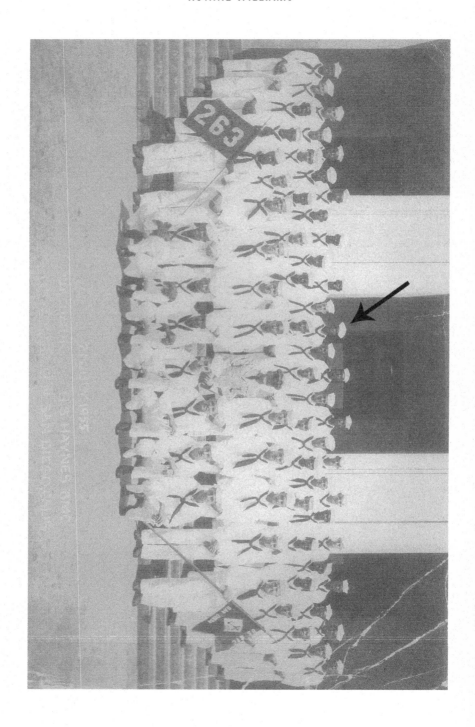

This is a photo of my parents with Geraldo Rivera during the filming of 20/20

Marvin's two children at a very young age

Sharon and Ricky, Marvin's two children, visit his gravesite in 1985

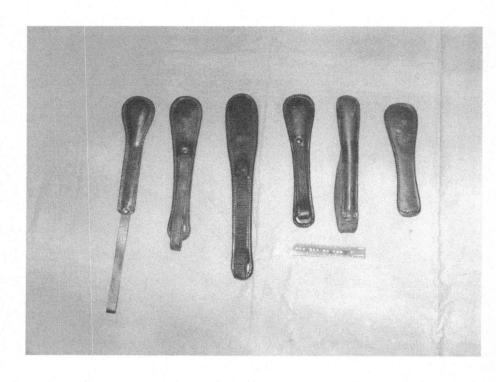

Slappers that were used by police officers when Marvin was murdered

The Sunset Cafe where Marvin was arrested